WHY SCHOOL BOARDS MATTER

WHY SCHOOL BOARDS MATTER

RECLAIMING THE HEART OF AMERICAN EDUCATION AND DEMOCRACY

SCOTT R. LEVY

THE MIT PRESS   CAMBRIDGE, MASSACHUSETTS   LONDON, ENGLAND

The MIT Press
Massachusetts Institute of Technology
77 Massachusetts Avenue, Cambridge, MA 02139
mitpress.mit.edu

The MIT Press would like to thank the anonymous peer reviewers who provided
comments on drafts of this book. The generous work of academic experts is essential
for establishing the authority and quality of our publications. We acknowledge
with gratitude the contributions of these otherwise uncredited readers.

This book was set in Stone Serif and Avenir LT Std by Westchester Publishing
Services. Printed and bound in the United States of America.

Library of Congress Cataloging-in-Publication Data

Names: Levy, Scott R., author.
Title: Why school boards matter : reclaiming the heart of American
    education and democracy / Scott R. Levy.
Description: Cambridge, Massachusetts : The MIT Press, [2025] |
    Includes bibliographical references and index.
Identifiers: LCCN 2025000336 (print) | LCCN 2025000337 (ebook) |
    ISBN 9780262552721 (paperback) | ISBN 9780262383592 (pdf) |
    ISBN 9780262383585 (epub)
Subjects: LCSH: School boards—United States.
Classification: LCC LB2831 .L46 2025 (print) | LCC LB2831 (ebook) |
    DDC 379.1/5310973—dc23/eng/20250225
LC record available at https://lccn.loc.gov/2025000336
LC ebook record available at https://lccn.loc.gov/2025000337

10 9 8 7 6 5 4 3 2 1

EU Authorised Representative: Easy Access System Europe, Mustamäe tee 50, 10621
Tallinn, Estonia | Email: gpsr.requests@easproject.com

For Mom, Dad, and Todd
And for my wife, Cynthia, and my children, Sydney, Andrew, and Jack

CONTENTS

PREFACE

When I embarked on writing this book, I thought a lot about my alma mater, Spring Valley High School, in the East Ramapo Central School District. East Ramapo, located just north of New York City, has garnered national attention during the past decade as the result of an ongoing education governance crisis.

Articles have chronicled the trials and tribulations of East Ramapo. In 2014, the *New York Times* ran an opinion piece titled "A School Board That Overlooks Its Obligation to Students" followed by a 2015 piece "When a School Board Victimizes Kids."[1] A recent *Education Next* piece by Vladimir Kogan titled "Locally Elected School Boards Are Failing" used East Ramapo as an "extreme example" of the "underlying representational problems and perverse incentives" of school boards in communities where "the interests of voters and public-school students are likely to be out of sync."[2]

The district is facing many grave challenges as its fiscal condition continues to decline, and its community remains divided. These issues are explored in depth when I discuss the topic of board accountability. But first, I want to share another story of East Ramapo that too often goes untold. It's about the East Ramapo that I experienced when I was a student in the district in the 1970s and 1980s.

Back then, the district served as a case study of public education at its best. The district was a beacon of strength and stability, earning the respect of the community and education experts across the state. East Ramapo consistently ranked as a top New York State district and was known for its academic excellence, positive culture, and extraordinary diversity. The district had rich course offerings and broad extracurricular opportunities. It achieved impressive outcomes despite lacking the economic resources of a private school or a public school in a wealthy zip code.

A 1997 *New York Times* article written seven years after I graduated highlighted East Ramapo's impressive results. The district achieved an 88 percent college matriculation rate, and its two high schools were ranked in the top 1 percent of all high schools in the United States regarding the number of AP courses offered. East Ramapo students were well prepared for the world after graduation. The district superintendent at the time stated, "We have students coming back from their first year of college telling us how easy their academic and social life have been," a sentiment I can corroborate based on my own experience.[3]

Another amazing aspect of East Ramapo was its diversity. In 1997, 65 percent of the students represented forty different nationalities.[4] There were large Haitian, Hispanic, Asian, and white communities from households ranging from upper middle class to below the poverty line.

Not only did my mother choose to work in East Ramapo as a kindergarten teacher, but like many others, my parents purposefully resided in the East Ramapo Central School District so that my brother and I could matriculate.

I am forever grateful for attending East Ramapo. My time in the district inspired me to be a lifelong learner and provided me with a strong foundation.

Through the years, I have expressed appreciation to teachers and classmates, but I must admit that I never thought much about the role of district leadership. I had limited interaction with the East Ramapo Board of Education.

Looking back, I have come to realize that the Board of Education played a central role in why East Ramapo consistently produced exceptional results. There is no doubt that it took high-quality administrators, faculty, and staff, but the board set the underlying conditions for the entire district to thrive.

District governance was consistent, stable, and strong. The Board of Education set a positive culture and climate, selected strong superintendents, allocated the budget wisely, demanded best-in-class offerings, and attracted the very best employees. The board created space for administrators and teachers to practice their craft and encouraged them to facilitate the teaching of civic responsibility before it became fashionable.

Many talented and altruistic individuals served on the East Ramapo board through the years, and they all deserve credit for their contribution and service. Yet there is one exemplary woman who went above and beyond. Georgine Hyde dedicated her life to East Ramapo and to the cause of school board governance more broadly.

Hyde, frequently referred to in Rockland County as an "icon," is probably the closest anyone comes to a public education governance rock star.[5] She won twelve consecutive elections and served on the East Ramapo Board of Education from 1969 to 2005, a total of thirty-six years.[6] She was the recipient of the prestigious Everett R. Dyer Award presented by the New York State School Boards Association for exceptional service to the public school students of New York State.[7] Her strength and desire to help the next generation provided stability to the school district.

Hyde's contribution went well beyond the district boundaries of East Ramapo. She served as the president of the New York State School Boards Association. She attended countless conventions of school board members where she lectured and contributed to the professional development of others. She was a source of counsel to Democratic and Republican politicians including Senator Daniel Patrick Moynihan and Congressman Benjamin Gilman.[8] According to Hyde's son John, Governor Mario Cuomo would call Hyde routinely in the 1980s to seek her perspective on state education policy.[9] Hyde also was chosen to participate in the Second White House Conference of Character Building for a Democratic Civil Society.[10] I knew of Hyde's sterling reputation, but I was unaware of her background until I discovered her life story when conducting research to write this book.

The USC Shoah Foundation recorded a testimonial of Hyde sharing her personal history.[11] Hyde was born in Prague, Czechoslovakia, on January 20, 1925. She came from a patriotic Czech family that was well integrated into the fabric of secular Czech society. She attended an excellent school and had loving parents and close friends, most of whom were non-Jewish.

At the start of World War II, Hyde's family initially felt secure. When the war first broke out, they had an opportunity to attain Ecuadorian citizenship but were reluctant to leave their beloved home, where they enjoyed a fulfilling life.

As Hyde's family learned of Hitler's aggressions, her parents became concerned for their safety. A cousin in New Rochelle, New York, secured them U.S. visitor visas, so her father went to the U.S. Embassy in Prague to complete the visa paperwork. There, long lines of people were waiting to be processed. In addition to Czech citizens attempting to secure passage to America, there were also refugees that had traveled to Prague from other countries.

Hyde's father mistakenly stood on the wrong line. After a very long wait, he discovered that instead of ending up at the window for visitors' visas, he was in front of a clerk who was processing immigrant visas. Subsequently, the clerk rejected his application, suspicious that his intent was to come to the United States permanently. Hyde remembers her father coming back from the embassy and telling her mother, "I have made the greatest mistake of my life."

After Germany invaded Czechoslovakia and took control of Prague, the family's business was taken away, and the Hydes were banished to a ghetto in central Prague, forced to hand over their home to the German army. Fourteen-year-old Hyde lived among four families sharing an apartment meant for one family. She was given a yellow star to wear on her sleeve. The Hydes were eventually moved to Theresienstadt, a transit camp for Czech Jews, and later Auschwitz.

Upon arrival at Auschwitz, Hyde recalls witnessing from the train two SS soldiers walking around a circle of prisoners with dogs, beating the prisoners on their backs. Blood trickled onto the ground, forming a red circle around where they stood.

After disembarking the train, prisoners were sorted, and 150 out of 1,500 were chosen for the work camp. The sorter was Josef Mengele, an infamous Nazi doctor who performed medical experiments on prisoners. Hyde was shuttled in the direction of the smaller group, while her mother was sent in the opposite direction.

Next, Hyde was ordered to remove her clothes and give up her remaining possessions. The SS shaved her head and provided a brief orientation to the concentration camp by pointing to the chimney. "That is the way you will get out of here."

Hyde asked the SS where the larger group that included her mother had been taken. The guard responded, "They already went through the chimney." Both Hyde's mother and father were murdered in Auschwitz.

Hyde's account of her Auschwitz experience epitomizes the darkest side of humanity and reminds us of the magnitude of the atrocities of Nazi Germany. She bore witness to constant fear, starvation, horrific sanitary conditions, disease, and suicide. She was able to sustain herself with the support of her friend Ruth, and eventually, Hyde and Ruth were among the few who made it out of Auschwitz alive. According to the U.S. Holocaust Museum, approximately 1.1 of 1.3 million people deported to Auschwitz between 1940 and 1945 were murdered.[12]

After brief stints in England and Australia, Hyde immigrated to the United States, got married, and ultimately settled in Rockland County, New York, within the boundaries of the East Ramapo Central School District. After having a son, Hyde decided to volunteer for the local public schools, the start of her lifelong commitment. She eventually ran for the East Ramapo Board of Education and became a public education leader.

When Hyde was asked how her Holocaust experience affected her choice of work, she responded, "I needed something that's future oriented where I can affect the lives of the next generations and education is one of the ways. . . . I truly enjoy very much looking back at the years I have spent on the school board. . . . It was a challenge. It has given me the opportunity to make a difference for a lot of people."[13]

The horror of the Holocaust motivated Hyde to dedicate her life to school board service. She was deeply committed to preparing the next generation for productive professional and civic lives. She also understood the importance of how school boards provide a forum for an engaged and empowered citizenry to participate in the process and how school boards strengthen our democracy.

An effective school board stays out of the spotlight. The board president doesn't usually seek extra attention or fanfare and doesn't serve as the face of the district day-to-day. Instead, a strong school board president elevates the superintendent, the entire administration, faculty, and staff, and sets the conditions for these professionals to do what they do best.

Hyde did not seek the spotlight. Instead, behind the scenes she tirelessly fought to keep East Ramapo strong. Under her leadership, generations of students, many of whom were first-generation Americans living in poverty, found opportunity, hope, and a steppingstone to a better life. John Hyde emphasizes that his mother's north star was to serve as a voice for students and to always have the "kids' interest at heart."[14]

Georgine Hyde passed away in 2015 at the age of ninety. I never had the opportunity to tell her that her life's work helped set my life trajectory in a profound way.

I owe so much of my professional and personal success in life to East Ramapo, and East Ramapo was exceptional in large part because of Hyde's leadership. Sometimes people you don't know make a big difference in your life. It is in that spirit, the spirit in which Hyde served, that I undertake to write this book.

INTRODUCTION

As I drafted this introduction, not a week went by without the media highlighting another battle at a school board meeting somewhere in America. Boardrooms have become the epicenter of contentious debates across a broad spectrum of controversial issues, reflecting society's deep divisions.

Across red, blue, and purple states, community members are attending board meetings late into the night and participating in public comment periods. While increased community engagement is healthy and positive for the democratic process, boardroom discourse has become angrier in tone. Board presidents have had to recess meetings that spiral out of control, and more frequently, a security presence is required in the boardroom to maintain order. There even have been reports of arrests and threats of violence:

- In Pennsylvania, a school board member was told she was a "treasonous pedophile who should get raped by undocumented immigrants." It was reported that she received emails that said, "You better grow eyes in the back of your head" and "you're going down." Another message stated, "Sleep with one eye open," and "we will never stop until you are done."[1]
- In Georgia, constituents told a board member, "We are coming for you."[2]

- In Nevada, a board president reported receiving messages saying she should be hanged or shot.[3]
- In New Jersey, two board members received letters with a photo of their bloodstained faces in the crosshairs of a gun.[4]
- In Connecticut, a fistfight broke out between a school board member and a resident.[5]
- In Virginia, a contentious school board meeting led to an arrest, an injury, and a trespassing summons.[6]
- In Utah, eleven people were charged with disorderly conduct after protestors disturbed a school board meeting and caused commotion.[7]

While these reprehensible incidents thankfully are still rare, the growing sense of frustration and anger is undeniable. Battles are by no means limited to community members versus the school board. Rifts occur among board members themselves, between the school board and district unions, and between the board and the superintendent.

Not surprisingly, school board members, most of whom are volunteers and often have day jobs, are quitting. An August 2021 Associated Press story on npr.org described a Nevada school board member who was harassed and subsequently had thoughts of suicide. He ultimately stepped down. A board member in Virginia resigned because she believed politics was trumping sound decision-making. Three board members from a Wisconsin district resigned. One said, "When I got on, I knew it would be difficult, but I wasn't ready or prepared for the vitriolic response that would occur, especially now that the pandemic seemed to just bring everything out in a very, very harsh way. It made it impossible to really do any kind of meaningful work."[8]

While some board members are choosing to step down, others are being challenged before the expiry of their term. Among the districts tracked by Ballotpedia, a nonprofit digital source of U.S. political information, recalls rose from 20 efforts in 2011 aimed at 48 board members to 92 aimed at 237 board members in 2021. Though recalls have trended lower in the past couple of years, they remain above pre-pandemic levels. In 2023, there were 48 efforts that named 97 officials. During the past thirteen years, recall success rates have ranged from 0.4 percent to 29.7 percent.[9]

Ballotpedia tracks election data in a subset of districts, including many of the nation's largest. Table I.1 illustrates a rise in contested elections and a decline in traditional incumbency advantage from pre-2021 levels.[10]

Table I.1 School board election statistics, 2018–2023

Year	States	School districts	Seats up for election	Unopposed seats (%)	Candidates per seat	Seats won by incumbents (%)
2018	28	405	1,215	40%	1.85	61%
2019	27	196	564	39%	1.86	57%
2020	28	358	1,025	36%	1.96	60%
2021	24	180	515	24%	2.09	51%
2022	28	372	1,169	25%	2.17	53%
2023	29	192	514	29%	1.92	51%

Note: Data sourced from Ballotpedia.

Whether you are an observer of school board meetings or a participant, it is easy to identify change since the COVID-19 pandemic began in 2020. Observers have witnessed intense battles over the contentious issues of the day that sometimes lack civility. Board members have the uncomfortable and difficult task of maintaining order in the boardroom and conducting district business amid protest. I know firsthand. Sitting at the boardroom table during the public comment period listening to speaker after speaker express disdain isn't pleasant. The increased frequency of contested elections requires board members to invest more time and resources in the reelection process.

But despite this sometimes messy, time-consuming, and awkward democratic process, airing differences in the open is healthy, productive, and quintessentially American. All the recent attention that school board meetings and elections have garnered serves as a reminder that school boards play a pivotal role in our public education ecosystem, and we have not sufficiently tended to them.

The big idea I'm expressing in this book is that we need to understand and elevate the importance of the school board. School boards are *the* vital organ for education decision-making and represent our best opportunity to improve public education in America. A well-functioning school board can make a district, and a dysfunctional school board can break a district.

A lot has changed in the nine years since I first ran for my local school board. Back then, most Americans did not think much about their local board of education, and if they did, they likely associated it with dullness. Indeed, just a few short years ago school boards were sleepy affairs, sometimes even literally. I remember running into a constituent soon after I was elected to my first term. He congratulated me and said, "I look forward to seeing you when I stream the board meetings. I often watch them when I have trouble falling asleep."

School boards conduct the mundane business of governing a school district. Meetings follow the arcane cadence of Robert's Rules of Order. The board president typically starts by saying, "The meeting will come to order" and "I move that the board approve the agenda." The motion must be seconded for the board to vote "Aye" or "Nay." Agendas often consist of the categories "Consent Agenda," "Unfinished Business," and "New Business." The board must approve each staffing change and every material contract over a certain dollar threshold. Budget discussions are often detailed and lengthy, and it is common to have exhaustive debates over intricate policy language. Not surprisingly, the highlight of the meeting is often when the president asks for "a motion to adjourn."[11]

Absent a scandal, school board meetings have generally gone underreported despite the open meeting laws requiring board business to be conducted publicly. Local news outlets, which are the traditional source of school board media coverage, have struggled to survive as Facebook and Google now collectively account for 77 percent of the local digital advertising market. In fact, over 65 million Americans live in counties with zero or one local newspaper.[12]

Furthermore, school board election turnout is generally dismal, with estimates often ranging from 5 to 15 percent, prompting some jurisdictions to resort to lowering the voting age to sixteen.[13] There are even districts that have lacked enough candidates and have board seats that remain unfilled.[14]

School boards have been relegated to the periphery of academia and scholarly research. Peruse the course catalog of any leading education school, and you would be hard pressed to find a course on school boards. Education scholars have conducted extensive research on topics such as state and federal education policy, principals, and teachers, but as noted by William Howell, editor, in *Besieged: School Boards and the Future of Education Politics*, "Unfortunately, scholarly studies on school boards and school board politics are startlingly sparse."[15] A review of journal articles in the Education Resources Information Center (ERIC) database found that only 108 of 40,419 articles tracked by ERIC in 2024 (0.27%) made mention of school boards in the subject.[16] A teacher or an administrator can easily find professional development opportunities on a broad range of topics from their choice of education schools, nonprofits, and consulting firms, but outside of school boards associations that exist nationally and at the state (and sometimes regional) level, continuing education options for school board members are limited.

Similarly, the school reform movement of the past several decades generally has overlooked local school boards. Reformers touted principles from the corporate world, such as competition, standardization, measurement, and accountability, which they believed would be easier to achieve through federal and state government oversight and mayoral control.

In the rare instances that reformers have paid attention to school boards, they have levied intense criticism. School boards are accused of being tools of teachers' unions special interests or agents of the progressive left or the conservative right, whose secret plot is to infiltrate public education and indoctrinate kids. Other times, they are viewed suspiciously by competing factions whose only commonality is to undermine the power of a given school board. With these preconceived notions, there is very little room left for trust or collaboration.

Over the past several decades, education reform policy, among other forces that will be explored later, has weakened school board power, shifting certain responsibilities to the state and federal governments. Many of the problems we have witnessed in recent years have often flowed from a disconnect of citizens thinking that they have a direct say in how their schools operate by voicing concerns to their district's school board, then finding, instead, that school boards are not as responsive as anticipated because the scope of their power has been reduced.

But for most of American history, school boards weren't overlooked. In fact, they quietly went about their work as the focal point of public education governance. School boards are uniquely positioned to provide district oversight. Unlike federal and state governments, school boards govern at the local level, which makes it possible to set district climate, hire a superintendent well suited to their district, and address local community needs. Unlike teachers' unions and other collective bargaining units with a vested interest in representing a single constituency, the job of a school board is to balance the needs of students and taxpayers while treating employees fairly and equitably. And unlike the perspective of an individual parent or student, school boards represent the collective parent and student body.

School boards matter because, in their best practice, they are the focal point where all important constituents meet—state policymakers, administrators, teachers, staff members, parents, community members, students— and where sensible decisions ultimately can be made that are consistent with the local community.

School boards are where theory meets practice, where federal and state requirements converge with local governance policies, and where constituents can express themselves and advocate for what they think is most important.

School boards also serve as one of the most direct forms of American democracy. If more Americans were productively engaged with their local school board and district, the nation itself would benefit from a greater sense of empowerment and purpose. Citizens would feel more connected to the government.

A HUMBLING EXPERIENCE THAT DROVE ME TO CARE ABOUT SCHOOL BOARDS

I admit that I too did not fully appreciate school boards until I became a school board member. Then and only then did I become aware of their potential.

On a crisp October evening in 2013, I entered a large auditorium packed with parents in Port Chester, New York. The Chancellor of the Board of Regents and the New York State Education Commissioner were hosting a forum on the state's rollout of Race to the Top, the Obama administration initiative designed to incentivize K-12 education reform, and the Common Core curriculum. With three young kids and a hectic full-time job that involved significant travel, I typically did not attend meetings of this sort, but I felt compelled to attend this one.

Before we go any further, I need to disclose my professional background. My journey in education started far afield. I am not an elementary or secondary school teacher and I do not have any pedagogical training. I am not a school administrator. I do not have a degree in education.

In fact, my background is like that of many supporters of the education reform movement. I spent twenty years on Wall Street as an investment banker. I read the *Wall Street Journal*. I believe in the virtues of our capitalist system. I think accountability is important.

I am aware that some readers, particularly those embedded in the world of public education, may view my background with skepticism or even as disqualifying. Educators are tired of business executives telling them what to do.

In her 2017 book *Reign of Error: The Hoax of the Privatization Movement and the Danger to America's Public Schools*, Diane Ravitch charged that the reform movement trying to fix public education is "a 'corporate reform' movement" funded by "major foundations, Wall Street hedge fund managers, entrepreneurs, and the U.S. Department of Education" designed to "cut costs and maximize competition among schools and among teachers."[17]

On the one hand, I am convinced that corporate-minded reformers do not have all the answers. Both No Child Left Behind, a federal initiative that put in place new testing and accountability measures, and Race to the Top, predicated on hallmarks of the corporate world such as standardization, data, measurement, and competition, had serious unintended negative consequences. But I also believe that those who dismiss applying any business principles to education ignore a meaningful opportunity. Who is right?

The Port Chester forum that night helped me answer this question in a more nuanced way. What prompted me to attend the forum was what I experienced as chairman of an education nonprofit with the mission of funding innovative initiatives in local public schools. Each year, faculty and administrators generate new ideas and present them to the nonprofit's board of trustees, which is composed of parents in the community. The board decides which ideas to prioritize and fund, a challenging task since compelling ideas typically exceed available funding.

But something changed in 2013. The process ground to a halt. When we investigated why the pipeline of creative ideas stopped flowing, we realized teachers and administrators could not focus on innovation because they found themselves overwhelmed by a series of reforms they were expected to implement. It was a negative unintended consequence of New York State's rollout of the Race to the Top initiative.

When Congress passed the 2009 American Recovery and Reinvestment Act, $100 billion was earmarked for education, and the Department of Education (DoE) targeted a subset of this money, $4.35 billion, for the new initiative Race to the Top. To allocate these funds, the DoE tapped into the business concept of competition by awarding money to the states that committed to implement reforms most aggressively.[18] New York State, facing acute budgetary challenges from the Great Recession and educational outcomes that disappointed state officials, submitted a compelling Race to the Top application and received nearly $700 million in federal funds as a second-round winner.[19]

As New York implemented the reform policy, something was awry. Supporters of Race to the Top touted how business principles embedded in the initiative, such as accountability, data monitoring, and standardization, could be applied to education. They believed it would dramatically improve the quality of education in the state.

I was not so sure. To me, the practices reformers espoused bore little resemblance to how my corporate clients ran their companies. What they were recommending recalled practices used in a 1920s Ford Model T factory, but they did not reflect the characteristics of a well-run modern-day corporation. The reforms were replete with top-down micromanagement, misjudgments regarding institutional capacity, a one-size-fits-all solution for districts facing vastly different challenges, and a lack of buy-in from those on the front line.

In light of this flawed reform approach, it is not surprising that in Port Chester that evening, parents from a highly diverse group of districts across the region articulated compelling examples of Race to the Top's unintended negative consequences.

Despite the obvious frustration in the auditorium and the well-reasoned evidence presented by audience members, parents were ignored, and the state did little to course correct. In fact, many pundits and policymakers mistakenly viewed parents who pushed back on Race to the Top as fringe, calling them uninformed middle-class suburbanites and pawns of the teachers' union. After all, the union was also adamantly against Race to the Top.

Astonishingly, despite unprecedented parent pushback, the New York State Senate and Assembly passed additional laws in April 2015 that doubled down on the reform effort. The legislation paved the way for standardized test score results to count for as much as 50 percent of a teacher evaluation.[20]

While the Port Chester forum seemingly had little impact on the actions of state leaders, it had a profound impact on me. I decided to leave a twenty-year career on Wall Street to study the rollout of Race to the Top. I am a product of New York State public schools as well as the proud son of a public school kindergarten teacher and son-in-law of a public school special education assistant teacher. Some of my earliest memories are of helping my mom set up her kindergarten classroom by stacking blocks and organizing books. I received a public education that changed the course of my life, preparing me for college and beyond. I could not stand by and watch these reforms damage New York's education system that served over two and a half million students, including my three children.

After conducting interviews and extensively analyzing the rollout of Race to the Top, I identified many issues that resulted from the reform effort. Some examples include:[21]

- The state rolled out the Common Core and a new teacher evaluation system but lacked the institutional capacity to implement so much change at once. Schools were required to teach the new curriculum before the state completed the instructional modules. There were mistakes in the released modules.
- District creativity and teacher autonomy took a back seat to prescribed standards. In fact, many teachers resorted to using word-for-word state-scripted lesson plans to teach to the test, and subjects such as social studies, music, and art were deemphasized since they were not tested. Parents across New York grew concerned that schools were narrowing instruction by teaching to the test.
- Third-grade standardized test length grew by 163 percent, and some elementary school students took up to 540 minutes (in comparison,

the SAT at the time was 225 minutes). There were reports that proper accommodations for students with disabilities were not honored.

- Concerns were raised regarding test quality and the usefulness of the tests. It took five months to receive student scores, and because the actual tests weren't released, there was a lack of transparency into what kids got right and wrong, making it impossible for students to learn from their mistakes and for teachers to use the tests to pinpoint individual student areas of development.
- Lawmakers and regulators from the state capital attempted to micromanage teacher evaluations by developing a formula to measure performance, in which the most important input was the growth scores of student standardized test results. A teacher in Long Island sued over the formula, which resulted in a New York State judge characterizing her evaluation as "arbitrary and capricious."
- Parents and guardians worried that the state did not have a cohesive plan to protect student data privacy.

After completing my research on Race to the Top and realizing how this brazen attempt at centralized reform had backfired, my attention turned to school boards for two reasons.

First, while I concluded that Race to the Top applied business principles to education in a flawed manner, I reject the notion that business principles have no place in education. After all, public school districts are organizations, just like hospitals, universities, nonprofits, and corporations. Each of these organizations succeeds or fails depending on common factors, such as governance, management, organizational climate, workforce recruitment and retention, resource allocation, innovation, and measuring success utilizing relevant benchmarks. When it comes to school districts, federal and state governments have limited control over these organizational factors. Rather, they fall squarely in the domain of boards of education and senior administrators, which are a school district's relevant governing and administrative bodies. Acknowledging this, in my view, is why applying business principles to education can be constructive, *but only if the principles are applied properly.*

Furthermore, I learned that reform efforts that usurp local control are doomed to fail. Teacher accountability is important, but it cannot be micromanaged through a state formula. It is more complicated and needs to be measured at the local, organizational level. State testing can play a meaningful role, but we must recognize its limitations and avoid excessive testing at the expense of creativity, innovation, and teaching to the whole child.

My second reason to turn to school boards is their ability to allow parents and community members to have a say. It ultimately took two years and a 20 percent testing opt-out rate for parents to convince New York State to reverse Race to the Top policies. Finally, in mid-2015 a group of New York State Regents publicly admitted that the teacher evaluation process was "malfunctioning," and by year end, Governor Andrew Cuomo called for a "total reboot" of the system. A task force was appointed that corroborated parent concerns and concluded the "one-size-fits-all" reforms caused "parents, educators, and other stakeholders to lose trust in the system." Ultimately, even the Obama administration admitted that Race to the Top policies had "unintended effects."[22]

The grassroots opt-out movement that started in the leafy suburbs of New York City upended Race to the Top statewide and contributed to a national movement to reverse course, paving the way for Every Student Succeeds Act (ESSA), a new federal education policy. ESSA toned down the federal government's role and shifted some power to states, but local districts still must follow a complex web of mandates.

After analyzing the rollout of Race to the Top, one element leapt out at me: the sheer amount of organizational effort and time it took for parents to have their voices heard. Parents expect they will be able to express their views directly to decision makers. It occurred to me that if these policies were within the authority of the school board instead of the state, parents could have accessed the decision makers faster and with less disruption.

Local governance provides a clear mechanism for parent influence. A parent with an issue can first talk to the teacher, then to the principal or the superintendent. If their concerns are still not adequately addressed, the issue can be elevated to the local board of education. If the board fails to act, that parent can run for a board seat in the next election.

Subsequent events have reinforced my view that the federal and state creep of control over public education does not map well with how American communities are set up, how Americans choose where to live (often explicitly for local schools), and how Americans pay local taxes, which again are tied directly to schools. Many Americans believe (and they are not wrong) that they pay for *their* schools.

While each citizen has their own view on the purpose and effectiveness of K-12 education, it is the blending of these views that has made our system successful. In a well-functioning democracy, we should make room for citizens to vigilantly monitor the quality of our educational systems rather than allowing a small number of state government officials to enforce a uniform solution. When power shifts from school boards to the state, parent feedback becomes more difficult to deliver.

These insights informed my understanding of the important role that school boards play in our education governance ecosystem and solidified my belief that many of our nation's educational issues would be best solved at the local level. And they are why I decided to run for a seat on the school board in my local community. After a successful election, my first term began in July 2015.

MY IMPETUS FOR WRITING THIS BOOK

Our public education system is at a critical juncture considering the pandemic and a national reckoning on race. Our system is frayed. Students are achieving subpar academic outcomes and experiencing a mental health crisis. Parents are frustrated. Superintendents and teachers are tired, and turnover is high.

Policymakers, education scholars, business leaders, and foundations have conjured just about every conceivable approach to try and improve public education in our country. They have looked high and low for solutions. Race to the Top was a federally driven approach. More recently, state-level policymakers across liberal and conservative states have been actively passing new legislation.

But a sustained focus on school boards as a mechanism for positive change has been noticeably absent. It's almost as if there's an unspoken consensus among experts that school boards simply do not matter.

The past few years have demonstrated that despite our focus on state and federal government, many of the most critical education policy debates are being adjudicated in boardrooms across the nation. Regardless of whether your view of school boards is favorable or unfavorable, regardless of whether you think they are functional or dysfunctional, school boards are an integral part of our system.

School board members are collectively the largest group of public officials in the United States. There are over eighty-two thousand school board members across more than thirteen thousand districts. Public school districts are responsible for the education of forty-seven million students, or 87 percent of American K-12 students, tapping into a collective budget of over $850 billion annually.[23] While we can tinker with different components of our education system and attempt new approaches, to positively impact the lives of the vast majority of K-12 students in this country, we should harness the power of school boards and focus on maximizing their effectiveness.

This book is a humble attempt to shine light on school boards and to explain how they can play a pivotal role in strengthening our nation's public school system. I do not purport to have answers to many of the most pressing questions regarding public school governance. I did not set out to write an academic textbook or compile a comprehensive review of scholarly education literature. Instead, my hope is that I can contribute to the education governance debate with a unique perspective, that of a four-time elected school board member who cares deeply about public education and has an extensive background in governance and management across the not-for-profit and for-profit sectors. Along the way, I draw on education history and scholarly research to provide context and support.

I am not suggesting a radical new approach that disavows a federal and state role in education. The federal government has provided funding to help economically disadvantaged students, supported policies to enhance academic achievement, and stood up for marginalized groups when some local school boards fell short. States need to measure progress and hold districts accountable since they are charged with the constitutional responsibility of educating their young citizens. The role of federal, state, and local authorities requires a delicate balance, with each exercising appropriate influence over public education.

What I am suggesting is that the pendulum has swung too far away from school board control to a world with excessive state, and sometimes federal, micromanagement. We have forgotten the value of investing in school boards and empowering them to strengthen their districts.

Swinging the pendulum back toward a better equilibrium can only be done properly when all participants in the governance process—from school board members to parents to policymakers to researchers—work collectively:

- State and federal policymakers should provide space for local districts to thrive. At the same time, they should hold districts to account for ultimate outcomes and intervene as a last resort when local governance efforts fail. They can also play a pivotal role in providing data repositories, benchmarking, and transparency to all stakeholders.
- Parents and community members should become more vested in the school board governance process by understanding the role of the board versus school administrators versus the state, exercising their right to vote and engaging with their local board members on wide-ranging governance issues, not just the controversial issue of the day.
- Academia and foundations should allocate more of their time and resources to studying school boards, teaching about governance, and providing more continuing education opportunities directly to board members.
- Superintendents should prioritize building constructive relationships with their boards to ensure alignment of district strategy and to set the tone for the rest of the district. It is important that they understand the boundaries between the roles of the superintendent and board.
- School boards should prioritize building constructive relationships with their superintendents and must be willing to seek continuing education to master the skills necessary to govern effectively, across policy, finance, leadership, strategy, and curriculum. They should use data to inform decisions and act as fiduciaries in the best interest of the overall district. They must serve as role models. Board members should stay in their lane and not encroach on the superintendent's day-to-day management responsibilities. They also need to listen to their constituents.

Part I will explore why there are so many battles in the boardroom and explain how the role of the school board has evolved. Part II will argue why school boards matter and how they can address some of the most intractable public education challenges. Finally, part III will describe how we can make boards stronger and invest in boards to strengthen our overall democracy. Let me now briefly highlight the contents of each part.

PART I: BATTLES IN THE BOARDROOM

Part I analyzes the current school board landscape and provides insight into why so many battles are occurring in boardrooms across the country. The pandemic and a national reckoning on race following the murder of George Floyd were the sparks that ignited many of the recent battles, but the philosophical underpinnings of those battles are not new. For generations, boardroom battles have centered on the tension between parental rights versus government control and the boundaries of curriculum versus perceived indoctrination.

What is different today is the emergence of a series of underlying societal factors that delocalize school boards and erode community trust, creating a tinderbox that has fueled these intense contests. Specific factors include the rise in polarization, the impact of the internet, the demise of traditional local news, and the influence of outside money.

While school boards share commonality with corporate and nonprofit boards, they have distinct structural features that make them natural and intentional battlegrounds, such as transparency requirements and the tradition of the public comment period. Battles are exacerbated by the gap between public perception and reality of school board power. Whenever something negative or controversial occurs, community members look to the board for answers and accountability, but they often misunderstand the limits of board power. Historically, school boards were delegated authority to serve as the primary governance authority, but during the past several decades, states and the federal government have increasingly inserted themselves. Lines are now blurrier between state and local control, contributing to public confusion and frustration.

Underlying societal trends, school board structure, and the gap between perception and reality of who controls school governance are all factors that contribute to battles in the boardroom and make board service more challenging. At the same time, there are serious negative repercussions to the pendulum swinging too far toward state and federal power. It is time to revisit the critical role that only school boards can play in improving our public education system.

PART II: THE CASE FOR SCHOOL BOARDS

Part II challenges conventional wisdom by trying to change the paradigm of how we think about education governance. Instead of putting school boards at the periphery, I make the case for why school boards matter and how they are well positioned to strengthen our public schools.

School boards are governance entities that sit *inside* of the school district, and they wield wide-ranging power to allocate resources; determine the tax levy; set priorities; make curriculum choices; hire, manage, and fire the superintendent; ratify material contracts; and set policy within the bounds of the law.

We must find a better equilibrium by granting school boards more authority and autonomy to govern districts and open our eyes to the fact that school boards are in a unique position structurally to solve many of our education system's biggest problems, including initiative fatigue, district climate, community engagement, accountability, and short-termism. Part II of the book explores each of these in turn and provides concrete action steps that school board members can take.

PART III: OUR SHARED RESPONSIBILITY

Many of the frustrations about school boards result from the fact that we haven't understood, elevated, or tended to school boards sufficiently. School board governance is far from perfect, and we must address issues such as low voter turnout, lack of board diversity, and board members who do not act as fiduciaries. These are surmountable challenges. Together, we can all contribute to the process of improving board governance. Board members particularly have a duty to seek professional development and networking opportunities to garner the set of skills required for them to excel in the role.

Despite school board shortcomings, it cannot be emphasized enough that in times of increasing factionalization and digital isolation, school boards are a linchpin of American democracy. School board meetings are one of the few places where citizens of the community can address each other by name and contend for ideas and outcomes of mutual deep concern—and then face each other the next day in the school parking lot, the soccer field, or the grocery store.

School boards are a vital lever not just of schooling, but also of American democracy itself. Contentious school board meetings may be at times uncomfortable, embarrassing, thorny, and difficult to manage. At their worst, verbal exchanges during these meetings can sometimes epitomize the ugliness of our broader society and the conspiracy theories that spread deep in the bowels of the internet. But at their best, these meetings can be an appropriate and excellent means to bring issues out into the open rather than having them lurk beneath the surface. School board meetings are a hallmark of our democratic system, worthy of pride and celebration, and they serve as a pleasant reminder of how passionate Americans are about educating their children. Well-attended board meetings where public comment periods run late into the night sometimes can be difficult to manage, but isn't that preferable to the public ignoring education governance altogether?

Investing in school boards and allowing them to tackle important educational issues is our best hope for improving our K-12 system of public education—and by extension, I believe, the country itself.

I

BATTLES IN THE BOARDROOM

1

ECHOES OF THE PAST

Thirty women representing a group called the Health Defense League attended a meeting of the Portland School Board in Oregon to argue against a compulsory vaccination requirement. The spokesman of the group addressed the board: "I stand here representing this delegation and the thousands of parents who believe that vaccination is most harmful. We respectfully and urgently request that this non-enforceable rule be withdrawn. As it is, hundreds of parents are being intimidated. We have been assured that you have no authority to make willingness to undergo vaccination a requirement for entrance into the public schools. We are prepared to contest the question in the courts, although we would not wish to bring action against the School Board."[1] Sound familiar? If it does, that is probably because these types of speeches were common during public comment periods in school boardrooms across the country throughout the COVID-19 pandemic. Many parents and community members were skeptical of vaccine safety and efficacy and expressed vocal opposition to imposing mandates on faculty, staff, and students.

However, the women of the Health Defense League were not speaking out against the COVID vaccine, and they did not deliver their speech to a twenty-first-century board of education. The comments were delivered at a board meeting that took place over one hundred years ago, in 1912, in opposition to the smallpox vaccine.

In early American history, schools played a de minimis role in the provision of healthcare, other than basic health curricula that was introduced during the eighteenth and early nineteenth centuries.[2] The smallpox outbreak put an end to this passive approach. In 1855, Massachusetts became the first state to require a smallpox vaccine for school enrollment, and by the early 1900s, many districts and states across the country followed suit.[3]

An 1899 *Arkansas Gazette* article reported on the Little Rock Board of Education's vaccination deliberations. The board held a "lengthy and weighty session last night, the main question before them being that of vaccination of public school pupils in accordance with the orders of the city board of health. This order as first issued required each pupil to be vaccinated immediately. . . . It was stated that the compulsory vaccination feature would encounter many obstacles, for many mothers have great faith in the efficacy of asafoetida and camphor to ward off smallpox. These parents are strongly opposed to vaccination and would fight to the last."[4]

Just as community members vocally opposed attempts to institute mandated public health measures to fight smallpox, it should come as no surprise that COVID-19 prevention protocols sparked epic boardroom battles. While the battles that ensued over polices in response to COVID-19 were particularly intense, they were not without precedent. They had historical precursors and contemporary parallels to tensions over curriculum. Since colonial times, parents have been concerned about what exactly schools are teaching their children. Parents have often accused board members and professional educators of overstepping their roles in efforts to indoctrinate kids.

While in every generation the specific issues are unique to the times, the thematic debate is timeless and universal. *Boardroom battles get to the heart of the age-old tension between parental rights and government control.* Disagreements over COVID policy and diversity, equity, and inclusion (DEI) are recent manifestations of age-old battles.

COVID-19

Niche.com, a website that ranks K-12 schools, describes Clovis as "one of the best places to live in California" with its "sparse suburban feel" and

plentiful parks. The website states, "Many families and young professionals live in Clovis, and residents tend to have moderate political views."[5]

Part of Clovis's appeal is its public schools. The Clovis Unified School
District (CUSD), with a growing student population approaching forty-
three thousand, is well regarded, and it reaps the rewards of a community that is supportive of public education.[6] Since 1986, the Foundation
for Clovis Schools has raised over $6 million to supplement the school
budget.[7]

But in August 2021, tension mounted in the CUSD boardroom. In theory, the August 25 school board meeting agenda looked like any other: a
confidential public employee matter, the recitation of the pledge of allegiance, the introduction of newly appointed administrators, the authorization of a debt service estimate, and the Opening of School Report.[8]
In practice, routine board business was overshadowed by the looming
debate over COVID-19 protocols and the public comment period in
which boardroom decorum quickly spiraled out of control.

As reported in *The Clovis Roundup* and *GV Wire*, parents pushed back on
mask mandates and the prospect of a vaccine mandate. While the board
had previously voted in favor of providing parents with mask exemptions
without physician verification, they reversed this decision to conform to
a new state mandate that all exemptions require medical documentation.

News reports of the board meeting described an intense atmosphere
and hyperbolic rhetoric: "Trustees were called Nazis, serfs, ostriches, and
lackeys of the state government's mandates requiring masks."[9] One community member, frustrated that the board followed the state mandate,
argued that if board members lived in the Netherlands during the Nazi
occupation, rather than helping Anne Frank and her family, they would
"obey and sign their death wish."[10] Another speaker said, "I believe in
freedom. I believe that we have the First Amendment, we're using it, and
God forbid we ever have to go to the next amendment because that's
what it was created for."[11]

According to the local newspaper, the board president summarized,
"This was an emotion-filled meeting once again. We feel the emotion like
you do and I hope that we can all give each other a little bit of grace."
The need for grace, and the challenge of experiencing it, were captured
by another board member, who stated, "A lot of things said tonight were

pretty outrageous, and it's pretty frustrating when this board has done quite a bit to try to afford parents as many choices permitted under the law and then to be compared to Nazis."[12]

Just one day prior to the Clovis board meeting, the Washoe County School District in Reno, Nevada, held a marathon board meeting on August 24, 2021, that lasted six hours and twenty-five minutes. During an extensive public comment period, parents expressed their frustration regarding COVID policies. Similar to the dynamic in Clovis, parents were dismayed at the board's compliance with state mandates, accusing them of being motivated by state and federal funding that had strings attached. During public comment period, one speaker declared:

The Washoe County School Board during the past 20 months has conspired with the tyrannical leadership of the state of Nevada . . . the board has failed to listen to and act according to the will of the people . . . it is absolutely forbidden to coerce, influence, or force any human being to be part of any experimental medical treatment. Let the citizens remind the board that the Constitution of the United States still reigns in this country. You have zero authority to infringe on our constitutional rights by mandating mask wearing and coercing children to be victims of an investigational medical experiment with unknown consequences. . . . [This is a] violation of civil liberties and an act of tyranny. When tyranny becomes law, rebellion becomes duty, and Nevada parents are on duty.[13]

Another speaker accused the federal government of covering up an allegation that 45,000 to 200,000 people had died from taking the vaccine. "This is a bioweapon to depopulate. This is a death jab. . . . this is our children . . . I am literally ready to go to war." Yet another speaker approached the podium to describe the testing regime as an agenda of "depopulation by the new world order" and touted Hydroxychloroquine, vitamins, and Ivermectin as the solution.[14] Others accused the board of violating the Nuremberg Code.[15]

These comments exemplify how strong views regarding COVID protocols ignited school boardrooms with heated rhetoric and contentiousness. With hindsight, it is evident that we found ourselves in uncharted territory during the pandemic. There were differences of opinion across demographic groups and political parties. Public health guidance constantly evolved. In many parts of the country, it was parents who recognized the tremendous toll remote education was having on American students in advance of many policymakers and public health officials.

COVID'S IMPACT ON PUBLIC SCHOOLS

The COVID-19 pandemic had a profound impact on America's K-12 schools. While the notion of shutting down schools for a protracted period was historically unfathomable, by March 25, 2020, instruction across the nation had shifted from in-person to remote.[16]

The country unified at the onset of the crisis, and at first, parents overwhelmingly supported school closures. A July 2020 Pew Research Center survey measuring which factors should be given "a lot of consideration" in the decision to reopen schools found that the majority of parents prioritized pandemic-related health issues. It did not take long for this unity to erode. While some parents were thankful to keep their children home, others realized the challenges of a remote education, and concerns mounted. By February 2021, policymakers were all over the map weighing the trade-off between the pandemic safety benefits of remote learning and the education benefits of in-person school, but as shown in figure 1.1, public sentiment shifted as the majority of U.S. adults began to prioritize learning loss over COVID prevention.[17]

While many of the costs of school closures were obvious (reduced academic learning, negative impact on social and emotional well-being, and lack of childcare), others were more subtle but no less important. One such issue was how closures exacerbated societal inequity. In August 2020, the *New York Post* reported that wealthy New York City parents

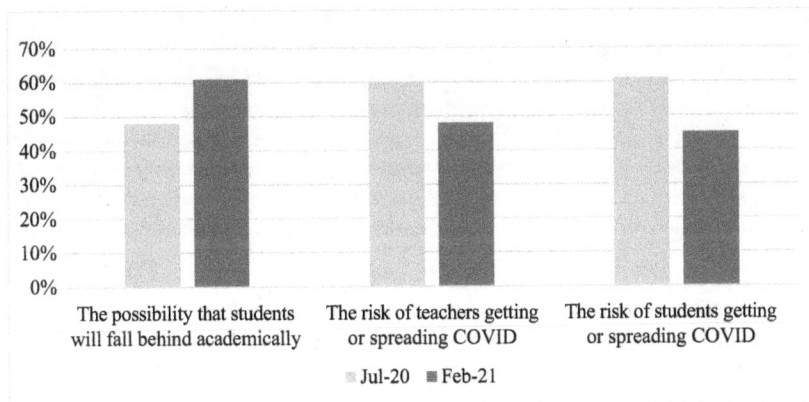

1.1 Percentage of respondents saying each of the following should be given a lot of consideration as K-12 schools teaching remotely decide to reopen (Pew Research Center).

sought outside tutoring to make up for classroom learning loss by form-ing "pods," or groups of four to ten students, at the cost of $70,000 per student for thirty weeks of school on top of $50,000-plus Manhattan pri-vate school tuition.[18] At the same time, there were New York City public school students struggling to find internet connectivity and devices to access asynchronous remote instruction, their only learning option.[19]

Further complicating matters, significant differences emerged across demographic groups regarding parent appetite for in-person school. According to a Pew Research Center survey, Black, Hispanic, and Asian adults were more likely than white adults to want to keep schools virtual until teachers had the opportunity to get vaccinated. A disproportionate number of lower-income adults and Democrats shared similar views. Figure 1.2 below highlights these differences.[20]

With time, the costs of remote school became more obvious, and the public grew increasingly concerned at the toll it was taking on American students. The Educational Recovery Scorecard, a collaboration between Professors Tom Kane at the Harvard Center for Education Policy Research and Sean Reardon at the Stanford Educational Opportunity Project, meas-ured pandemic learning loss. They found that the average U.S. student in public school grades three to eight lost a half year of learning in math and

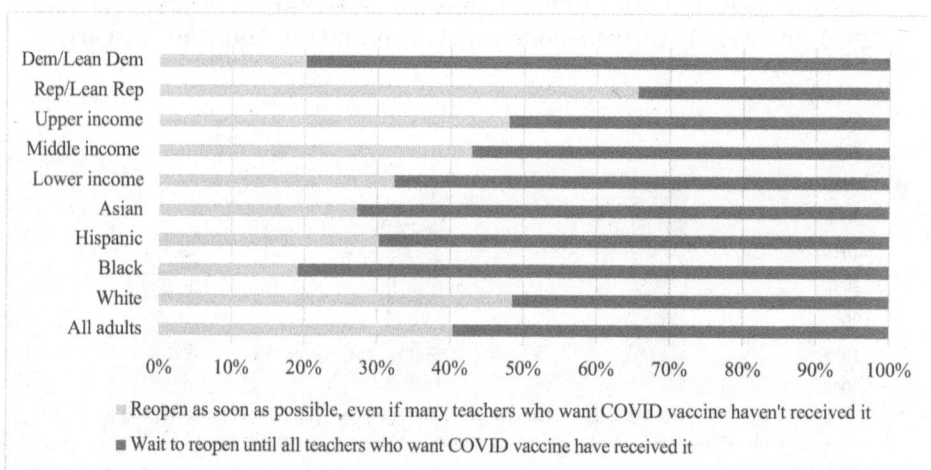

1.2 Percentage saying what K-12 schools not open for any in-person instruction should do as of February 2021 (Pew Research Center).

a quarter year of learning in reading and that the gap between high and low poverty schools widened.[21]

Another study conducted by McKinsey & Company looked at 1.6 million elementary school students across more than forty states and found that students fell an average of five months behind in math and four months behind in reading. Furthermore, the achievement gap widened, with majority-Black schools falling six months behind and low-income schools falling seven months behind in math.[22]

McKinsey also conducted a national survey and found that roughly 80 percent of parents exhibited at least "some level of concern" about their child's mental health or social and emotional well-being since the start of the pandemic. There was a five-percentage point increase in reported anxiety and a six-percentage point increase in reported depression from pre-pandemic levels.[23]

A study conducted by Tali Raviv, Christopher Warren, and Jason Washburn of Northwestern University found that caregiver reports of student signs of loneliness grew from 4 percent pre-shutdown to 32 percent. Students considered "agitated or angry" grew from 4 percent to 24 percent. White children were found to fall particularly low on being "hopeful or positive," with pre-pandemic levels of 56 percent dropping to 25 percent.[24]

The shutdowns resulted in more students dropping out of high school and fewer students attending postsecondary school. McKinsey researchers found that 17 percent of seniors who planned to pursue college changed their mind. They estimated the consequences of school closures to be a loss of earnings that on average fall in the range of $49,000 to $61,000 over each student's lifetime, which equates to a collective hit of $128 billion to $188 billion per year to our economy by the year 2040.[25] Additionally, working parents grappled with childcare issues, particularly for young children who could not attend virtual school without close supervision.

The wide-ranging variability of district reopening fueled further stakeholder outrage. If some schools managed to reopen, why couldn't all schools reopen? An analysis of fall 2020 district reopening plans across the nation shows that 24 percent were planning to be fully online, 51 percent were employing a hybrid model, and 17 percent had in-person instruction. Fifty-one percent of districts were planning to restart school athletics.[26]

Many school boards found themselves adjudicating reopening decisions amid sparring factions. While many teachers across the country collaborated to resume in-person instruction swiftly, others resisted. In some districts, reopening policies fractured historically strong relationships between parents and teachers, with many school boards and superintendents mediating parents pushing for in-person school and teachers' union resistance.

Each state responded differently. From September 2020 to April 2021, one study estimated that 98 percent of students in Florida and 75 percent in Texas had access to full-time in-person learning, compared to 2 percent in Maryland.[27] Most states provided high-level guidance and directives but afforded local school boards the ultimate responsibility of putting together a reopening plan. With few reliable studies on COVID transmission in schools, conflicting guidance from experts, an evolving U.S. Centers for Disease Control and Prevention (CDC) position, and no national consensus, districts found themselves in a quandary, forced to make difficult decisions with imperfect information.

Some large cities had a difficult time reopening schools. In New York City, teachers protested reopening by marching to the Department of Education headquarters while displaying "handmade coffins and a guillotine."[28] Chicago Public Schools narrowly avoided a strike. According to reporting by *The 74*, the Chicago Teachers Union deleted a tweet that said, "The push to reopen schools is rooted in sexism, racism, and misogyny."[29]

The Los Angeles Unified School District closed for more than one year. *The 74* also reported that in addition to COVID protections, United Teachers LA included Medicare for All, a charter moratorium, and defunding the police as conditions for in-person school to resume. Some unions, including the United Teachers of Dade County, Florida, sued the government to try and prevent school reopening. A petition posted by the Fairfax [Virginia] Education Association asked for schools to remain remote until a vaccine was widely available and there were fourteen days with no community spread.[30]

Some of the largest and most diverse, lowest-income districts kept their doors shut the longest, and the union was only one of several variables that drove decision-making. A lack of resources, larger class sizes, and aging physical plant in many underresourced districts made reopening more challenging, and in some cases, community members were generally more supportive and accepting of remote schooling.

Once schools decided to reopen, COVID policies regarding masking, quarantining, social distancing, and test-to-stay were just as contentious and not uniform. To make matters even more complicated, some states deferred decisions to the local district level, while others instituted mandates. Florida, Oklahoma, Georgia, and Utah, for example, banned mask mandates, while other states such as New York, New Jersey, California, and Massachusetts instituted mask mandates.[31]

Researchers Michael Hartney and Leslie Finger analyzed predictive factors for whether schools convened in person or remained remote in the fall of 2020. By way of background, most states hold nonpartisan school board elections, meaning school board candidates do not run with a party affiliation. They observed that "nonpartisan local school district governments are far more institutionally insulated from partisan and nationalizing influences and freer to make policy decisions based on the best scientific evidence and public health concerns than are public officials in many other political institutions." They are the "least nationalized, and least partisan governments." Nevertheless, the study found that Trump vote share and union strength were strong predictors of how likely a district was to stay remote, as well as the existence of parochial schools in a local community as a viable transfer alternative from the public system.[32] Interestingly, Vladimir Kogan's research finds that "one of the strongest predictors of attitudes toward in-person learning is whether one's own school has reopened."[33]

By the summer of 2021, a KFF poll indicated that 63 percent of American parents supported mandatory masking for unvaccinated students, but only 31 percent of Republicans supported masking compared to 88 percent of Democrats and 66 percent of Independents.[34] In public comment periods across the nation, parents vehemently expressed concerns that mandatory masking was government overreach, encroaching on the parental right to choose.

All these COVID-related battles, whether over the merits and drawbacks of masking, COVID testing protocols, or vaccinating children under Emergency Use Authorization, follow a long tradition of debate regarding the line between parental and government control. This tension is at the heart of the American experiment, and when these debates are civil, they are the epitome of our democracy.

In the postmortem analysis of COVID protocols, all of us in decision-making roles should have a sense of humility. We were in uncharted territory, and many mistakes were made. The lack of randomized control trial data regarding school masking policy created confusion and eroded public confidence.

Unfortunately, too many legitimate policy debates over COVID devolved into conspiracy theories and accusations directed at school boards and other government leaders claiming they were intentionally abusing children.

There was also one unanticipated byproduct of remote education, the ability of parents to see directly into the classroom. They didn't always like what they observed. Parents were galvanized by perceived instances of teachers inserting their political or ideological beliefs or addressing controversial topics in lessons, setting the stage for future curriculum battles that many districts across the country would experience.

CURRICULUM BATTLES

Records of the nation's earliest school board meetings provide evidence of tension between parental and government control, often over curriculum. Some of the very first school districts in New England were organized around a particular church community rather than geographic town lines. In fact, some towns split into multiple districts not only to make it logistically easier for students to travel to school, but also to conform to mores and religious beliefs specific to a subset of the community. Unsurprisingly, with so many parents holding differing views, they were skeptical of board power, particularly when boards expressed a desire to teach kids the "right" values in school.

These tensions came to a head in Gloucester, Massachusetts, a thriving coastal town known for its shipbuilding and fishing. Gloucester had multiple small school districts that were governed by a school committee (still to this day, Massachusetts and Connecticut use the term "school committee" in lieu of school board). Smaller districts were often more expensive to run given the lack of economies of scale, but Gloucester parents resisted consolidation and remained skeptical of school board power and leery of government overreach. An 1844 report by the Gloucester School Committee touches on parent versus school board tensions. The school committee provided a surprisingly blunt critique of parents, claiming that some view school as a babysitting service and threaten "personal violence and insult" when their child is accused of wrongdoing. Based on the following passage from the report, the school committee understood parents viewed them skeptically:[35]

Some unwelcome facts must be told; facts which neither flatter parental authority, obedience to the laws, nor show a solicitude for the well being of their offspring. . . . Who would have supposed that in an intelligent community there were persons who regarded the visits of the School Committee to the schools as obtrusive; as going where they had no right and were interfering with the rights of a free people? Such is reported to be a fact. Reform of the defects already mentioned, is necessary; and who attempts it, will be rewarded with hearty opposition if he dare boldly to express an opinion of his own, or go contrary to erroneous or popular doctrines of the public.

Just north of Gloucester in New Hampshire, the Portsmouth School Committee boldly addressed curriculum tensions with parents and the line between content taught at home and at school. Their 1833 "Annual Report of the School Committee of the Town of Portsmouth" argued that the mission of the district is not just to impart academic knowledge, but also to instill "virtue" through "moral instruction." The school committee went on to explain that some students learn this from parents at home, but other students do not because they are "bereft of parents" or because their "parents are vicious." Thus, "It is for the benefit of these [particular students] that our laws are chiefly designed." The school committee was quite cognizant of the fact that there was parental fear and skepticism regarding the teaching of moral instruction: "It may be feared that the door will thus be opened for the introduction of sectarism, and for fettering the infant mind with false doctrines of religion."[36]

The mid-1800s brought intense battles over the teaching of the bible, yet another controversial curriculum issue. In 1838, the Pennsylvania legislature passed a law requiring the use of the Protestant King James Bible in all public schools.[37]

Four years later, the Board of Controllers for the Public Schools of Philadelphia received a letter from Bishop Francis Patrick Kenrick, asking that Catholic children be granted the option to read the Catholic bible instead of the Protestant bible. This request reflected widespread sentiment across Philadelphia's Catholic community, and in 1843, the Philadelphia Board of Controllers voted to pass a resolution that permitted the reading of a substitute bible.[38]

This highly charged board decision had grave consequences. In early 1844, a rumor surfaced that Hugh Clark, a director of public schools who was Catholic, asked a teacher not to read from the Protestant bible. Though accounts of the precise exchange differ, word of mouth traveled quickly and contributed to unrest and violence, resulting in the death of at least forty-five people and significant property destruction, including the burning of Catholic churches and other buildings.[39]

Throughout American history, there has been constant debate regarding an appropriate school curriculum. Issues that have sparked controversy go far beyond moral instruction and religion. Other examples include the teaching of evolution versus creation, mandating "loyalty oaths" for educators in the 1950s in response to fear of communist indoctrination, and the teaching of sex education.

In 2020, history repeated itself with another curriculum battle, this time over DEI and critical race theory (CRT).

DIVERSITY, EQUITY, AND INCLUSION

While the nation was grappling with the COVID-19 pandemic and tensions were already high, the May 25, 2020, murder of George Floyd resulted in an increased focus on racial injustice and inequity in our nation, and many advocated that K-12 schools adopt DEI initiatives to help support marginalized communities. As DEI was introduced into curriculum, training, and policy, certain aspects of these changes sparked contention in many communities. At the center of the DEI debate was whether schools were teaching CRT, and the answer to this question depended on which media outlet you chose to watch.

Consider MSNBC host Stephanie Ruhle's interview of John King, former Secretary of Education in the Obama Administration:

RUHLE: CRT is not being taught to kids, but Republicans are out there pumping these lies everywhere. Should Democrats be out there using those same social media channels to set the record straight?

KING: What we have to address is this dog whistle around critical race theory that's really being used to send a false message about what's happening in our classroom.[40]

Laura Ingraham shared a different view on Fox News: "Because public schools have become cesspools of far-left political thought, many parents whose views don't align and who can't afford private or parochial schools, rightly feel that their children are trapped. . . . Why should we send our tax dollars to schools that end up teaching our kids to hate the country? So by choosing an aggressive secular humanist focus which is now laced with CRT, teachers and administrators have created their own taxpayer funded fiefdoms of radicalism . . . they want complete and total control no questions asked while the parents, forget it, be damned."[41]

Forbes Magazine tried to give context to the varying perspectives of CRT across media outlets. "As is too often in the case of education, we are not really talking about what we're really talking about." *Forbes* goes on to explain how the right erroneously labels everything CRT, whether it is or not, while the left glosses over ways in which teacher training and educational curriculum materials have been informed by CRT.[42]

Communities are deeply divided over multiple facets of DEI-driven school policy, leading to emotionally charged exchanges. A more in-depth analysis of boardroom battles, however, reveals that the CRT debate alone does not provide the full picture of why there is so much tension. Debates spanned many aspects of school life, including accelerated coursework, admissions to magnet schools, curriculum, disciplinary policy, and hiring practices.

Once central to America's defense and economic strategy, gifted and talented education and tracking (sorting students into different level classes by performance) have become highly controversial DEI topics.[43] According to the Fordham Institute, Black and Hispanic students are underrepresented in gifted programs. Black students make up 15 percent of the student population and 10 percent of gifted student enrollees, while Hispanic students represent 28 percent of all students and 21 percent of the gifted student enrollees. Black and Hispanic students are 49 percent and 23 percent less likely than their peers to matriculate in AP courses, respectively.[44]

These racial imbalances prompted some school boards to explore the elimination of acceleration and gifted and talented programs. Additionally, districts reexamined the use of entrance exams for admission to selective public high schools. For example, in 2020, the Fairfax County School Board in Virginia revised its policy regarding admissions criteria for Thomas Jefferson High School for Science and Technology, ranked one of the top high schools in America by U.S. News and World Report.[45] Instead of relying on results of a competitive entrance exam, new admissions criteria involved a holistic review process that took into account family income, English language learner status, and whether the applicant comes from a historically underrepresented school.[46]

The new policy had a significant impact on Thomas Jefferson's student body. Following its adoption, in 2021 the percentage of Black students rose from less than 2 percent to 8 percent, while the percentage of Asian American students dropped from almost three-quarters of the student body to just over half. The shift in policy proved highly controversial among parents and even precipitated litigation. Some lauded the move as a step toward better racial desegregation and more opportunity for historically disadvantaged students, while others believed it harms academically advanced students, discredits academic achievement, reduces objectivity and meritocracy, and discriminates against Asian Americans and whites.[47]

Recent calls for the elimination of advanced coursework sometimes originated at the state level but eventually made their way to the boardroom. For example, California proposed a new math framework in 2021 that encouraged districts to discontinue math acceleration and the aggressive push to calculus in twelfth grade in favor of keeping students at the same level in middle school, with the goal of reducing inequity.[48]

A Pathway to Equitable Math Instruction, whose "dedicated partners and collaborating organizations" include the Association of California School Administrators, put out a report alleging that a white supremacy culture exists in math instruction. This report includes suggestions for schools that are based on widely accepted principles, such as encouraging students to "use mistakes as opportunities for learning" and asking instructors to "teach rich, thoughtful, complex mathematics."[49]

Other recommendations in the report, however, sparked controversy across California, such as the call for educators to "dismantle white supremacy culture" in mathematics by creating a goal "that incorporates specific antiracist practices" in math lessons. The framework labels "individualism" and "objectivity" as white supremacy characteristics and argues that educators should "center ethnomathematics" which is defined as the relationship between culture and mathematics. It encourages teachers to "identify and challenge the ways that math is used to uphold capitalist, imperialist, and racist views" and to "expose students to examples of people who have used math as resistance."[50]

The teaching of American History likewise came under fire. Some boards wanted to revamp the history curriculum by adopting the 1619 Project, which was designed to "reframe the country's history." The 1619 Project sets the date of America's founding as 1619, the year the first African slaves arrived in Jamestown, rather than 1776, the year of the Declaration of Independence. Further, the 1619 Project claims that one of the primary reasons the Revolutionary War was fought was "to protect the institution of slavery."[51] In some communities, parents expressed vehement opposition to the 1619 Project, and several history scholars published letters criticizing the accuracy of certain arguments in the work.[52]

More generally, DEI training programs for teachers and students also came under criticism. *The Atlantic* published a story with the subtitle "A curriculum inspired by the Black Lives Matter movement is spreading, raising questions about the line between education and indoctrination." It describes a book read in kindergarten class that shows a devil holding a "contract binding you to whiteness" where you get "stolen land, stolen riches, and special favors, to mess endlessly with the lives of your friends, neighbors, loved ones, and all fellow humans of COLOR, and your soul." One parent who was uncomfortable with this curricular approach said, "They present every issue with such moral certainty—like there is no other viewpoint. And we're definitely seeing this in my daughter. She can make the case for defunding the police, but when I tried to explain to her why someone might have a Blue Lives Matter sign, why some families support the police, she wasn't open to considering that view."[53]

In addition to curriculum related to race, the teaching of sexuality in school has sparked complaint. Parents and school boards grapple with the age at which sexuality should be taught, if at all. There are also differences of opinion regarding transgender bathroom and athletic participation policies.

Even school security policy has become intertwined with race. School Resource Officers (SROs) are sworn law enforcement officials assigned to districts to provide security to public school campuses. While SROs were historically rare, a spate of school shootings prompted the federal government to invest over $1 billion, increasing the penetration of SROs from 1 percent of schools in 1975 to 58 percent in 2018.[54] Some board members and parents view SROs as essential to keeping campuses safe, while others believe that SROs harm students of color, lead to discrimination, and contribute to the fact that minority students experience higher rates of exclusionary discipline and arrest.

Furthermore, districts have vigorously debated the merits and drawbacks of strict zero-tolerance disciplinary policies, including suspension, which disproportionately impact Black students and urban students with low socioeconomic status.[55] Some districts advocate in favor of restorative justice, which emphasizes repair instead of punishment. Others believe that less strict disciplinary policies can make classrooms less conducive to learning and amplify the risk of school violence at a time when it is all too prevalent.

While debates over COVID and DEI are unique to our time, tensions between parental versus government control and curriculum versus indoctrination have existed throughout education history. But something has changed. Boardroom battles seem to be growing louder, more frequent, and more intense. For all the historical parallels that can be drawn between recent sharp contests among parents and boards, there are identifiable factors that exacerbate the discord and make it a very challenging time to be a school board member.

2

EROSION OF TRUST

It is quintessentially American for two individuals, living in the same community, to have dramatically different approaches to education issues. There is nothing more democratic than vigorously debating these differences in a public forum. But over the past decade, these debates have grown more intense and less civil. A root cause is an erosion of trust.

As a school board president in the suburbs of New York City during much of the pandemic, I witnessed many community members in our region speak out against COVID prevention protocols with passion, eloquence, and a genuine concern for the children in their community. Some expressed anger and outrage as local districts complied with the New York State mask mandate. However, at times, heated rhetoric at school board meetings across New York and the country at large has crossed the line of decency.

Responding to out-of-control school board meetings nationwide, the Anti-Defamation League (ADL) released a statement on December 26, 2021, that called out an increase in "threats, harassment, and doxing targeting school board members around the country," the latter being the public posting of names and contact information of individuals without their permission. The release attributes much of the "deteriorating discourse" to individuals who are not members of an extremist group but have strong opinions on the contentious policy debates around COV-ID-19 prevention protocols and CRT.[1]

By no means is it only community members who have a monopoly on poor boardroom decorum, nor is the public comment period the only forum where controversy abounds. Sometimes board members fail to conduct themselves in a professional and civil manner and express inappropriate comments to their community, to administrators, and to each other.

In one example, the members of the Oakley Union School District Board of Education experienced a hot mic moment. Under the impression that they were having a private conversation, they made inappropriate comments about parents in the community who were pressuring them to reopen schools. In response to a disparaging letter from a community member, one board member said, "If you're going to call me out, I'm going to f*** you up." Another said, "They want to pick on us because they want their babysitters back."[2] The incident went viral, prompting the entire board to subsequently resign.

The ADL determined that there were some instances of extremist group involvement in board meetings for the first time in recent American history. The most chilling aspect is evidence of "direct threats" to school board members.[3]

In an ideal world, two individuals with policy differences would approach a debate with the open-minded view that the other person may in fact have good intentions. But lately, individuals on each side of an argument too often believe that those on the other side are intentionally trying to do harm.

To illustrate the point, consider masking policy during the COVID-19 pandemic. In a world where we maintain mutual respect for different viewpoints and understand that individuals may have varied beliefs of what is in the best interest of children, it is perfectly plausible to understand well-intentioned differences of opinion. Some believe that proper masking is beneficial to help prevent the spread of COVID, particularly to help protect children and adults with underlying health issues. Others believe that masking is harmful, because it may contribute to mental health and child development issues. Individuals on both sides could legitimately have the best interest of children at heart but hold different policy views.

Yet in a world where there is an *erosion of trust*, many believe that supporters of mandatory masking policies want to intentionally abuse children, and that those against mandatory masking do not care about harming others in the community. People view each other's intentions as sinister.

What follows is a breakdown of civility, a reliance on conspiracy theories, a blindness to fact, and a lack of hope for a productive resolution. The result is that school board meetings become more difficult to manage and less productive, with battles more commonplace. And we set a bad example for our kids.

Five societal trends that this chapter will discuss have helped fuel an erosion of trust:

1. Societal polarization and anti-institutionalism;
2 School board meetings going viral;
3. Social media connecting like-minded people across the country;
4. The shift from local news to national news;
5. Influence of outside money.

These forces collectively have contributed to a "delocalization" of school board governance. Boardrooms are becoming more influenced by regional and national forces. The book *Outside Money in School Board Elections* by Jeffrey Henig, Rebecca Jacobsen, and Sarah Reckhow appropriately describes this dynamic as the "nationalization of local education politics."[4]

There is a new realization that local participants in the board governance process can help shape the national agenda and vice versa. Not long ago, several layers of insulation existed between school boards and broader national trends. Local news outlets covered school board meetings. Elections were community affairs. School boards had broad decision-making authority when it came to their own district.

Now, local, regional, and national issues are highly intertwined, resulting in the following dynamic: What happens in the school boardroom has the risk of spreading to the entire country instantaneously, and what happens in the rest of the country can easily penetrate the boardroom.

SOCIETAL POLARIZATION AND ANTI-INSTITUTIONALISM HAVE BECOME MORE PREVALENT

We are living during a time in which intense polarization has become commonplace. A recent study conducted by the Carnegie Endowment for International Peace attempts to measure "pernicious" levels of partisan polarization (defined as "the division of society into mutually distrustful political camps in which political identity becomes a social identity") by analyzing data since 1950.[5]

Using a five-point scale, with zero representing very little polarization and 4 representing the most extreme polarization, the United States historically matched the average level of polarization in the rest of the world, scoring about a 2.0. By 2020, the world average rose to 2.4, and the U.S. level rose to 3.8. The U.S. score was even more of an outlier when compared to full democracies, with the study's authors sadly concluding, "The United States stands out today as the only wealthy Western democracy with persistent levels of pernicious polarization."[6]

The pandemic seems to have further exacerbated the divide. A recent Pew Research Center poll showed that 77 percent of Americans said the country was more divided than before COVID-19, compared to a median of 47 percent in the thirteen other surveyed nations.[7]

We see clear evidence of this polarization in our national politics. In 2020, only Maine voters split their ticket across the presidential and Senate races.[8] Political gerrymandering in red and blue states alike has contributed to candidates in House races who are more worried about primaries than general elections. Candidates appeal to the extreme left and the extreme right, ignoring more moderate voters in the center.[9]

Increasingly, there is less desire to compromise, and bridging our divides seems out of reach. Divisions in the boardroom go well beyond ideological polarization to affective polarization, which occurs when members of a political party distrust those from the other party. Individuals hold strong views on groups themselves, not just their underlying policy preferences.[10] According to Pew, a month before the 2020 election, roughly eight in ten registered Republican and Democratic voters characterized their differences with the other side as about "core American values," and roughly nine in ten worried that an election loss would result in "lasting harm" to the country.[11] A 2016 survey found that 60 percent of Democrats and 63 percent of Republicans do not want their child marrying a spouse in a different political party.[12]

Polarization has seeped into public education. While the level of satisfaction with U.S. education used to be quite similar between Democrats and Republicans, survey results have more recently diverged. According to Gallup's 2022 survey, 51 percent of Democrats, or those who lean Democrat, report being "completely" or "somewhat satisfied," compared to only 30 percent of those who are Republican or lean Republican.[13]

In addition to polarization, Americans have become increasingly skeptical of our nation's institutions, with 57 percent of respondents in a 2021 survey that includes a cross section of the U.S. population describing "public confidence in civic institutions" as declining. Additionally, only 28 percent of respondents said they trust their state government, only 19 percent trust the federal government, and only 22 percent trust broadcast media outlets.[14]

Public education has not eluded these strong anti-institutional forces. In the past, local public schools were somewhat shielded. No longer. According to the results of Gallup's "Confidence in Institutions" poll conducted annually, confidence in public schools has been falling over the past fifty years. In 1975, 62 percent of respondents reported having a "great deal" or "quite a lot" of confidence in public schools. In 2022, only 28 percent of respondents fall into that same category.[15] Sadly, a PDK poll found that just 37 percent report wanting their child to become a public school teacher in their community, down from 75 percent in 1969.[16]

School boards, serving as the local epicenter of public education governance, have become a lightning rod for affective polarization and anti-institutional sentiment, both of which contribute to an erosion of trust between school districts and the public.

SCHOOL BOARD MEETINGS GO VIRAL

Not long ago, if there was an inflammatory comment or heated exchange at a local school board meeting, it is likely that few people beyond those present in the boardroom would find out about it. While school board meetings are designed to provide transparency to the community, there may have been a story in the local newspaper, or it might have been a topic of conversation on the supermarket line, but there was a limit to how far news would travel.

Now, this transparency extends to the entire world. Any given moment of a school board meeting could potentially end up on social media, quickly garnering hundreds of thousands of viewers across the country and around the world. Furthermore, this viral distribution engine has the potential to work quickly, in a matter of days, hours, or even minutes. The video clip could also end up as a lead cable news story, being broadcast to a large audience nationwide.

The stakes have risen for school board members and community members alike. Literally every word and facial expression during a public meeting may be posted in perpetuity for the world to see. Here are some examples:

- 4.9 million views of a teacher's resignation submitted to the Grosse Pointe, Michigan Board of Education;[17]
- 2.7 million views of a disorderly meeting at the Caldwell School District in Idaho;[18]
- 2.0 million views of the Oakley Union Elementary School District (California) Board of Trustees "hot mic" moment;[19]
- 1.5 million views of a father speaking out at the Cabarrus County School Board meeting in North Carolina;[20]
- 1.5 million views of a community member addressing the board regarding library books they deem to be inappropriate in Cherokee County, Georgia.[21]

In some cases, individuals may intentionally use the public comment period to incite controversy that can later be posted on YouTube or similar sites, drawing attention and publicity to their cause.

Whether intentional "gotcha!" moments or not, these episodes can prove uncomfortable for all involved. In the Cherokee County, Georgia, video aired on Fox News, a mother starts reading from a book during a public comment period that she does not think is appropriate for the school library. The school board president tries to stop her, stating, "Excuse me, we have children at home. It's live streaming. And it's really not appropriate for you to read that," to which the community member responds, "Don't you find the irony in that? You're saying exactly what I'm telling you."[22] Regardless of each participant's intentions, indisputable is the fact that the ability to live stream a local board meeting—potentially to the entire world—ups the ante on the potential consequences and makes it more difficult to focus on building trust locally with one another.

SOCIAL MEDIA SITES CONNECT LIKE-MINDED PEOPLE

Because school board politics have always been local, individuals with opposing viewpoints serendipitously meet across the community at local events such as the high school football game or the Parent-Teacher Association (PTA) meeting. Differences have typically been hashed out face-to-face. In many communities, that continues to happen, only now with a difference. Courtesy of social media, it is increasingly the case that an individual is expressing opinions reflective of and shaped by a large and not always local group of like-minded people.

Forums on social media provide an alternative platform for community members to debate and discuss issues. Most communities have unofficial networks on Facebook or other social media platforms where individuals express opinions on the state of district affairs. At their best, these sites allow for the sharing of accurate information and provide opportunities for engagement, debate, and interconnectedness. At their worst, these sites can spread misinformation, can be infiltrated by trolls, and can provide a forum for irresponsible discourse that spirals out of control. After all, it is easier to say something hurtful on social media than it is to say it to somebody's face.

Districts struggle over what to do when they see misinformation spread. If a board member or district official steps in to correct a misstatement, what happens the next time if they don't notice a misstatement or if a legal issue prevents them from intervening? Will their silence be interpreted as confirmatory? It's a slippery slope to respond and set a precedent, even though it is painful to ignore rumors and misinformation.

The proliferation of social media has also created an additional complexity. Board members themselves may have digital footprints on social media, and the line between personal and school district business continues to be more precisely defined. During the 2023–2024 term, the U.S. Supreme Court considered *O'Connor-Ratcliff v. Garnier*, a case in which two California school board members wrote posts related to district business on their personal Facebook pages and used blocking features to delete comments and block future comments. A lower court found that these school board members were "state actors" engaging in "viewpoint discrimination."[23] The Supreme Court vacated the judgment and remanded the case to the U.S. Court of Appeals for the Ninth Circuit for further review, taking into account the related Supreme Court decision in *Lindke v. Freed.*[24]

In the *Lindke v. Freed* case, Freed, the city manager of Port Huron, Michigan, was accused by Lindke of acting in his official capacity when he silenced Lindke's speech on social media. The Supreme Court recognized that government officials sometimes "use social media for personal communication, official communication, or both—and the line between the two is often blurred." In delivering the opinion for the Court, Justice Amy Coney Barrett wrote that "such speech is attributable to the State only if the official (1) possessed actual authority to speak on the State's behalf, and (2) purported to exercise that authority when he spoke on social media."[25] Judges must look at the specific facts and circumstances of each case mapped against this two-pronged approach.

Even when board members post on social media in their capacity as private citizens on issues completely unrelated to school district business, the public doesn't always appreciate the distinction. Posts viewed by members of the community as controversial could have a direct impact on the individual board member and on the district overall.

Another byproduct of social media is the ability to connect like-minded individuals across communities seamlessly. Instead of individuals in the same community who think differently spending time with each other, citizens have the option to live in a virtual world surrounded by people who think the same way. Individuals with similar views *across* localities can share information, coordinate actions, and try to effect change.

Through these connections that span different geographies, the new media landscape not only has made it easier for what happens in the boardroom to be broadly distributed to the world, but also has enabled outsiders to influence a local school district.

Regardless of your politics, from far left to far right, you can find a social media group or website that shares your views. You are no longer limited to the confines of the public square on Main Street. Now, you can develop a specific world view and interact with the horizontal slice of America that agrees with you. The web can serve to reinforce your ideology instead of challenging it. By interacting in an echo chamber, outsiders can help you develop a roadmap of how to change your community. Consider the curious case of surety bonds.

On January 18, 2022, at a Wake County School District Board of Education meeting in North Carolina, a community member stood at the podium during the public comment period and outlined a series of demands, including the immediate cessation of the mask mandate and COVID PCR testing, the parental right to review and approve all curriculum materials, and the return of federal Elementary and Secondary School Emergency Relief Fund (ESSER) money.

School districts get sued frequently for a host of reasons including the provision of special education services, bullying incidents, and employment issues. Board members are sometimes named as part of a suit. But in Wake County, a community member referenced something more out of the ordinary: "I am here to inform you of the 26 laws that you, every single one of you, have violated. Both state, federal, and international laws . . . a public official bond is a type of surety bond . . . requiring faithful performance, fidelity, and integrity of a public official's duties to the public. . . . I along with other parents are serving each one of you a letter of intent *to file a public official surety liability claim*" [my emphasis].[26]

A parent threatening "to file a public official surety liability claim" was not an everyday occurrence. Yet this threat wasn't isolated to Wake County.

A few weeks later, during the February 8 public comment period at the Elmhurst Community Unit School District 205 in Illinois, an impassioned community member made their way to the podium and explained how masking was leading to behavioral problems and anxiety, then referred to the same strategy of filing a surety bond claim that arose at the Wake County meeting. "This has infuriated me for a long time . . . screw this . . . why are you indoctrinating all of our children? You need to stop it. And you, *I have sent you a FOIA [Freedom of Information Act] request for your surety bond. People need to look up what we can do when we put a claim against your surety bond and I'm starting that process now. . . . Once we put a claim against your surety bond, you cannot ever run again* [my emphasis]."[27]

On the same evening, just over eight hundred miles away, there was a heated public comment session at the Chesterfield County School Board meeting in Virginia. Local media reported that a group of parents announced a plan to file claims with the surety bond company unless the district removed materials that parents deem inappropriate, amended the transgender bathroom policy, and eliminated COVID prevention protocols. One community member stated, "I'm here to publicly serve the board this *notice of intent to file a claim* against your risk management plan" [my emphasis].[28]

The following week, at the Ankeny Board of Education meeting in Iowa, a similar speech was made:

I'm here to serve you all a notice of cease and desist. This letter is to serve you due to policies, regulations and mandates that you are in violation of regarding constitutional law, oath of office, Iowa Code for Public Health, FDA, HIPA, Nuremberg Code, segregation, disabilities medical and mental, discrimination based on color, religion, and gender, child abuse, sexual abuse, as well as the Iowa state and US Constitution. . . . *You guys are required to have bonds. I have a letter from a lawyer that says you are not bonded. If you are not bonded, you can't be on a board* [my emphasis]. I've done FOIA requests. By law you need to give me your bond information . . . I will have the sheriff remove you all.[29]

Seemingly out of nowhere, in early 2022 this unusual pattern emerged during the public comment period in boardrooms across the country. Community members expressed their discontent by putting their local school board on notice that if certain demands were not met, usually relating to curriculum issues and COVID-19 protocols, then they would file a claim against board members' surety bonds for the many laws that they allegedly violated. Ultimately, these community members' goal was for the board member to be removed from office, either prompted by the surety bond provider or for their own fear of personal liability.

This approach is outlined at BondsForTheWin.com, a website designed to mobilize a national effort to fight school boards. Accessible to any citizen with internet access, it provides a step-by-step guide to teach parents how to influence their local school board.[30]

Bonds for the Win instructs community members to follow three steps. First, obtain the school board member's surety bond and oath of office. Second, serve the school board member with a Letter of Intent that if demands are not met within a certain timeframe, a claim will be filed against that member's surety bond. Third, develop a list of violations that will form the basis of the claim, such as the member breaching their oath of office by violating the Geneva Protocol (a treaty prohibiting the use of biological weapons believed relevant due to asphyxiation from mandatory masking), abusing power by acting without authority (Color of Law or Color of Office: Section 1983), or violating the Nuremberg Code.[31]

It is true that in some states school board members have surety bonds. However, according to a report by NBC News, insurance companies and the FBI have stated that Bonds for the Win's claims are "not legitimate."[32] That didn't stop individuals across the country from attempting to threaten and intimidate board members with this approach.

Another website, SchoolBoardWatchlist.org, is a project of Turning Point USA, a 501(c)3 organization with a mission of "Exposing radical and false ideologies endorsed by school boards and pushed in the classroom." The organization "finds and exposes school board leadership that supports anti-American, radical, hateful, immoral, and racist teachings in their districts, such as CRT, the 1619 Project, sexual/gender ideology, and more." The website explains the purpose of its watchlist:

School boards across the country hold a massive sway over the education of our children and the future of our country. For too long, they have operated silently under the radar, with no organization holding them accountable for their actions. Turning Point USA's latest initiative, the School Board Watchlist, works tirelessly to fight the corruption and blatant indoctrination of our children occurring in our K-12 public education system. . . . In short, school boards determine how our children's minds will be shaped—and by whom and with what. The School Board Watchlist is at the frontlines in the battle to reclaim our schools.[33]

The School Board Watchlist website provides a list of what it deems to be the "most radical board members." It highlights district controversies and provides direct contact information. In addition, a guide is posted that provides pointers on how to speak up at board meetings, encouraging parents to play a vocal role in the process.[34]

Another website, No Left Turn in Education, is focused on preserving parental rights. Here is an excerpt from their materials:

For years, school boards have enjoyed unconditional trust from the parents and the public in general. In fact, most were uninformed about school boards (composed of local elected officials) or understood the direct impact they have on our daily lives . . . The public now realizes that our local school boards have in fact a great impact on our lives and the well-being of our communities.

Left unchecked, many of these entities have imposed rules, regulations, and curricula on the schools with no regard to the wishes of the communities they serve. They have acted with little transparency, disregarding the values of their constituencies to foist their own on the students, all the while minimizing the primary role of parents in their children's education.[35]

Moms for Liberty, an organization formed to defend parental rights, also has received significant press coverage. It was founded by two former Florida school board members who believe that the line between parental and school district authority has blurred.[36] The organization has built a nationwide network with 195 chapters across 37 states and has garnered support from political leaders including Florida governor Ron DeSantis.[37]

Other groups work to help create and strengthen the pipeline of conservative school board candidates. Citizens for Renewing America is one such organization.[38]

Parents Defending Education is another organization trying to fight against what they deem to be "indoctrination" in the classroom and schools that have "ideologically driven curriculum" trying to divide children into "oppressors" and "oppressed." They publish guides that explain parental rights, including how to utilize public comment periods and the open meeting laws.[39]

While the organizations previously mentioned are generally conservative, progressives have also created national resources aimed at influencing school boards. According to a May 31, 2022 National Public Radio piece titled "Progressives Take a Leaf out of the Conservative Playbook to Target School Boards," the group Run for Something focuses on recruiting and training progressives and liberals to run for school boards, providing funding and resources.[40] Another organization, Red, Wine & Blue, is a left-leaning national effort that has featured Julia Louis-Dreyfus and Amy Schumer. Their goal is to distribute a "parent playbook" regarding school boards, and they host sessions to teach people how to run for school board seats.[41]

In Florida, two mothers started the Florida Freedom to Read Project to fight against book banning. They have endorsed school board candidates as a key strategy. One thousand miles north, in Fishkill, New York, two mothers started Defense of Democracy, supporting school board candidates who favor diversity programs, transgender accommodations, and books regarding LGBTQ issues.[42]

As many special interest groups harness the power of the internet and social media, their efforts to raise school board awareness, impact school board elections, and provide tools to influence school board decision-making contribute to the rising number of boardroom battles. They also underscore the trend that what happens in the boardroom not only can quickly spread to the rest of the country, but also the rest of the country can more easily make its way into the boardroom.

THE SHIFTING MEDIA LANDSCAPE HAS FURTHER NATIONALIZED THE NEWS

Historically, local newspapers have been a place where school board elections and decision-making were covered with some degree of journalistic integrity and, as important, extensive familiarity with the community. However, the local newspaper business lacks the breadth and resources it once enjoyed. Newspaper industry advertising revenue has fallen from $44 billion in 2002 to just under $10 billion in 2022.[43] The number of newspaper newsroom employees has dropped from 71,070 to 30,820 between 2008 and 2020.[44] These reduced staffing levels have led to declines in coverage and reader trust and interest, further propelling a cycle of disinvestment.

Does it really matter if newspapers disappear or no longer have the same resources to provide comprehensive local news coverage? The MacArthur Foundation believes that the decline in local news is "inextricably connected" to problems such as low turnout in elections, increasing partisanship, a lack of consensus regarding "facts and science," and reduced levels of civic engagement. On its webpage, the foundation highlights how one-fifth of Americans reside in "news deserts" and that many other communities have at-risk news sources. The lack of local news is particularly acute in poorer communities, and the local newsrooms that do exist do not always reflect the diversity of the local population.[45]

Consistent with the MacArthur Foundation thesis, research conducted by Meghan Rubado and Jay Jennings shows that a reduction in local newspaper staffing is associated with mayoral elections that have lower voter turnout and fewer candidates.[46] Another group of researchers found that without local news coverage, voters become less likely to split their vote between two parties in presidential and senatorial elections.[47] With more reliance on national news sources, including cable and digital media, there is increased likelihood of high exposure to partisan conflict, disengagement from local democratic life rises, and achieving local accountability is more challenging.[48]

An analysis by Lee Shaker of newspaper closures in Seattle and Denver suggests that the demise of a local newspaper leads to lower levels of civic engagement.[49] Another study by Pengjie Gao, Chang Lee, and Dermot Murphy found that newspaper closures may have negative financial consequences for local government, including less efficiency, a larger tax burden per capita, higher deficits, and up to an eleven basis point increase in borrowing costs.[50]

Local TV stations, another historical source of local news, have also consolidated. In 2004, twelve companies owned 304 TV stations, rising to 589 stations by 2014.[51]

When local news disappears, citizens turn to national media sources. Cable news and internet access have been shown to contribute to social polarization and sorting. As interest in national news grows at the expense of local news, it becomes more difficult to find information regarding specific local issues. Furthermore, national media exposure has been shown to change opinions on local elections even if the specific local elections are not directly covered.[52]

During the pandemic, cable news media covered school board controversies more frequently.[53] Additionally, websites and social media play a more central role in local news.[54] Online media sources often do not substitute for traditional local news since their content is not always locally sourced and investigated using journalistic standards. There are some national education online news services, but they often skew toward serving education professionals with universal topics of interest rather than local community coverage.

The demise of newspapers and the rise in cable news and the internet have profoundly influenced school boards by changing the nature of how they connect with the outside world.

OUTSIDE MONEY INFLUENCES LOCAL RACES

Another highly publicized factor since the pandemic has been a rise in the number of political action committees (PACs) that are donating to school board races. The political right is particularly active. The 1776 Project PAC raised $437,000 during the second and third quarter of 2021 to support fifty races.[55] Their website explains their mission, which includes fighting against CRT and DEI and promoting parental rights and academic accountability. They also actively endorse school board candidates.[56] The PAC announced on Twitter that from November 2021 to November 2022, they flipped 100 school board seats, proclaiming, "the parents revolution is winning across the country."[57]

Patriot Mobile, a wireless provider promoting Christian and conservative values, created Patriot Mobile Action PAC and has spent over $600,000 on school board races in the Fort Worth suburbs. At the Conservative Political Action Conference, the group reported how they fought for eleven seats and managed to take over four boards in an election cycle. Their mission is to bring conservative values back to school and to fight against "woke" ideologies and "political agendas" and ban books they deem to be socially inappropriate. According to *NBC News*, they have expressed ambition to expand across the nation. They hired GOP consulting firms that worked on the Ted Cruz senate and Glenn Youngkin gubernatorial campaigns, "bringing sophisticated national-level political strategies to local school board races."[58]

Historically, foundations and wealthy individuals focused on reforming public schools have made outsized contributions to local races to influence policy, particularly to support pro-charter school candidates. Just as the Supreme Court's *Citizens United v. Federal Election Commission* decision facilitated corporate and union money flowing into federal and state political contests, school board races were impacted as well. In five districts analyzed in the book *Outside Money in School Board Elections*, 22 percent of all dollars given to school board candidates by individuals were from out-of-state.[59]

Money flowed across state lines from individuals closely aligned on philosophy and typically connected through service on boards such as the New School Venture Fund and Teach for America. For example, Michael

Bloomberg committed $1 million to the 2013 Los Angeles Unified School District school board race.[60] These large donors generally leaned Democrat, but it should be noted that their views on education policy diverged from pro-union Democrats since many of them supported reform efforts that unions opposed, including accountability measures.

In addition to individuals, organizations are important donors. While they are fewer in number, their donations were found on average to be comparatively 125 times larger. Though it is sometimes difficult to determine the geographic base of these organizations, one analysis of fourteen elections suggests that 42 percent of organizations that donated to school board races were from outside the district.[61] Finally, unions fund campaigns of individual board members. For example, in 2017, the National Education Association (NEA) Advocacy Fund spent $950,000 on state and local races.[62]

Outside Money in School Board Elections persuasively argues that in addition to national issues becoming a more important component of local races, outside money is increasingly becoming a factor.[63] While still a highly local undertaking, school board members now work on an ever more national stage. And while just a few short decades ago the most important factor was the trust shared among neighbors and parents who had the best interests of their children in mind, outside influences, whether via social media or campaign funding, have become increasingly relevant.

Taken together, these five societal trends have eroded trust in school districts and have made it more difficult for school board members to govern. As if navigating these trends isn't enough, school board members have an additional challenge. While they perform a function very similar to corporate and nonprofit boards, they must follow specific rules regarding transparency, further amplifying their role as lightning rods for public controversy.

3

THE FISHBOWL

In August 2021, the late summer air was filled with the usual frenzy of the back-to-school season. As a school board member, I found much of it familiar. The beginning of a new school year brings responsibility and excitement, including updates on summer capital projects and assurances that the buildings and grounds are student-ready. Board members determine a set of annual goals that will help prioritize initiatives and provide organizational focus.

But this year was different in my region and across the country. Still in the midst of the pandemic, the country was engaged in an intense and divisive discussion regarding COVID prevention protocols, a difficult topic riddled with evolving science and a heavy dose of politics.

On the last day of that August, as board president I presided over a meeting before an audience full of parents expressing deeply felt concerns about the way in which COVID prevention protocols were impacting their children. They were passionate, determined, and they were not happy with the situation.

As I listened to them speak, I thought about how different serving on a school board is compared to the other boards on which I serve, including a hospital board, a nonprofit board, and a private company board.

Without a doubt, boards of all types of organizations faced challenges navigating COVID-19. The pandemic brought difficult and sometimes contentious policy decisions. Hospitals were particularly challenged to navigate an operational nightmare. Closure for even a day was simply not an option, and patients and staff were directly in harm's way. Medical supplies were limited. Before it became clear that the government planned to provide support, most hospitals experienced a substantial revenue decline. Staff members were stretched, and labor shortages made it difficult to hire more people.

Yet when you turned on the news during COVID, while there were stories about the hospital front lines, it was rare to hear anything about high-stakes hospital boardroom drama. Despite hospital boards making consequential, life-and-death decisions that had implications for the communities they served, they got virtually no coverage compared to school boards. Why such a difference?

School boards are designed to conduct their business with a high degree of transparency. Meetings are purposeful forums to air policy differences publicly. The public can attend board meetings and speak directly to board members before votes are cast. Speakers during the public comment period can say almost anything they want. Citizens can look board members in the eye. This helps facilitate direct communication channels with the public. News reports and videos of angry citizens voicing their concerns to school boards are so common we can forget how *un*common a practice it is.

On corporate and nonprofit boards, decisions most often get made without constituents in the room when deliberations take place, and sometimes with limited stakeholder input. There is latitude for corporate and nonprofit board members to debate contentious issues behind closed doors or to build consensus prior to a public meeting. Sensitive issues can be handled delicately and discretely. Most boards conduct as much business outside of the boardroom as they do inside. The CEO or chairperson fields phone calls and builds consensus before a meeting even takes place.

School boards do not have this luxury. To accomplish the goal of transparency, school boards have a different set of rules and structural characteristics from other types of boards. The textbook definition of a "fishbowl" is "a place or condition that affords no privacy."[1] School boards are intentionally designed to be just that. Though meeting minutes are a general requirement for most governance boards, school board transparency rises to a different level. With a few narrow exceptions for items such as ongoing litigation, contract negotiations, or disciplinary action regarding a specific student or employee, open meeting laws dictate stringent requirements for full transparency. Business is conducted in front of community members, and meetings are either live streamed, televised, or recorded and archived on the district's website for anyone to view.

Harvard Business School Professor Linda Hill and George Davis, an executive, interviewed corporate board members about innovation. They observed that "many board members reported a reluctance to ask their most-pressing questions, because they don't want to be perceived as 'micromanaging' or 'second-guessing management' or as criticizing the CEO in front of his or her team."[2] Imagine the dilemma a school board member faces when they want to question the school district superintendent but know their conversation will be visible to the general public, perhaps even ending up on YouTube or cable news.

There are some additional key differences between school boards and other types of boards that contribute to the uniqueness of school board-room battles and heated exchanges. School board meetings most often occur at night, which can be particularly taxing and exhausting for board members and community participants who work a full-time job or manage a household or both. Tensions often run high at ten o'clock in the evening when school board meeting participants have been up for sixteen hours and still have to run home to put their kids to bed.

Another difference in public school board structure is the board member recruitment and selection process. Nonprofits and private corporations have nominating committees that often handpick board members, a process that allows the existing board to maintain control of board composition. Public company nominating committees generally work behind the scenes to make interim appointments or identify suitable candidates, including those with skill sets that the current board may be lacking. While public company shareholders elect board members and activist shareholders can have tremendous influence, in most circumstances, existing public company board members maintain some semblance of control.

By comparison, public school board members have no substantive control over which candidates file petitions, campaign, and ultimately

Table 3.1   Comparison across different types of boards

	Public companies	Private companies and nonprofits	Public school districts
Typical meeting time	Day	Day/Sometimes night (for certain nonprofits)	Most often at night
Transparency	Minutes	Minutes	Live streamed, or video is made available via the web after the meeting
Control over new board member selection	Medium	High	Minimal

seek votes from the community. Table 3.1 compares school boards to corporate and nonprofit boards.

PUBLIC COMMENT PERIOD

Perhaps the most distinct feature of a public school board meeting is the public comment period. You don't have to look very far to find poignant examples of inflammatory public comment periods. A casual observer of school board meetings may find the public comment period perplexing, and many participants find it deeply frustrating.

The public comment period traditionally is not the place for debate or two-way dialogue, even though many wish it were. Simply put, it is a forum for the public to state concerns and viewpoints and the board to listen. The experience can be deeply unsatisfying for a community member who wants to elicit an immediate response from the school board. On the other hand, it is understandably difficult for board members, most of whom are volunteers, to listen to rhetoric that at times may be inflammatory or false. Board members also struggle at times because they may want to respond but are constrained by protocol.

Citizens often take the public comment period for granted, mistakenly thinking that it is constitutionally protected. The public is always entitled to attend board meetings, but the right of the public to speak at the meeting varies by state statute. Some states make the public comment period mandatory, some make it mandatory for certain defined matters such as a budget hearing, and others leave it up to the district to decide.[3] But whether a public comment period is codified in law or not is overshadowed by the fact that it is steeped in tradition, and its elimination would be met with resistance in the court of public opinion.

As a technical matter, when a school board allows the public to comment, it creates a "designated public forum," which means the public generally has the right to speak. The board may place reasonable restrictions as to the time, place, and manner of the speech, but these rules must be enforced consistently and without bias. The board cannot restrict viewpoints or discriminate against speakers for their view. Abiding by a consistent set of rules is of tantamount importance.[4]

When boards start to treat citizens differently and fail to uphold content neutrality, there are repercussions.[5] A New Jersey parent was given the gavel just thirty seconds into his negative comments about a particular athletic coach. Other speakers during the same public comment period exceeded the five-minute per speaker allotment. Though the board stated that personnel matters were not to be discussed during the public comment period, in practice the district had permitted positive feedback regarding personnel. The New Jersey Supreme Court confirmed the school board's ability to institute content-neutral restrictions (such as a consistent time limit) as long as other channels, such as emailing the board, remain open. However, treating disagreeable speakers differently is expressly forbidden, with the only exception being if the restriction meets the threshold of a "significant governmental interest."[6]

Sometimes individuals use a public comment period to speak about the latitude they have as citizens to express their view. A former board member of the Pennsbury School District in Pennsylvania used the public comment period to address the current board: "You snowflakes apparently have a bigger problem with public comment . . . I've got news for you, school board president Benito Mussolini. Your power does not supersede that of the U.S. Constitution and the First Amendment rights of the citizens of this great nation. . . . I don't have to be nice to you."[7]

He went on to cite the landmark 1964 U.S. Supreme Court decision *New York Times Co. v. Sullivan*. In this opinion, the Supreme Court stated that the justices considered this case "against the background of a profound national commitment to the principle that debate on public issues should be uninhibited, robust, and wide-open, and that it may well include vehement, caustic, and sometimes unpleasantly sharp attacks on government and public officials." A public official could succeed in a libel suit against the press only if statements are false and are made with "actual malice," or the knowledge that it is false at the time, and the burden of proof is on the public figure.[8]

OPEN MEETING LAWS

Open meeting laws, or sunshine laws, provide the U.S. media and the public access to meetings of government agencies. These laws were not always in place, and they cannot be found in the Constitution or the Bill of Rights. In fact, in seventeenth- and eighteenth-century England, revealing the substance of debates in Parliament was punishable. Even as recently as 1950, no state had an open meetings statute except Alabama. Yet by 1976, all fifty states had statutes applying to state and local government bodies making it mandatory to meet in public. Statutes also typically require a meeting notification requirement. Furthermore, the public has the right to obtain copies of government records. Certain exceptions, including issues regarding certain employee matters, student disciplinary matters, union negotiations, and litigation, can be discussed in an executive session so long as the public is made aware of the general topic.[9]

Open meeting laws prevent school boards from conducting business outside of the boardroom. If a quorum of the board meets at a school concert, they cannot sit next to each other with the intent of discussing or debating district business. Over time, case law has shed light on what this means in practice, particularly considering technological advances.[10] The full board cannot conduct business by deliberating or discussing issues electronically. Regular email correspondence that does not constitute deliberation is traditionally permitted, though it is subject to a FOIA request by the public. Statutes vary by state. For example, Connecticut's FOIA defines "meeting" to include "any communication by or to a quorum of a multimember public agency, whether in person or by means of electronic equipment, to discuss or act upon a matter over which the public agency has supervision, control, jurisdiction, or advisory power."[11]

Another point that has been adjudicated is whether the superintendent can meet with subgroups of the board in rapid succession to avoid triggering a quorum. State courts have ruled differently, and the facts and circumstances of each case, including intent, becomes critical.[12]

True in nearly all instances is that board members carry an explicit responsibility to follow state law and conduct business in a manner that allows for citizens to comment and observe.

SCHOOL BOARD RESPONSIBILITIES

Though open meeting laws and public comment period give school boards a different feel from boards in the for-profit and nonprofit sectors and at times make serving on a school board particularly challenging, school board members have similar roles and responsibilities to those on the board of any organization.

The pandemic made especially visible the pivotal role that boards play in adjudicating school district decision-making. Boards are responsible for hiring, managing, and firing the superintendent, the day-to-day chief executive of the school district. Boards set wide ranging district policy. They adopt textbooks and approve curriculum. They approve material contracts and ratify personnel changes, including tenure decisions. They set district goals and overall strategy. They embark on capital projects, such as building additions or new school buildings, and determine school closures. They draw attendance boundaries within the district. School districts either determine the budget or propose a budget to be approved by voters or the town or county boards. Boards also ensure the district's facilities are adequate and provide oversight of safety and security protocols. The board can only act as a group.

These wide-ranging responsibilities help explain why when someone is unhappy with district policy or when something goes terribly wrong in a school district, community members reflexively turn to the board of education and hold school board members accountable. Recent notable examples include:

- After a fourteen-year-old girl in New Jersey was tragically bullied and committed suicide, her father called for the "whole school board gone."[13]

- In Virginia, when a six-year-old shot his teacher, community members told the board that "trust has been lost," that the board was at fault for not having a stricter disciplinary policy, and its members should resign.[14]
- After the Uvalde, Texas, mass shooting, community members called for the school board to resign. During the public comment period, comments included: "Our babies are dead. Our teachers are dead." "You are not going to sweep this under the rug. All of you are accountable."[15]

In tragic situations, discussion and debate in boardrooms not only focus on accountability but also on important policy issues to prevent future tragedies. Behind questions of accountability and policy, of course, stands another question: what is the extent of school board power?

Political scientists classify school boards as a special-purpose government entity. Said another way, they differ from general government bodies responsible for a broad range of services from healthcare to public safety to zoning to infrastructure. While the board is the only local school district governance authority (as opposed to a county, state, or federal government with a legislative, executive, and judicial branch), its power is limited by highly prescriptive statutes, regulations, and boundaries set by the state.

To understand how school boards derive their power, it is important to first understand that school districts are autonomous corporate entities. Ninety percent of districts are legally and politically independent of general-purpose local governments such as counties or municipalities, and approximately 80 percent have distinct boundaries, not always following town boundaries.[16]

School districts have the power to execute contracts and sue. School districts can also be the subject of a lawsuit, though depending on the state, some degree of sovereign immunity may narrow the circumstances in which they can be sued. They are also a public body of government with the power to issue municipal bonds, and they are responsible for adhering to constitutional constraints such as freedom of speech and due process.[17]

Most school boards have five or seven members, though the average number of board members per district by state ranges from three to ten. Most board trustees are elected, although a minority of boards function by appointment.[18] Board terms range, but according to a National School Boards Association survey, the average is approximately four years.[19]

Board members confront a tension between the traditional role of a school board and the more recent rise in central government power that has encroached on their authority. While the allocation of responsibilities to boards and state government used to be quite clear, states and the federal government have become increasingly more active in micromanaging districts. This shifting power distribution has had consequences, most obviously in the blurring of lines denoting where power and responsibility lie. In chapter 4 we turn to exploring these blurring lines, which at times causes confusion and frustration, exacerbating battles in the boardroom.

4

BLURRY LINES

School boards differ from municipal or county-level government. School districts derive their power from the state, and in most states, the concept of "home rule" does not apply.[1] Providing a free secular education is embedded in most state constitutions or is mandated statutorily at the state level. Board members are *state* officers, and they must follow *state* law and mandates. They take an oath of office to uphold the *state* constitution upon getting elected. According to Jon Wiles and Joseph Bondi's book *The School Board Primer*, "District school boards are part of the machinery of state government, and their powers may be enlarged, diminished, modified, or revoked at the pleasure of the [state] legislature."[2] What that means in practice is most parents miss an essential component of how to assess a potential neighborhood's public schools.

I am no different. Following the birth of our third child in 2009, my wife and I decided to move from an urban community to the suburbs. As we searched for a place to live, school district quality was a priority.

We were hardly unique. According to the National Association of Realtors, 53 percent of all homebuyers with children under age eighteen view school district quality as an important factor when purchasing a home.[3] A Brookings Institution study analyzing the 100 largest metro areas found that the cost of housing is 2.4 times higher in areas with high-performing public schools.[4]

We evaluated several districts in New Jersey and New York. We toured school buildings and spoke with district leaders. We looked at recent educational outcomes data. We assessed the quality of school leadership and the degree of community involvement.

In retrospect, we conducted a perfectly thorough due diligence process if we were in nineteenth-century America, but for the twenty-first century, we missed the mark. To compare school districts across two states we should have extended our analysis well beyond the local district. To truly understand differences between an educational experience in a New York and a New Jersey public school, we should have reached out to education committee members of the state legislature. We should have had conversations with the governors at the time, Chris Christie in New Jersey and David Paterson in New York. We should have spoken with the New Jersey State Board of Education and the New York State Board of Regents.

Although this ideal due diligence clearly wasn't possible for us, or any parents, for that matter, it would have emphasized the fact that states have broad authority when it comes to education. While forty-nine states (with Hawaii being the one exception) choose to delegate power to local school boards, each state retains ultimate authority.[5] All states have some type of chief school officer, usually with the title of commissioner or state superintendent. Thirteen states elect individuals to this position, while the remainder are appointed.[6]

Court cases have reinforced state power. In 1957, the Oregon State Supreme Court ruling in the case of *Monaghan v. School District No. 1* stated, "Education is a function or duty not regarded as a local matter. It is a governmental obligation of the state. Few of our administrative agencies are creatures of organic law. But, as to schools, the constitution mandates the legislature to provide by law 'for the establishment of a uniform and general system of Common schools.' It is a sovereign power and cannot be bartered away." The opinion goes on to say that "A school district, as a legislatively created entity, enjoys closer proximation to the state than to the community it serves."[7] In essence, the state has the power but delegates certain responsibilities to local district governance.

In *Besieged*, edited by William Howell, Richard Briffault outlines two forces that have impacted education case law. The first is the "formal approach" that views the school board as "a legally subordinate arm of its state." Briffault goes on to say that, in practice, districts have "less formal autonomy and are subject to far more state mandates and oversight than other local governments" and that ultimately they are a "creature of the state." The state can "amend, abridge, or retract any power it has delegated," including matters of school policy, arbitrating disputes between the district and another party, and reducing local board authority.[8]

As stated by Chief Justice John Forrest Dillon of the Iowa Supreme Court in 1868, "Municipal corporations owe their origin to, and derive their powers and rights wholly from, the legislature. It breathes into them a breath of life, without which they cannot exist. As it creates, so may it destroy. If it may destroy, it may abridge and control."[9]

You may think that the school board and superintendent lead the district and are answerable directly to the community, but state education laws dictate much of what a local district does, including the structure of the board. While you may move into a neighborhood thinking your kids will attend a particular district, the state may have power to force district consolidation or redraw lines, unless such action violates U.S. Constitutional law.

A state can also abolish a school board altogether, choosing to place a district under direct control of local municipal government or the state itself. While this may be more familiar to residents of some of America's largest cities that are governed by mayoral control, most parents don't realize that it can happen anywhere.[10]

Briffault goes on to explain a second, "informal approach" that recognizes "districts have enjoyed a de facto autonomy that has received intermittent legal recognition."[11] Though states currently exert significant power through laws and regulations that micromanage districts, adding to community frustration and confusion, for much of American history, states granted school boards virtually complete autonomy. The line between state and local power was not always blurry.

School board history, and de facto school board autonomy, can be traced back to colonial times. In 1647, the Massachusetts Bay Colony passed the Ould Deluder Satan Act, requiring every town to establish a school principally to teach children Puritan values. Though this act was passed at the colonial level, it delegated responsibility to the local community with the goal of encouraging participation, responsiveness,

efficiency, and a sense of community. While initially school-related decisions were made at general town meetings, urban and rural dynamics
contributed to the need for a new decision-making body, the "school
committee" (also known as "school board").[12]

In urban Massachusetts, one specific factor that led to the formation
of school committees was the fact that Boston lacked representative government during colonial times. Instead, Boston governed itself through
a series of general meetings of its citizenry. Running Boston schools by
general meeting proved burdensome and impractical. By the early 1700s,
the city delegated this responsibility to a visitation committee charged
with school oversight.[13]

In rural Massachusetts, a different issue prompted the formation of
school committees. Just as in Boston, schools in less densely populated areas
were initially governed through town meetings. Yet over time, "school districts" evolved as residents moved to the outskirts of towns. Districts were
able to follow the boundaries of religious parishes and population clusters
that formed further from town centers, easing practical transportation
logistics and facilitating the governance of schools among localized residents with shared values. Districts and towns having divergent boundaries required a distinct education governance body, creating the need for
a school district and school committee.[14]

When the Founding Fathers designed the American political system,
there were competing philosophies about how school governance should
work. John Adams feared the mob and wanted a well-educated elite to
be in charge, while Samuel Adams believed in the power of the people.
Among the Founders, there was healthy skepticism of a distant, centralized
authority.[15]

Ultimately, Samuel Adams's philosophy prevailed in the context of
education governance. The provision of education is not mentioned in
the U.S. Constitution and therefore it became a power reserved for the
states. In turn, individual states typically delegated this authority to
local governance. Furthermore, if a group of citizens disagreed with their
local governance body, there were instances when they could convene
their own committee and start their own school.[16]

In 1789, an ordinance in Boston called "The System of Public Education" delegated power to the "school committee" that would be made up

of twelve members elected directly by the people. Responsibilities included hiring teachers, determining salaries, maintaining physical space, setting the calendar, deciding on instructional methods, and monitoring classes.[17]

That same year, the 1789 Act in Massachusetts codified the concept of school districts and even provided them with the power to subdivide into smaller districts. It mentioned the duty of the school committee to hire school personnel and highlighted the need to levy local taxes to support schools. The 1789 Act helped create a system that facilitates citizen participation, fosters a sense of community, and reflects shared values.[18]

While town selectmen remained in charge of school finance responsibilities, school committees became responsible for operations and policy. These committees were very active and responsive to the town. They ran the schools from a governance and administrative perspective.[19]

In the early 1800s, Massachusetts took additional steps to provide districts with the power to control their own destinies. Because towns had competing fiscal priorities and did not always properly fund education, a law was passed in 1800 that provided districts with the ability to raise funds directly from citizens. In 1817, districts were codified as distinct corporate entities that can sue or be sued.[20]

Town government still played an active role in education funding in the 1820s, but often came up short. Thus, in 1827, Massachusetts legislation imposed a requirement that all schools be governed by separate school committees with a dedicated funding stream and direct citizen representation.[21] Instead of creating a department or agency at the state or municipal level, school committees were purposefully designed with significant authority to make decisions independently.[22] They were given the power to tax so that a separate and steady revenue source could be secured.[23]

The Massachusetts school governance model spread across the country, eventually becoming universal, though with some degree of variation. According to Navad Shoked of Northwestern University, the school district came to be "the smallest, and most voluntary, unit of self-government in the political system." For example, in each Midwestern town, there were an average of nine school districts.[24]

While states remained responsible for the provision of public education, at this point in American history virtually all power was delegated to school boards, and a series of state court cases reaffirmed the board's role. In 1872, the Supreme Court of Ohio explained that the "management and control" of schools has been placed "exclusively in the hands of directors, trustees, or boards of education."[25] Two years later, the Supreme Court of Michigan found that school districts have the power to form high schools and that the power to appoint a superintendent is vested in "the full control which by law the board had over the schools of the district, and that the board and the people of the district have been wisely left by the legislature to follow their own judgment."[26] From a practical standpoint, early in American history the school board enjoyed almost full autonomy.[27] When my wife and I were doing our due diligence to move into a new school district, we thought this was how things worked.

During the past 120-plus years, we have strayed far from this original version of American public education governance. A series of events moved the country away from this system of local control to our modern-day complex ecosystem of shared power across multiple levels of government. Several key events contributed to a slow but steady decline in school board power.

PROGRESSIVE ERA REFORMS

By the late 1800s, business leaders, politicians, and professors pushed to professionalize schools. As industrialization swept across America, the approach of Progressive Era reformers, like modern-day reformers, attempted to apply business concepts to education. They looked to infuse industrial ideas such as standardization, centralization, professionalization of management, and efficiency into the education system.

Above all, Progressive reformers were leery of the general citizenry having too much control over school district affairs. At first, they viewed school boards skeptically, concerned that they might be too political. Eventually, they realized that school boards could help facilitate their core reform ideas. They advocated for two major governance changes.

First, the Progressive reformers astutely realized that in the corporate world, boards served as a governance body only, appointing a professional foreman to run the enterprise day-to-day. School boards, by contrast, performed both governance and administrative functions. The growth of manufacturing that took place during the Progressive Era required an executive team with the expertise and focus to manage a company top-down, scaling the operations and maximizing efficiency. Now that America was experiencing rapid growth of its school population and scaling educational opportunity became a priority, reformers believed that just as corporate boards appointed an executive leader, so too school boards could appoint a superintendent. The board of education retained its governance responsibilities, including the hiring and firing of the superintendent, but it delegated the day-to-day responsibility of managing the district to a trained professional.[28]

Second, reformers believed that districts were too small to be efficient and they moved aggressively to encourage, or even mandate, consolidation.[29] In addition to achieving operational synergies, they believed that larger districts would be more likely to elect people who (at least in the reformers' minds) were better qualified school board members. Progressive Era reformers were leery of ward-based school board elections (in which a board member is elected from individual neighborhoods rather than district-wide) for the very same reason, and they believed that at-large elections would better protect against special interests by providing larger pools of candidates and broadening constituencies.[30] They wanted to put power into the hands of individuals they deemed to be accomplished and capable leaders.

Along with consolidation, Progressive reformers also pushed to reduce the size of school boards, now that their role was more focused on oversight rather than day-to-day decision-making.[31] Fewer board seats, they believed, would raise the bar, helping to ensure that the accomplished and capable leaders they hoped for would be elected.

In cities, school board size dropped from an average of 21.5 members in 1893 to seven members twenty years later.[32] All in all, the changes made by Progressive reformers were the start of a historical trend to place limits on school board power.

FEDERAL GOVERNMENT PROTECTION OF INDIVIDUAL RIGHTS

Prior to the 1950s, the federal government played a limited role in education policy that is consistent with the Tenth Amendment of the Constitution, which reserves any powers not specifically granted to the federal government to the states or to the people. Beginning in the mid-twentieth century, a new wave of federal activism was ushered in under the premise of the Fourteenth Amendment, which says that no state shall "make or enforce any law which shall abridge the privileges or immunities of citizens of the United States" and that no one should be denied "equal protection of the laws."[33]

The federal judiciary has ruled on seminal cases related to schools that focus on the protection of individual rights, specifically those of marginalized community members. The court system is more inherently insulated from the political process and public opinion than school boards and has intervened when boards fall short of their duty to serve and protect the interests of all children, regardless of race, gender, socioeconomic background, or disability. These decisions have served as a counterbalance to board power.[34]

The 1954 *Brown v. Board of Education of Topeka* (Kansas) case is the most well-known example of how the courts challenged the power of local governance. During the 1950s many local school boards resisted the integration of schools. In *Brown v. Board of Education*, the Supreme Court deemed the "separate but equal" doctrine, established in *Plessy v. Ferguson* (1896), unconstitutional in the field of public education.[35]

Federal involvement in school desegregation did not end with the *Brown v. Board of Education* decision. On September 24, 1957, President Eisenhower addressed the nation to explain his decision to send federal troops to Little Rock, Arkansas, to assist with the school board's desegregation plan that locals were obstructing. He stated that America is a "nation in which laws, not men, are supreme" and that presidential action was required given the failure of local authorities to uphold the Supreme Court ruling.[36]

Over a decade later, the federal judiciary branch continued to rule on the matter of desegregation by finding certain school board plans unlawful. In the 1968 case of *Green v. County School Board*, the New Kent County of Virginia school board's "freedom of choice" plan was found to be insufficient to desegregate schools.[37] In the 1971 case of *Swann v. Charlotte-Mecklenburg Board of Education*, the Supreme Court decision supported busing students as a means of achieving desegregation.[38]

In 1974, Judge Wendell Arthur Garrity Jr. ruled against the Boston
School Committee for their efforts to create and preserve a segregated
district. He forced the district, against the will of the school board, to
bus students across town to achieve racial integration.[39] Subsequently,
after Garrity heard reports of Black students being beaten and ignored, he
placed a school in federal receivership.[40]

Other court cases opined on issues such as the role of religion in
schools and school board authority in curricular decision-making.[41]

Federal interest in education continued under President Lyndon Johnson, with a focus on improving the quality of education for students from
families with low incomes. The 1965 Elementary and Secondary Education Act (ESEA) under Title 1 created a federal aid program to assist low-
income students.[42]

Federal involvement continued to expand with Section 504 of the
Rehabilitation Act of 1973, which mandates that schools provide reasonable accommodations and a free and appropriate public education (FAPE)
to disabled students. Section 504 does not provide funding but serves as
civil rights legislation that any institution receiving federal funds must
follow. The federal government went a step further in 1975 by passing
the Education for All Handicapped Children Act (currently known as the
Individuals with Disabilities Act or IDEA), which proved to be an inflec-
tion point for federal influence. IDEA establishes regulatory requirements
and provides funding aimed at protecting disabled students.[43]

These initial pieces of legislation set the stage for a steady expansion
of federal power, and the Department of Education was officially created
through congressional legislation in October 1979. While in 1965 the
Office of Education had more than 2,100 employees and a budget of $1.5
billion, by mid-2010 it had nearly 4,300 employees and a $60 billion
budget.[44]

Areas of federal focus include antidiscrimination statutes, gender and
sports issues, English as a second language, and academic accountability.[45] Though the federal government has become more and more active
in public education, states continue to play the central role. To this day,
most federal public school funding flows to the states for distribution,
not directly to districts.[46]

SCHOOL FUNDING

Federal and state judiciaries have played an active role in curtailing school board power. One area of state judicial activity has been public education funding. Initially, schools predominantly were funded by local property taxes, which proved to be a stable and reliable revenue source. However, underresourced communities were at a disadvantage.

By the early 1900s, many cities were thriving and had ample means to fund schools, but many rural areas struggled with an inadequate property tax base. In the wake of several lawsuits, in 1923, George Strayer and Robert Haig, as part of the Educational Finance Inquiry Commission, constructed a "foundation program" that attempted to provide grants to underfunded communities. Since then, there have been many legal battles over funding and attempts by states to develop a variety of redistribution mechanisms.[47]

One example is the 1973 *Robinson v. Cahill* decision in New Jersey, which encouraged the legislature to address state education fiscal equity by instituting a state tax that would help support underresourced districts. In May 1976, the New Jersey Supreme Court lost patience with legislative inaction and ordered the public education system to shut down until the state solved the funding issue.[48] In another 1973 case, *San Antonio Independent School District v. Rodriguez*, the Supreme Court upheld the requirement for a minimum funding level but decided that unequal funding driven by wealthier districts raising more money in property taxes is not discriminatory.[49]

As a result of these cases, by 1980 state aid surpassed local tax revenue as the single largest source of public education funding. More recently, the federal government has stepped up its funding efforts as well. Figure 4.1 illustrates the change over the past century in public education revenue by source of funds.[50]

As states have increasingly controlled a meaningful portion of the purse strings, it is unsurprising that governance power has shifted from local boards of education to state legislative and executive branches, as well as state boards of education and state education departments. Exerting their will, states aggressively pushed rural districts to consolidate, and over the course of several decades, as illustrated in figure 4.2, the number of school districts nationwide dramatically declined.[51] The consolidation

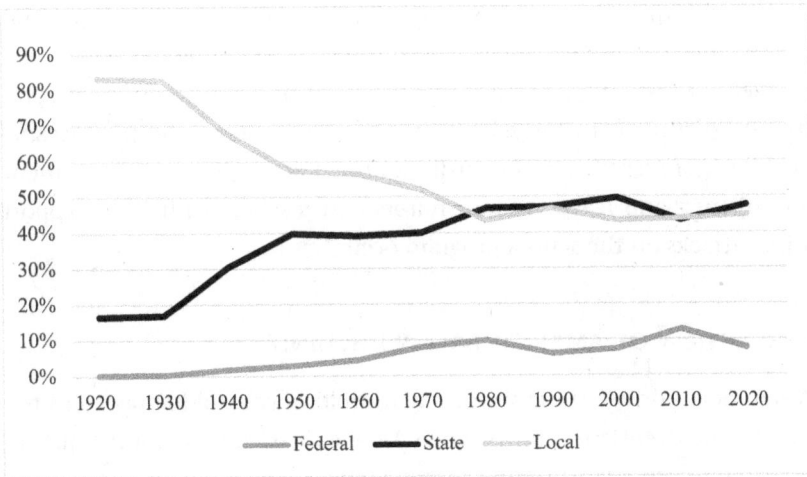

4.1 Public education revenue by source.

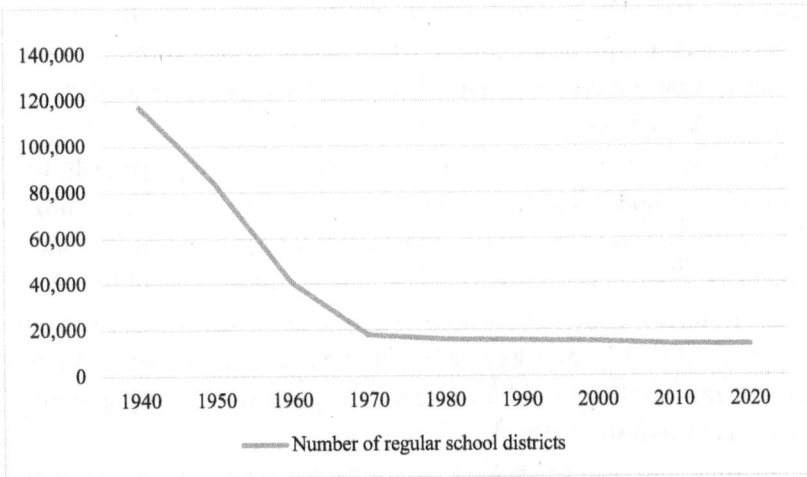

4.2 Number of regular school districts.

of districts and the rise in private school enrollment contributed to a weakening of the link between local schools and the community.

Additionally, until the second half of the twentieth century, most adults maxed out at a high school education and stayed in the same town. There was a generational sense of ownership between community members and local school districts. After World War II, more adults chose to pursue postsecondary education and exercised greater mobility. As Wiles

and Bondi explain in their 1985 book *The School Board Primer*, "Since educators have always been viewed with some suspicion by the public, the
problem of fostering a positive identification of parents and other community persons with the schools has become acute in the past decade.
Such lack of identification contributes to an atmosphere of detachment
and distrust and leaves administrators and teachers with little support
when attacks on the school program occur."[52]

PERCEPTION OF AMERICA FALLING BEHIND

A significant driver of the shift away from local control happened in the
mid-to-late twentieth century when America started to doubt the quality
of its public schools. The 1957 launch by the Soviet Union of the Sputnik
satellite led to a growing sense that America was falling behind, particularly in science and mathematics. Concerns also emerged regarding the
growth of school district bureaucracy and the power of unions, an unintended consequence of the consolidation and professionalization of public schools during the Progressive Era. Both forces were counterbalances
to local school board power.[53]

For most of American history, the federal government played a de minimis role in public education. When in 1867 President Andrew Johnson
created the federal Department of Education to gather statistics about
America's schools, fear arose that the new department would have too
much influence over local districts. A year later it was downsized to the
Office of Education, and its role was limited to a narrow set of matters
such as the granting of public land for the purpose of opening schools.
That changed in the 1950s.[54]

Sputnik prompted the federal government to take a closer look at the
nation's public education system and to commit to investing in science
education. The National Defense Education Act of 1958 focused on the
enhancement of science and math education in elementary and secondary
schools.[55]

The sense of urgency regarding America's educational inadequacy
seeded in the 1950s grew, and cumulatively, the effects were decisive.
Power was starting to shift away from local districts. A journal article written by J. Myron Atkin in 1980 summed it up well by stating, "Increasingly

local school administrators and teachers are losing control over the curriculum as a result of government action." There was fear that political
decisions were driving the curriculum and that "the local administrator
becomes less of an educational leader and more of a monitor of legislative
intent."[56] The trend to increase state and federal involvement in education, however, was soon to increase yet again.

The 1983 *A Nation at Risk* report claimed that America's schools were
falling behind, and that the country's economic and geopolitical strength
were dependent on fixing the problem.[57] This provided federal and state
officials an impetus to take an even more proactive approach to public
education.

The 1980s and 1990s were a time when politicians at the state and
federal levels discussed education with increased frequency. The three
presidents that served after *A Nation at Risk* was published emphasized
education in speeches at two and a half times the rate of the seven previous presidents.[58] At the state level, governors recognized the political
benefits of making education a top issue. The topic resonated with voters,
and the growing scope of the education sector, which at the time had over
four million public school employees and represented a large proportion
of the GDP, became irresistible for politicians looking to amass power.[59]

Improving America's schools became inextricably linked to America's
ability to compete on the world stage from an economic and national
security perspective. Politicians weren't alone in paying attention. The
business and philanthropic communities generally supported the National
Governors Association's push for standards and accountability.

That there was (and still is) great variation in outcomes among American school districts, rhetoric regarding American students falling behind
was often a characterization of overall results. Strong local pockets of positive outcomes were often glossed over or ignored when critics discussed
statewide and national performance. A result was that reform efforts were
applied universally to districts.

THE STANDARDS AND ACCOUNTABILITY MOVEMENT

While the trend toward the federal and state governments having a
heavier-handed role in local school district affairs has been evident since

Sputnik, during the past thirty years momentum has increased. For much of this period, Democrats and Republicans were broadly in lockstep. Republican President George H. W. Bush and Democratic Governor Bill Clinton, the former chair of the National Governors Association, convened the 1989 Education Summit in Charlottesville, Virginia. The bipartisan Education Summit sparked a call to action, setting the stage for future federal and state initiatives.

One such federal initiative was President George W. Bush's 2001 No Child Left Behind (NCLB) legislation, which allowed states to maintain their authority but for the first time imposed a federal government requirement to administer standardized tests. NCLB imposed a new layer of accountability. Its goal was to achieve "proficiency" for all students in math and English language arts (ELA) by 2014. The law, however, allowed each state to define its own standards and set its own "proficiency" level.[60]

The business community generally cheered on the shift in power to centralized authorities, under the assumption that it would be easier to influence fifty governors than thousands of school boards when lobbying for significant reforms. Business leaders wanted to see reforms happen quickly, through state legislation rather than the drawn-out process of local community deliberation. These prospective reforms included charter school expansion, privatization, the proliferation of standardized testing, mayoral control, and school vouchers, all of which have gained some degree of traction.[61] Additionally, reform agenda items that may threaten the autonomy (or even the existence) of public school districts were easier to discuss and implement without local district interference.

In 2009, the Obama administration doubled down on testing and accountability with Race to the Top. The federal government lured states with large sums of money, at a time when budgets were tight, in exchange for a commitment to institute changes in policy and practice. By instituting Common Core standards and tying teacher evaluations to student test scores, Race to the Top took substantial power away from local districts.

Many states embraced their new activist role in education policy. After all, education is simply too big to ignore. According to U.S. Census data, state and local governments spent $1.1 trillion on education generally in 2021, representing 25.4 percent of total expenditure.[62] The political allure of controlling education policy is intoxicating. Furthermore, depending

on the region, it can be politically useful for candidates and elected officials to support (or oppose) education unions.

Increased state involvement has resulted in a complex and nuanced system. Boards still wield significant power, but the state places limitations on
their authority in virtually every aspect of governance decision-making.

THE CURRENT ROLE OF CENTRALIZED GOVERNMENT

The shift of power from school boards to centralized government happened incrementally. Yet the cumulative result has been dramatic. States,
and to some extent the federal government, have instituted voluminous
requirements that districts must follow. The regulatory role that centralized government traditionally played has shifted in some cases into the
realm of micromanagement. From school lunch to math curriculum to
teacher certification, there are few facets of public education that have
escaped federal or state influence.

The result of this micromanagement has been a blurring of the lines
between the local school board and state/federal government power. Yet
much of the public still believes school boards control their own destiny.
This gap between perception and reality frustrates community members
and board members alike. During school board campaigns, candidates
sometimes run on making changes beyond the scope of what boards have
the power to do. During board meetings, the public often complains to
board members about state and federal mandates.

Consider that today just about every basic school board function is
entangled in state regulation. For example, hiring decisions are made at
the district level, but strict state credentialing requirements and tenure
rules must be followed. While boards retain curriculum oversight, they
must comply with voluminous state regulatory standards that cover specific subject matter, including legislation related to specific topics and
lessons. Boards adopt the annual calendar but must adhere to a specific
number of school days set by the state and must honor state holidays.
Some states have requirements that influence the start and end date of
each school year. Boards can issue a bond and manage their assets and
liabilities but must adhere to restrictions on cash reserves and carry-over
balances. Boards can raise revenue by levying taxes, but in some states,

their ability to do so is limited by state-imposed tax caps. Boards can determine salary scales, but many states require districts to opt into the state-run pension system, over which they have no say regarding contributions, benefit levels, or funding strategies.

Table 4.1 highlights important areas of board activity and how roles and responsibilities are generally divided between states and districts.

When my wife and I were searching for a new place for our family to live, with schools we were eager to send our children to, assessing the school board was an important component of our process. This was because we understood that at any point, if we were dissatisfied with district policy, we could show up to a board meeting and participate in the public comment period. That, after all, is an American tradition.

But today, even if our local school board is sympathetic to our view, it may or may not have the authority to act. The board may be powerless if the matter falls into the realm of the state.

In addition, it's often unclear to board members, superintendents, and state officials which of them has the power to do what. For the average American citizen who does not spend their spare time reading education statutes or consulting with education attorneys, it can be even more perplexing.

Roles and responsibilities have blurred, with the unintended negative consequence of contributing to battles in the boardroom. When COVID-19 and the national reckoning on race hit our nation, angry citizens complaining to boards grew more frustrated when they didn't see boards act. Yet, in many cases, boards did not have the requisite power.

There is no better example of jurisdictional confusion than masking. During the heart of the COVID-19 crisis, arguments over masking took place during school board meetings. Yet ironically, many boards did not have clear legal authority to take independent action. During the 2021–2022 school year, twenty-two states allowed districts or local governments to develop independent policies, eighteen states and Washington, D.C., instituted a statewide mask mandate, and eleven states prohibited mask mandates (Virginia went from a requirement to a ban during the school year).[63]

For example, Florida imposed an executive order prohibiting any district from mandating masks. However, several local districts, including

Table 4.1   Roles and responsibilities

	Typical state	Typical school board
Financial	• Allocates state funding • Imposes restrictions and regulations • Conducts audits	• Sets budget and tax levy • Determines need to issue bonds • Approves contracts over certain $ threshold
Strategy/priorities	• Launches state initiatives and mandates through legislation and regulation	• Sets district strategy and goals within state statutory and regulatory parameters
Curriculum	• Sets standards and sometimes specific curriculum topics • Determines graduation requirements	• Adopts curriculum material • Selects courses
Personnel	• Sets teacher certification requirements and employment law framework • Legislates collective bargaining rights • Mandates pension participation	• Hires, manages, and fires superintendent • Approves staff hirings/firings and granting tenure • Engages in succession planning
Policy	• Sets parameters on many policy issues	• Sets district policy within state parameters
Calendar	• Sets number of instructional days, mandated holidays, and sometimes start/end dates	• Sets calendar within parameters set by state
Safety/Security/Discipline	• Establishes regulations to determine permissible disciplinary actions and safety protocols	• Decides whether to have a school resource officer • Sets district discipline policy within state parameters

Broward County, defied the mandate, prompting public confusion and litigation.[64] In New York, Governor Andrew Cuomo and his successor Governor Kathy Hochul issued an executive order mandating masks. Yet Nassau County Executive Bruce Blakeman attempted to undermine the state's authority by passing a local law that allowed school boards to vote on a masking policy in their respective districts. Parents pursued litigation against the state mandate, and courts stepped in to determine which governmental body had jurisdiction.[65]

Night after night across America, parents participated in public comment periods to voice their opposition to mandatory COVID vaccination requirements. However, it is standard practice (and in many states a matter of law) for student vaccination decisions to be made at the state level, with local districts having no authority to deviate. Time and time again, community members argue for change that boards are powerless to deliver.

Sometimes even when community members explicitly understand that a mandate comes from the state, they nevertheless implore board members to defy the state rule. This is particularly ironic, because when board members get sworn in, they take an oath to uphold the U.S. Constitution and the state constitution. When school boards refused to defy state masking mandates, some community members accused boards of being pawns of the state, lured by state and federal funds.

There were some instances when federal and state officials attempted to tie money to controversial mandates such as masks, which fed into more general conspiracy theories. For example, in Washington State, the superintendent of education stated that a failure to comply with the state mask mandate could result in federal or state funds being withheld.[66] Despite some of the public believing that boards were following mandates because they were afraid of losing district funds, most of the time, districts followed the rules simply because they were legally obligated to do so.

While battles in the boardroom always seem to be all about community members versus school boards, they often reflect the frustration and distrust community members have with state and federal power. A close look at public comment periods across the country reveals example after example of battles in the school boardroom that at their core are about federal and state distrust and broader conspiracy theories. Examples include:

- In Grand Blanc, Michigan, a speaker argues that Dr. Anthony Fauci is leading an effort to experiment on children and that the school board is helping.[67]
- In Seminole County, Florida, a parent tells a school board that COVID vaccines are a "deep state conspiracy."[68]
- In Washoe County, Nevada, a community member claims that mask mandates are in place because Governor Steve Sisolak's wife has family members who own a mask company in China. The school board is accused of being part of the "New World Order," in reference to a conspiracy theory.[69]
- The *Akron Beacon Journal* in Ohio reported how community members were accusing Stow-Munroe Falls City Schools of mandating masks for the express purpose of receiving federal funds, an accusation denied by the U.S. Department of Education and the district.[70]
- The *Post Independent* reported how Garfield School District Re-2 in Colorado denied protestor accusations that federal CARES Act funding was predicated on mandatory masking at local public schools.[71]

Given how strident our boardroom battles have become, it is appropriate to take a step back and determine if our current division of power between federal, state, and local authorities serves us well. Has enhanced state and federal power made our system stronger? Or does it create a system that is unwieldy and broken? Do we need to restore school board power as the primary place to make education governance decisions? Or should we gravitate even further to federal, state, or mayoral authority?

We will address these questions in chapter 5.

5

SEARCHING FOR A CEASEFIRE

During the past fifty years, policymakers have searched high and low for a formula to improve public education, experimenting with virtually every conceivable reform permutation to drive better outcomes. Mayoral control. Site-based teams. Vouchers, charters, and school choice initiatives that encourage more competition and privatization. Standardized tests administered to foster accountability. Constant curriculum revamping to match ever-evolving standards. Countless state mandates and bans. Conditional or competitive grants as a tool to encourage "desired" behavior.

For quite some time, reform efforts were bipartisan. Policy positions of the Clinton, Bush, and Obama administrations shared common themes. More recently, education policy has become a political lightning rod, with stark differences in approach visible in red and blue states. Democrats tend to support curriculum mandates—most recently focused on social justice issues and DEI—and policies that are friendly to unions and the public school status quo. Republicans generally push for changes to public school structure (including school choice initiatives and more charter licenses) and have increasingly supported curriculum bans, particularly around race and gender issues. It's two different worlds that bear little resemblance to each other.

The one commonality that both parties share is that their solutions to improving public education look more to states, municipal, and federal governments because they view school boards skeptically. Many Democrats worry that school boards are increasingly being taken over by conservatives looking to ban books and curriculum topics and that they lack diversity. Republicans lament that too often school boards are agents of progressivism and teachers' unions, standing in the way of parental rights. Both parties have realized that mandates and bans are easier to push with centralized control. Local authority is fragmented and involves the complexity of grassroots decision-making.

Even board members and superintendents sometimes express relief when decision-making shifts to centralized government. After all, state control makes it easier for local officials to deflect responsibility when making controversial decisions. If community members are unhappy, local leaders can point their fingers in the direction of the state capital or Washington, D.C., and say, "Don't complain to me, complain to them."

Are we better off with a system that favors more centralized control? To see why school boards should be at the forefront of our policy discussions, we need to first confront why other solutions—federal control, mayoral control, or additional state control—have serious limitations.

FEDERAL CONTROL

Ideally, schools in America teach kids how to think critically. Ideally, they prepare students to, among other things, contribute to our democratic society. Unfortunately, this mission can be undermined by schools abusing their power and teaching kids what to think instead of how to think. When any level of educational governance—whether local, state, or federal—crosses this line, it sets off alarm bells. Local control, however, contains the damage to one community instead of an entire state or country, which could have far more devastating consequences.

To better appreciate concerns over federal control, and the appeal of local control, let's take two big steps back, first in time, then in comparison among nations.

In his seminal book *Democracy in America*, Alexis de Tocqueville views local government as a protective layer of democracy. He astutely observes that the lack of administrative centralization serves as a buffer from tyranny and despotism. "If the law were oppressive, liberty would still find some shelter from the way the law is carried into execution."[1]

Tocqueville further argues that "local institutions are to liberty what primary schools are to science; they put it within the people's reach . . . without local institutions a nation may give itself a free government, but it has not got the spirit of liberty."[2] Tocqueville believes that local volunteerism is part of the fabric of democracy and helps sustain the entire American republic. For these and other reasons, Americans have expected to have a say in the affairs of their public schools since the earliest days of our republic.

In addition to our nation's historical commitment to local institutions, there have always been underlying concerns regarding what can go wrong with a centralized authority in charge of instructing our children. There are many disturbing images and stories that have come out of the Russian invasion of Ukraine, but one of the most chilling involves education. In occupied Ukraine, Russia has engaged in "a comprehensive reeducation program" of Ukrainian school children by mandating curricula that rejects the notion of the Ukrainian nation and bans Ukrainian textbooks.[3] It is an attempt by Russia to indoctrinate the next generation of Ukrainians.

Prior to the fall of the Soviet Union, it was common to use schools as a mechanism to indoctrinate children, and this practice has reemerged not only in occupied Ukraine, but also in Russia itself. As reported by the *New York Times*, Sergei Novikov, a Kremlin bureaucrat, addressed thousands of teachers during an online workshop. He explained the new imperative of the Putin regime: "We need to know how to infect them with our ideology. Our ideological work is aimed at changing consciousness."[4]

The Russian government has instructed schools to incorporate propaganda war movies and virtual tours of Crimea starting in the first grade. Lectures include "traditional values" and the geopolitical narrative set forth by the government, emphasizing Russian "rebirth" under Putin's leadership. Legislation has been passed encouraging children to join a new patriotic youth movement led by Putin.

In its reporting, the *New York Times* describes how there are efforts underway to accomplish the "reprogramming of Russian society" to end openness to the West and eliminate dissenting opinions. A ninth grader in Russia reported her computer class was replaced by a lecture emphasizing that state media is the only source of trustworthy information. In history class, the standard curriculum depicts Putin's twenty years in power as a "historical turning point" with the "rebirth of Russia as a great power in the 21st century."[5]

Education was also used deliberately and effectively in Nazi Germany to achieve political goals. Just three months after Hitler became chancellor, the 1933 Restoration of the Professional Civil Service Act took control of the teacher credentialing process, disqualifying Jewish teachers and teachers with certain political beliefs. Additionally, teachers were mandated to attend a one-month Nazi training course. The curriculum also was revamped with particular emphasis on sports, history, and racial science. Textbooks had to be approved by the Nazi party and incorporated racist ideology.[6]

While these are extreme examples of weaponizing education for political purposes, and in no way should we conflate Russian and Nazi governance with the situation in the United States, it is not far-fetched to believe that disturbing things, even when subtle, can happen when centralized political power and education policy converge.

There's another reason why a federally controlled education system is unrealistic for America. The United States is larger and more diverse than many other nations. Additionally, we are a product of our own unique history, which has celebrated a tradition of local control and a reluctance to place excessive power in the hands of the federal government.

Lamar Alexander, a long-time chair of the Senate Education Committee, has expressed that the federal government has a "limited" but important role to play as it relates to education. While he provided examples of productive federal involvement such as "setting standards, highlighting examples, contributing some funds, providing flexibility in return for accountability," he was leery of excessive federal power. In September 1992, Alexander warned House minority leader Bob Michel about a piece of pending legislation that in his view would create a "national school board that could make day-to-day school decisions on curriculum, discipline, teacher training, textbooks, and classroom materials . . . such decisions belong with communities, parents, teachers, and local school boards. A federal recipe book dictating how to operate a local school does not make schools better."[7]

Americans have long been in sync with Lamar Alexander's view of federal power as it relates to public education. Time and time again, federal government perceived or actual involvement in local educational affairs has triggered a clear, predictable, and concerted backlash.

A recent example of this dynamic is the reaction to the National School Boards Association's (NSBA) attempt to address the boardroom skirmishes during the COVID-19 pandemic. To address the safety and security of school board members across the country, on September 29, 2021, the NSBA penned a strongly worded letter to President Biden that included the following passage:

As these acts of malice, violence, and threats against public school officials have increased, the classification of these heinous actions could be the equivalent to a form of domestic terrorism and hate crimes. As such, NSBA requests a joint expedited review by the U.S. Departments of Justice, Education, and Homeland Security, along with the appropriate training, coordination, investigations, and enforcement mechanisms from the FBI, including any technical assistance necessary from, and state and local coordination with, its National Security Branch and Counterterrorism Division, as well as any other federal agency with relevant jurisdictional authority and oversight.[8]

In response, Attorney General Merrick Garland issued a Memorandum on October 4, 2021, directing the Department of Justice (DOJ) to use its resources, including the FBI, to combat a "disturbing spike in harassment, intimidation, and threats of violence against school administrators, board members, teachers, and staff."[9]

The NSBA letter and the DOJ's response generated intense criticism, particularly related to the charge of "domestic terrorism." On October 18, 2021, a group of state attorneys general accused the DOJ of violating the First Amendment rights of parents by "seeking to criminalize lawful dissent and intimidate parents into silence." They argued that the federal government's action "has all the characteristics of McCarthyism" and "intrude[s] on the well-recognized First and Fourteenth Amendment rights of parents and guardians to direct the upbringing and education of their children by intimidating parents away from raising concerns about the education of their children."[10] Shortly thereafter, the NSBA issued a formal apology.[11]

In late 2021 and 2022, multiple state school boards associations severed ties with the NSBA, and a second national organization called the Consortium of State School Boards Associations (COSSBA) was formed.[12] The challenge of keeping red, purple, and blue states together in a unified association is further evidence of how difficult it is to forge a national consensus on education issues.[13]

More recently, the NSBA has appointed new leadership and taken steps to repair relationships. As reported in the *Washington Post*, the organization has emphasized its nonpartisanship and approved policies supporting local control and parent engagement.[14] Notably, both the NSBA and COSSBA provide professional development and networking opportunities to school board members from member and nonmember states across the country.

Another example of Americans pushing back on federal involvement in local schools is the doomed rollout of the Common Core State Standards Initiative. By 2011, forty-five states and Washington, D.C., committed to the rollout of the Common Core and corresponding high-stakes tests from either the Smarter Balanced Assessment Consortium or the Partnership for Assessment of Readiness for College and Careers. Though borne out of state cooperation—it had the backing of the Council of Chief State School Officers and the National Governors Association—the Common Core became perceived as a federal initiative when the Obama administration made it a central part of its Race to the Top initiative.[15]

Support for Common Core eroded across the political spectrum. Voices on the right grew concerned that the federal government was encroaching on curriculum and exerting too much influence in the classroom. Voices on the left viewed the effort as "corporate school reform," expressing concern that a common curriculum and the associated standardized tests were intended to enrich large for-profit education companies.[16] A 2014 *Education Next* survey found that 64 percent of respondents (a representative sample of American adults) who were familiar with the Common Core thought "the federal government requires all states to use the Common Core standards," and 85 percent believed the federal government would receive detailed testing data. From 2013 to 2015, teacher and parent support for Common Core dropped by 36 and 16 percentage points, respectively.[17]

Postmortems on the reform suggest that the lack of effort expended to achieve local community buy-in upfront proved problematic:

The Common Core standards and their aligned assessments drew many support-ers from the federal and state governments, from the philanthropic community, and from reform advocates, but most members of these groups do not have a personal stake—a vested interest—in what happens in schools at the ground level. Therefore, their support alone is not enough to sustain education reform over time. . . . Efforts have largely focused on lobbying policymakers, not build-ing the kind of broad-based coalitions needed to reengineer the K-12 system around high standards, quality assessments, and accountability for results.[18]

Jay Greene at the University of Arkansas argues that foundations inter-ested in reforming K-12 should include local communities in the process, since they are the most vested and can be a powerful ally or formidable opponent.[19]

In the wake of the failure of Race to the Top and the Common Core, Congress passed the December 2015 Every Student Succeeds Act (ESSA), which shifts some control back to the states. While this landmark leg-islation sets forth a less aggressive role for the federal government, it has not stopped people from leveling accusations that the federal govern-ment continues to meddle in local school district affairs.

The role of the CDC during COVID is yet another example of contro-versial federal involvement in education. In story after story, federal health authorities were accused of bowing to the influence of teachers' unions when setting COVID prevention and school reopening recommendations. These accusations were vigorously debated. The Republican-controlled House Committee on Oversight and Accountability reported that "senior agency officials shared a draft copy of the Operational Strategy with the American Federation of Teachers (AFT)." The AFT asked that the CDC add a "trigger" to the guidance that recommends school closure if COV-ID-19 positivity rates reached a certain threshold. According to the House Committee, the CDC inserted language that said updated guidance may be necessary upon higher levels of community transmission.[20] Democrats and the AFT argue that the facts fail to prove any inappropriate influence and that the CDC consulted about fifty other organizations for feedback even before the AFT knew about it.[21]

As discussed in chapter 4, the federal government has played a pivotal role in upholding the Fourteenth Amendment when school boards have fallen short. Through congressional legislation, executive power, and case law, the federal government has addressed the segregation of American schools, discrimination against students with disabilities, and the lack of resources available for schools that serve students from low-income families. While we should recognize the importance and legitimacy of federal involvement along these lines, it is also critical to recognize the reasons why federal overreach has typically backfired.

MAYORAL CONTROL

Another popular concept among education reformers is to place power in the hands of general-purpose government at the local level, most typically the mayor's office. Reformers argue that a strong executive can take quick and bold decisive action to enact reform. Because voter turnout is sometimes greater in municipal elections than school board elections (though it is often still woefully low) and election issues encompass more than just education, advocates of mayoral control suggest that this will make it more difficult for special interests to control the election outcome.

But mayoral control has multiple shortcomings. First, the idea is impractical on a grand scale because many districts have borders that do not align with one local municipality. Second, mayoral control reduces the ability of the public to exert direct influence. Individuals cast their vote for mayor based on a set of criteria that extends beyond education. For example, I might dislike a mayor's education policy, but the mayor might still get my vote if I like their economic development agenda and choose to prioritize that issue. Third, mayoral control can be very disruptive. Each time a mayor gets defeated, there could be an abrupt change in initiatives and agenda.

Fourth, education is just one of many issues that would compete for mayoral attention. Mayors need to balance a broad set of responsibilities that include crime, economic development, poverty, housing, healthcare, transportation, sanitation, and recreation. Fifth, although some mayors have been successful school district stewards, there have been other cases where mayoral control has been disappointing. There is no consensus on outcomes.

Last, compared to mayoral control, school boards have more underlying stability and longevity because it is rare for an entire board to turn over at once. Terms are typically staggered. And, although politics undoubtedly can seep into school board elections, education and politics directly collide with mayoral control.

STATE CONTROL

With all the challenges of federal or mayoral control, the more salient question is whether a continued shift toward centralized state government would be beneficial.

At the heart of the matter is a shift that has occurred during the past few decades resulting in states becoming ever more granular in their education mandates, straying far from our original system in which legislators and governors delegated the bulk of the authority to local school boards. What we're seeing is states taking a more active role in the governance of all school districts state-wide, regardless of performance, at the expense of local control.

On the surface, you might think of heavy-handed state involvement as more of a blue state phenomenon. After all, conservative philosophy typically dictates a more hands-off, small government approach, but lately, many red states have been active in passing curriculum legislation.

Consider the matter of DEI as an example. In 2021, Governor Phil Murphy of New Jersey signed a bill mandating K-12 DEI instruction, including the impact of unconscious bias and economic disparities. California, Connecticut, and Vermont, among other liberal states, passed bills requiring ethnic studies.[22]

Those blue state examples have their red state parallels. On the opposite side of the spectrum, conservative states including Idaho, Tennessee, and Texas have passed legislation banning certain DEI-related discussion. Examples include prohibitions on training involving unconscious bias, privilege, and discussion that the U.S. is inherently racist.[23] Florida went a step further, announcing that the College Board's Advanced Placement (AP) African American Studies course is not approved by the state because it violates state law.[24] The state also instructed schools that offer

AP Psychology not to teach the topics of gender and sexuality, which are part of the AP curriculum, though the state education commissioner followed up with a letter to superintendents stating that AP Psychology "can be taught in its entirety in a manner that is age and developmentally appropriate."[25]

Indiana state government passed HB 1608, which mandates schools to notify parents if a student requests a name or pronoun change.[26] Meanwhile, the New York State Education Department issued guidance to schools that they should not require parental permission or professional proof when a student requests a pronoun change or determines they want to transition their gender, nor should they share the information with the parent if the student does not consent.[27]

Table 5.1 provides examples of legislation that crosses the line from the traditional state role of setting high-level "standards" to very granular laws that sometimes coincide with the politics of the party that controls the statehouse. It is important to keep in mind that the table does not contain state education department regulations, which are often more detailed and voluminous; rather, the list is limited to actual legislation.[28] Whether you agree with the various bills or not, the point is that states have become very granular in their education legislation.

There is a serious downside to the recent trend of states trying to micromanage districts through increased regulation and legislation. The

Table 5.1   Recent education bills

State	Legislation
CA	SB 369—Mandates to teach about the Vietnamese American refugee experience: Cambodian American history and heritage
CA	AB 1078—Requires school boards when adopting materials to include materials that accurately portray the contributions of people of all genders and the role of Latino Americans, LGBTQ+ Americans, and other ethnic, cultural, and socioeconomic status groups
CT	HB 6880—Mandates that play-based learning must be part of professional development requirements
FL	HB 1069—State department of education must approve any materials used to teach reproductive health or HIV/AIDS, gender identity, and sexual orientation instruction

first problem is that legislation tends to be sticky. Once a bill becomes a law, the system is not always nimble enough to be reversed if it triggers negative unintended consequences. The process is complex and requires consensus among many politicians.

Second, states often do not have the bandwidth to oversee schools, even when the legislature and governor have the will to impose change. By contrast, local governance has significantly more capacity to oversee schools than states or federal regulators, and it is good practice to align responsibility with capacity.

Third, real-world evidence does not support the notion that states would be better than local boards in helping students achieve superior academic outcomes. States do not have a strong track record of performing even their most basic duty, which is to hold districts accountable and intervene when outcomes are unacceptably low.

Beth Schueler, an education scholar at the University of Virginia, has written extensively on the Massachusetts takeover of Lawrence Public Schools in 2010 as an instance where turnaround was successful. However, Schueler and Joshua Bleiberg analyzed an extensive dataset on state takeovers across the nation over time. The frequency of these takeovers has increased in response to underperformance. Takeovers include instances in which the state takes over a district by either replacing the entire board or the majority of the board with appointees or inserts a state-appointed superintendent receiver. Their research found that, on average, state takeover of a school system does not lead to enhanced academic performance. In fact, takeovers were found to disrupt achievement in reading, particularly in the early years of the state takeover.[29]

States play a pivotal role in our education governance system, and they must continue to provide essential funding, set standards, and uphold ultimate accountability. At the same time, the nature and reach of state authority needs to be revisited. In recent years, legislative activism and regulatory micromanagement have prompted the question of whether the pendulum has swung too far.

Despite the shortcomings of federal, mayoral, and state control of our public schools, policymakers and reformers have been skeptical of school board governance and have not given up their search for a better alternative. School boards remain at the periphery of education policy discussions.

There are many reasons why. Compared to a more centralized system, reformers understandably view the fragmented universe of school boards as a stumbling block to implementing reforms rapidly and efficiently. There are worries that board members do not have the expertise to govern the complexity of a district and sometimes lack the diversity of their underlying communities. Perhaps the single largest criticism is low voter turnout and a lack of community engagement, paving the way for special interests to exercise disproportionate influence and prompting concerns that there is a lack of school board member accountability.

In addition to these classic arguments, the recent boardroom battles described in chapter 1 exacerbate concerns. As parents loudly express their opinions in boardrooms across the country regarding a range of policy issues, not everyone likes what they are seeing and hearing.

Some observers of these battles find the views expressed by parents during public comment periods as too conservative or too progressive. Others worry that fights about gender pronouns, critical race theory, public health matters, and other controversial cultural issues are supplanting much needed discussion about improving student outcomes. Still others look at these battles with dismay because of the negative tone they set for their respective districts and communities.

On top of these concerns, there is no doubt that the societal trends outlined in chapter 2 coupled with school board transparency requirements explained in chapter 3 make the job of the school board member harder than ever before. School board races have become more contentious, and incumbents are challenged more often.

We cannot have it both ways. We cannot criticize school board governance for low voter turnout and community apathy and then dismiss parent concerns when they are expressed.

The intent of the public comment period is to create a forum for citizens to express their personal beliefs and to encourage all of us to listen carefully. It is not to stick to a specific script or reaffirm one viewpoint. Maybe, just maybe, we can learn a thing or two about diverse perspectives if we maintain humility and an open mind, regardless of our personal ideology.

School boards may no longer be boring, and societal trends and transparency requirements make board service more challenging than ever before.

Battles have become more frequent, intense, and sometimes vitriolic. However, these battles provide tangible evidence that parents care deeply about our education system and can find the boardroom. The boardroom may be quiet and voter turnout may be low when parents are comfortable with the status quo, but when community members disagree with district policies and practices, they seem to be quite capable of exercising their democratic right to make sure their voices are heard.

While both political parties have been skeptical to embrace school boards from an education policy perspective, it is telling that they have decided it is a priority to leverage school board battles to energize voters and galvanize their base, with the hopes of gaining momentum in state and national elections.[30]

Just as political operatives know they can no longer afford to ignore school boards, neither can we. We should all look at recent boardroom battles as the impetus to revisit the potential for school boards to help strengthen our public education system. How we do that is suggested by what has happened without many of us noticing: the pendulum of school governance has swung in the direction of state power at the expense of local control. Seeing the problem points us toward a solution. Part II will explain how school board governance is uniquely suited to address some of public education's greatest challenges and therefore why it is urgent that the pendulum swing back. We can unlock board potential by balancing local and centralized authority to allow each to exercise appropriate responsibilities and accountability. Reaching a better equilibrium, I underscore, requires us to collectively invest in school board capacity through additional research, professional development opportunities, awareness, and participation. We all have a role to play.

II

THE CASE FOR SCHOOL BOARDS

6

FROM WALL STREET TO
A SCHOOL BOARD SEAT

It is time to challenge conventional wisdom and change the paradigm of how we think about education governance in America. School boards matter. For decades they have been an afterthought, a distant third in the triad of state, federal, and local authority. They should assume their rightful place alongside these centralized actors.

In the chapters that follow, I will make the case for why school boards are critical to the success of a district and to the public education system overall. It is a conviction I arrived at through experience and research as I transitioned from a job on Wall Street to a school board seat.

On obtaining that seat, I began my service with humility and plenty of blind spots. I had no familiarity with education law, and I was completely naive about New York State politics. I lacked a background in curriculum and pedagogy. I relied on fellow board members who had more experience, and I tapped into the larger network of board members and administrators across my region and state.

At the same time, I brought professional experience to the table that provided me with a relatively unique perspective. For years, I worked as an investment banker, advising boards and management teams of large and medium-sized corporations on governance, strategy, and finance.

As discussed in the Introduction, many in the education world regard Wall Street executives skeptically. Some view any idea borrowed from business as a back-handed attempt to profit from testing, curriculum materials, and technology. Fears are exacerbated when Wall Street executives fund school reform initiatives that threaten to dismantle public education, while sending their own children to private school. For many who spend their careers within public education there is fatigue from the unintended consequences of mandates related to applying business principles such as standards, accountability, and competition to education.

Without question, the purpose and mission of a public school is fundamentally different from the purpose and mission of a for-profit corporation. That said, the more I immersed myself in school board service, the more I became convinced that there are critical insights the education world can gain from the private sector.

The first point of contrast I noticed relates to how the education world views school boards and how the business world views corporate boards. While school boards are an afterthought in education policy circles, corporate boards have long been considered to be fundamental and central to the success or failure of a corporation.

The lack of focus on school boards seriously hampers ongoing efforts to improve education governance. Consider that there is a substantial amount of academic research, press, regulatory attention, and professional dialogue within corporate executive circles aimed at trying to make company boards better. You do not have to travel far in the corporate world to hear active debates about the many pressing governance issues that modern day corporate boards face. In the education world, however, school board governance issues garner little attention beyond board members themselves and school boards associations. There are times when reformers and policy makers have pushed to eliminate school boards, but never have I witnessed a serious debate regarding an alternative to corporate boards.

The very idea that a corporate board is not pivotal to a corporation would be completely absurd to anyone on Wall Street or in corporate America. When making an investment decision, the quality of the board is often part of the analysis. When an activist shareholder believes a company is moving in the wrong direction, they frequently campaign for a board seat. When a company contemplates a strategy shift, bankers and consultants present their ideas to the board. When there are new regulatory risks that arise, the Securities and Exchange Commission contemplates the board's obligations to address any shortcomings.

Just as boards have served as an extremely effective mechanism to govern corporations since the 1600s, they similarly govern nonprofit organizations, such as universities and hospitals. My experiences advising corporate boards and sitting on nonprofit boards prompted me to ask a simple question: *Don't school boards matter just as much?*

There is another important parallel worth noting between the business world and the public education universe. Just like corporations, school districts are organizations. After all, an "organization" is defined most simply as "a group of people who work together in an organized way for a shared purpose."[1] School districts certainly are composed of a "group of people" with a "shared purpose." Their funding sources, constituents, and mission are unique, but just like a company or a nonprofit, at their core, school districts are organizations.

Historically, the school reform movement has been focused on leveraging business concepts outside districts. Examples include greater regulatory and statutory micromanagement, the desire to encourage more competition, and standardization to facilitate system-wide comparisons for purposes of accountability.

What has been forgotten are the business concepts that relate to the dynamics *inside* organizations, including the role of strong and empowered organizational governance and management teams.

These inside forces are paramount. America's school districts are incredibly diverse. Each faces its own unique set of challenges. A school board, sitting *within* a district, has the capability of applying customized solutions to specific problems rather than a one-size-fits-all top-down regulatory approach.

School boards have broad and consequential organizational responsibilities, wielding power that can often determine the success or failure of a district. These responsibilities generally include:

- Hiring, managing, and firing the superintendent;
- Setting policy on matters ranging from discipline to school safety;
- Making budget allocation decisions, and in many jurisdictions, proposing or determining an annual tax levy;

- Determining district goals and strategic direction;
- Approving curriculum;
- Signing off on material contracts and ratifying personnel decisions;
- Setting the organizational tone and climate.

For all these reasons, school boards matter, and we must reframe our thinking not only to recognize the critical role they play but also to embrace them as a critical lever for school improvement.

We have reached a fork in the education governance road. Our current path places boards in the peripheral vision of policymakers as red and blue states alike continue to invoke centrally enforced mandates and bans that further erode board autonomy. Little by little, states have transitioned from their traditional regulatory role to proactive micromanagers, inserting themselves into just about every facet of district life, crushing political will at the local level. This is the wrong path, and it is imperative that we follow a different one.

There are two important elements that need to be addressed before we can harness the capability of school boards to improve our educational system. The first is structural. While state and federal oversight undoubtedly needs to play an important role in providing funding and ultimate accountability, the pendulum has swung too far in the direction of state micromanagement, and with urgency, we must find a better balance so that states maintain their important oversight role but purposefully delegate more authority and latitude to local boards of education.

The second is to ensure that school board members practice good governance. Even without structural change, there are many actions boards can take today under our current system to make their districts function better. Boards should have thoughtful onboarding processes and encourage continuous professional development. They should be contemplative and follow governance best practices. Put simply, board members must, as many of them do, take their responsibilities seriously, and this includes seeking out training, mentoring, and developing governance expertise.

Part II discusses how empowered and well-functioning boards have the capability of addressing five key challenges that public schools face and provides suggested next steps. The acronym "IDEAS" serves as a reminder of these challenges:

1. Initiative Fatigue
2. District Climate
3. Engagement with the Community
4. Accountability
5. Short-termism

Chapters 7–11 will tackle each in turn. Each chapter will start by explaining why addressing the respective challenge is critical to improving our system. Then, it will pivot to why school boards, not state or federal government, are uniquely positioned to solve the problem and what action steps school board members can consider and implement. When appropriate, insight from the corporate world will be gleaned.

The stakes couldn't be higher. For the foreseeable future, regardless of what comes next on the school reform agenda, most American kids will receive their education from a public school. America's future, from economics to politics to scientific discovery to civic life, is dependent on how well we educate the next generation. We cannot afford to overlook our opportunity to empower school boards to address some of the biggest challenges facing public education. The potential scope of influence that school boards could exert cannot be overstated.

7

INITIATIVE FATIGUE

When I first was elected to the board of education, I naturally sought advice regarding district leadership. I could have reviewed scholarly education literature. Instead, I turned first to my trusted source for all things education—my mother.

Mom taught kindergarten for thirty-five years, which earned her the right to share her opinions on education. She provided me with important insights into school governance from a teacher's perspective. Foremost on her mind was initiative fatigue: "Teachers have become conditioned to expect initiative after initiative. A new initiative is rolled out from above, and before long, another initiative is introduced. Sometimes, if you wait long enough, a new initiative ends up being the opposite of a past initiative. My advice to you is to tell the teachers in your district that you care about their perspectives and that you value them being highly engaged. It will do wonders."[1]

I had worked in large corporations for most of my adult life, and I was familiar with the concept of initiative overload. It is a common phenomenon across all types of organizations. But as I familiarized myself with the world of public education, I realized that the initiative fatigue my mom described was on a totally different scale. There is a constant flow of new initiatives in the public school universe far beyond anything I experienced in the for-profit and not-for-profit world. Table 7.1 illustrates a sampling of initiatives that many schools have adopted recently.

Table 7.1   Selected recent education initiatives

Adaptive testing	Financial literacy
Anti-bullying	Flipped classrooms
Authentic assessment	Inclusive classrooms
Block schedule	New math standards
Childcare services	New science standards
Civics education	New social studies standards
Coding and robotics	New world language standards
Community schools	One-to-one devices
Cybersecurity	Online learning
Data dashboards	Performance-based assessment
Differentiated instruction	Phonics instruction
Digital divide	Reevaluating the role of homework
Digital literacy	Restorative justice
DEI	Social and emotional learning (SEL)
Electric buses	Student directed learning
Equitable grading	Twenty-first-century "soft" skills
Executive functioning skills	Universal meals
Extended learning	Universal pre-K

The issue isn't whether any individual initiative has merit, but rather, how many there are. The implementation of too many initiatives at once can be daunting for even the best-run districts.

THE PROBLEM

Education scholars have long recognized the problem of initiative overload. In 2002, Douglas Reeves explained how the "Law of Initiative Fatigue" sets in when limited time, resources, and physical and emotional energy of staff are spread across a growing number of initiatives. As more initiatives are introduced, there is less time available to dedicate to each, and initiative effectiveness "declines exponentially" as employees "grow weary and cynical when confronted with leadership that does not understand the difference between what is new and what is simply more."[2]

Ironically, despite the endless array of initiatives schools embrace, they are often criticized for being stuck in the past. Ken Robinson, an expert on schools and creativity who delivered the most popular TED Talk ever, argued that schools still look much as they did in the early twentieth century when they were standardized and scaled to accommodate the rapidly growing population and the labor requirements of the Industrial Revolution. These systems, developed over one hundred years ago, he stated, "are inherently unsuited to the wholly different circumstances of the twenty-first century."[3] Examples include grouping students by age, organizing lessons by subject, administering traditional quizzes and tests, and separating periods by ringing a bell.

How is it possible that schools have overloaded themselves with initiatives but in some respects remain antiquated? Much of it depends on whether initiatives are executed well, fit into the overall picture, and stand the test of time. Jeffrey Henig observes that "in a seeming contradiction, school systems are portrayed both as rigidly resistant to new ideas and as fickle consumers that embrace every last trend."[4]

In fact, a great deal of change has happened over the past century. If you walk into a well-run school today and compare the experience to 100 years ago, it wouldn't take much to notice positive and meaningful differences. Many classes no longer use textbooks but rather a compilation of curated materials. There are computer science and engineering classes. Traditional lecture formats have given way to more engaged, hands-on learning. The Advanced Placement (AP) and International Baccalaureate (IB) curriculums are accessible, and the tests themselves are less about the memorization of facts and more about analysis and synthesis of ideas, a reaction to the fact that we have search engines at our fingertips. Some high schools have transitioned to block schedules that allow teachers more time for in-depth learning. Reading is taught differently. So is math. There are social and emotional learning and mental health resources.

When new initiatives are thoughtfully sourced, prioritized, and executed with focus and discipline, they can be transformative. Conversely, haphazard and rushed new initiatives can be detrimental to teacher satisfaction and student outcomes.

In 2022 and 2023, surveys of over one thousand U.S. public school teachers each year were conducted by Merrimack College and *Education Week* and compared against historical results of the *MetLife Survey of the American Teacher* (administered through 2012). The most recent survey found that the percentage of teachers who said they are "very satisfied" with their jobs has declined precipitously from 59 percent in 2009 to 20 percent in 2023, and the percentage of teachers "fairly or very likely" to leave the profession to pursue a different occupation has risen from 17 percent in 2009 to 35 percent in 2023.[5]

More granular survey results provide a window into what is driving dissatisfaction. Fifty-five percent of teachers felt that the public "respects them and sees them as professionals," down from 77 percent in 2011. Less than half of respondents "strongly agree" that they have a lot of control and influence over their teaching/pedagogy, while only 25 percent "strongly agree" they have a lot of control and influence over the curriculum and 5 percent "strongly agree" they have a lot of control and influence over school policies.[6]

The 2022 survey provided a profile of teacher satisfaction, focusing on the group of teachers who reported feeling "very satisfied" with their jobs. One hundred percent of this group reported that they "feel respected/ seen as a professional" within their own school, 99 percent said they have "a lot of control/influence" over teaching pedagogy, and 65 percent said they have "a lot of control/influence" over school policies.[7]

The 2022 survey report explained that results suggest "concerns among some respondents that teaching is being deprofessionalized, i.e. converted to a job like cashier or warehouse worker, where employees have limited control over their work." One Connecticut middle school teacher with thirty-plus years of experience explained:

My district incorporated a robotic curriculum for my subject, and all teachers must be on the same page doing the same assessments. It's horrible. . . . Creativity has been killed in the classroom. . . . Sadly, it feels like [the] good times are gone with people [who rarely set foot in a classroom] making crucial decisions that directly affect teachers and students. . . . The mass exodus from the teaching profession is just beginning. This country and its children will be casualties of these flawed policies and lack of respect for professional educators who simply want to teach and inspire their students.[8]

This loss of autonomy has been happening for decades. Joseph Murphy of Vanderbilt University observes, "It is difficult to examine reform initiatives across time and fail to notice that teachers are sometimes devalued and treated as second class participants, as subjects, technicians, and as hired hands."[9]

During a Harvard Graduate School of Education webinar reported on in the *Harvard Gazette*, Professor Heather Hill explained that the increase in accountability expectations has led to "heavy regulation of teaching" and described how "all the mandated things are taking away agency from teachers to make decisions, and that is at the heart of what teaching actually is." The webinar lamented a loss of teacher autonomy, further exacerbated by the pandemic.[10]

Researchers Amanda Olsen from the University of Texas at Arlington and Erica Mason at the University of Illinois Urbana-Champaign define autonomy as "a teacher's perception about the degree to which they can make decisions (i.e., their influence) related to their work."[11] With the teaching profession increasingly characterized by a lack of autonomy and initiative fatigue, the profession becomes less desirable for highly motivated and talented college graduates. In *Forbes Magazine*, Ethan Siegel succinctly explains the problem. "The reason, as much as we hate to admit it, is that we've disobeyed the cardinal rule of success in any industry: treating your workers like professionals."[12]

Another cause of initiative fatigue in education is the combination of high expectations and a lack of patience. Often, a new initiative is introduced by those who proclaim it will solve all our problems, and when they don't observe rapid change, they quickly become disillusioned and disappointed. They give up and switch course before we even know with certainty that a particular initiative has a positive, neutral, or negative impact. Schools are complex environments, and it is difficult to isolate the impact of any one variable when conducting a study. Often research shows correlation, but policymakers or practitioners view it as causation.

As illustrated in figure 7.1, districts get caught in an all too familiar cycle that compounds problems of eroding teacher autonomy and the general lack of patience for evidence of results.

It is not unusual for any organization to lack focus and spread itself too thin, but why is initiative fatigue so pervasive in education? A significant contributing factor is the structure of education governance, in which there are many unique layers of decision makers that converge on the classroom.

Jeffrey Henig, in his book *The End of Exceptionalism in American Education*, notes the large number of initiatives in urban school systems that have "been like a series of spinning wheels." Henig attributes these competing initiatives as not only "the latest in a string of disparate, ephemeral, and herky-jerky enthusiasms that will come and go," but also the outcome of school board governance structure changing from a system

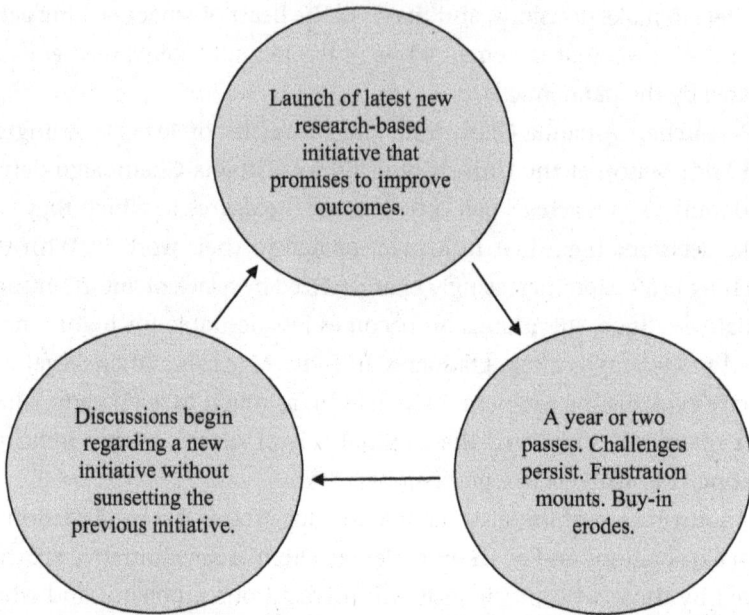

7.1 The initiative cycle.

centered on local, single-purpose governance (the school board focused exclusively on education) to "multilevel, general-purpose government and politics."[13]

It is not surprising that our complex and multilayered educational governance ecosystem promotes dysfunction and lack of coordination. Just think about the number of external parties that direct what happens every school day. Congress, the president, and the U.S. Department of Education tout a set of initiatives and priorities that often are a prerequisite to receiving federal funding. At the state level, governors, legislatures, education commissioners, and state boards all have a heavy hand in launching initiatives, regulations, mandates, and bans.

Other outside influences, including academia, foundations, think tanks, and the business community, play a role in generating ideas for new initiatives. Similarly, parents and community members advocate for initiatives by participating in advocacy groups and organizations or by expressing their opinions directly to the school board. Finally, there is governance and administrative leadership at the district level and administrators at the school levels launching initiatives of their own. As illustrated in figure 7.2, these layers exist even before you get to the teachers and students who are in the classrooms doing the actual work.

Joseph Murphy writes how school reform partners, including researchers, policymakers, corporate executives, and foundation leaders, lack in-depth knowledge of what it is like to operate and work in a district and that "teachers and school administrators routinely judge solution strategies developed by their partners as discordant and unhelpful."[14]

Because there are so many disparate players introducing initiatives, there is a lack of coordination, and at times, initiatives conflict with one another. As a result, initiatives rarely are holistic and often are constantly changing depending on who has the most power at any given time. It is like an orchestra where every member diligently plays music but there is no conductor or uniform score.

The lack of coordinated decision-making within the education governance ecosystem results in what researchers call the "multiplier effect," which occurs when multiple priorities are set by different people in isolation,

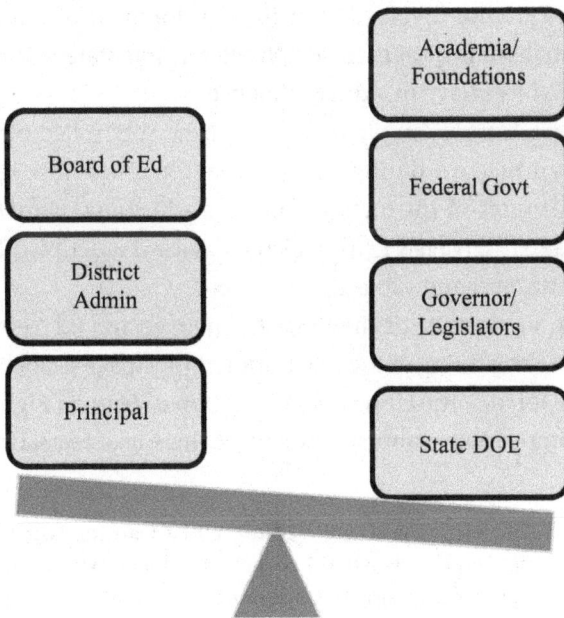

7.2 Sources of initiatives.

without regard for the capacity and specific circumstances of other parts of the organization.[15] Each initiative may be sound, but when taken as a whole, the collective priorities become unrealistic and uncoordinated.

The multiplier effect can occur in any organization where the board and CEO lead in an unfocused, overambitious manner, but it is common in education, where outside forces at the state and federal levels exert significant influence and often have strings attached to funding. A state senator who drafts a new education mandate has no way of knowing how every individual district in their state is going to manage that mandate in the context of their other organizational requirements and priorities.

Furthermore, mandates often do not come with the requisite funding, nor are they accompanied by the sunsetting of prior mandates. The list of required initiatives just grows, making resource allocation even more difficult.

In addition to state and federal governments lacking context for the broader picture regarding the priorities and challenges facing an individual district, there is another clear downside to centralized mandates. This top-down system runs in an overly prescriptive way where all too often practitioners are not involved with the development of initiatives, or a relatively small number of them are placed on large statewide committees where their voices have marginal influence.

There is no better example than when New York rolled out the Common Core curriculum during Race to the Top. New York developed a comprehensive set of instructional materials to support teachers. These modules, called "EngageNY," provided a day-by-day scripted lesson plan for each grade level and subject.

Consider an example of the English language arts (ELA) materials by reviewing the beginning of the five-hundred-plus-page Grade 5 ELA Module 1 on the topic of the Universal Declaration of Human Rights (UDHR). The following passage summarizes part of the suggested script from the module:

Minutes 0–10: The teacher is asked to read the first learning target to the class: "I can follow our class norms when I participate in a conversation." Then, the teacher states that learning targets are important and asks students to provide synonyms of the words *follow* and *participate*. Next, the teacher is instructed to have a student read the second learning target: "I can define human rights." The students are then instructed to discuss the meaning of the words *human* and *rights* and they are reminded to pay attention to the class norms.

Minutes 11–15: The teacher is instructed to use the Fist to Five strategy to have students rate how they did on the first learning target. The teacher is told to: "ask students to indicate with their fist if they did not attend to the class norms at all, or five fingers if they attended to all class norms consistently. They can choose to show one to four fingers to indicate that their attention to norms was somewhere in between."

Minutes 16–20: The teacher distributes copies of the UDHR to each student and says: "This is a really cool primary source called the Universal Declaration of Human Rights, sometimes called the UDHR. We will learn more about this document in the next few days. Look it over. What do you notice about the way this document is structured or laid out on this page?" Then, the teacher is instructed to say "The UDHR has 30 different articles, or specific sections. Each article identifies a different right, or claim, about something that the people who wrote this document believe should be true for all human beings." It then instructs the teacher to write on the interactive white board "articles in the UDHR are claims about things that the authors of this document believe should be true for all human beings."[16]

Districts were not forced to use the scripted EngageNY materials. However, despite widespread reports of state educators finding the modules to be overly scripted, lacking in creativity, and containing errors, many districts made the decision to rely heavily, if not exclusively, on EngageNY. Ken Slentz, deputy education commissioner, said, anecdotally, "There are more [teachers] using them than not." Robert Lowry, Deputy Director of the New York State Council of School Superintendents (NYCOSS), said administrators were concerned that teachers were using the modules like scripts and were afraid to deviate, fearing they would not be aligned with the state assessments.[17]

In *What School Could Be*, Ted Dintersmith chronicles his trip to 200 schools across all 50 states in the span of one school year to find examples of local innovation. He concludes: "In education, our experts know what to do. The problem is, we listen to the wrong experts. Our innovative teachers, not those at the top of the education pyramid, are the ones who know."[18]

We must recognize that grassroots ideas will often have the most authentic enthusiasm and buy-in, which are essential ingredients when implementing a new initiative. Teachers and staff should be asked for their input and ideas early on, before an initiative is rolled out. If district employees do not have their hearts in an initiative, implementation will be more difficult and less effective. There is a difference between "going through the motions" and executing an initiative with genuine enthusiasm. Students should also be consulted. They can be a source of ideas and can assist in the implementation process.

In *Outside Money in School Board Elections*, Henig, Jacobsen, and Reckhow argue that the principal-agent theory and implementation research suggests that local districts play the role of a "gatekeeper" and can "reinterpret, adjust, co-opt, or stymie directives" of centralized policymakers, ultimately determining what gets done and what dies in the implementation process.[19]

At the organizational level in public education, implementation gatekeepers are board members in their governance role and superintendents in their managerial role. State mandates are only as good as the quality of the implementation on the ground. The words and actions of these school district leaders matter and will ultimately influence whether the organization goes through the motions or rigorously embraces a new edict from regulators. If a school board does not believe in the mandate, they may be reluctant to implement it with fidelity, and the initiative will likely flounder. The very outcomes that innumerable top-down initiatives aspire to produce depend on local effort, and for this reason alone, more deference and responsibility should rest with the agents who are going to be depended on to carry out centralized directions.

Without local buy-in, education research has pointed out the tendency for federal or state initiatives to falter and sometimes die. Researchers Heinrich Mintrop and Gail Suderman observe that of all the attempted restructuring strategies related to No Child Left Behind federal legislation, "none stand out as universally effective or sufficiently robust to overcome the power of local context."[20] The same initiative may not be relevant to address the needs of each school. Furthermore, implementation may vary significantly depending on the capacity, culture, and context of each district.[21]

Instituting new initiatives and striving for innovation requires flexibility to course correct when mistakes are inevitably made. At the local level, it's easy for a board and superintendent to course correct. At the state level, legislation is not particularly flexible, and if it backfires, it is hard to repeal.

Eric Abrahamson, in *Change without Pain*, highlights symptoms of what he calls "repetitive-change syndrome," which includes "initiative overload, change-related chaos, and widespread employee anxiety, cynicism, and burnout." He explains how this syndrome causes new initiatives to fail and can negatively "impinge on routine operations." Though Abrahamson stipulates that there are times when highly disruptive change is needed, he encourages organizations to pursue "creative recombination," which involves looking at what an organization already has and determining how to "reuse, redeploy, or recombine these existing elements of the firm into new configurations."[22] Recombination is something that would be difficult for a centralized authority to do since it is predicated on detailed knowledge of the specific organization.

In addition, we should be honest that we can't legislate the precise winning formula because we don't have one. Reformers have been at it for decades but have yet to develop the universal solution to all our education problems. Look at almost any aspect of schooling and you will likely find a history of conflicting best practices. If we foster innovation at the district level, we create a laboratory of ideas and experiments. Centralized government can play an important role in monitoring these experiments, determining what moves the needle, and then sharing best practices to facilitate scaling.

Another reason that local innovation is optimal is because one size does not fit all. In their book *Tinkering Toward Utopia*, Tyack and Cuban observe that "American public schools have been and are extremely diverse. This helps explain the uneven penetration of reforms, though policy talk about education reform sometimes conveniently neglects variability."[23]

There are dramatic differences in our education system, even within the same state. Districts within the same state vary in their rates of absenteeism, graduation, and academic proficiency. In fact, a well-resourced suburban district in one state likely has more in common with a well-resourced suburban district in another state than an underresourced urban district within the same state.

State policy often tries to solve an overarching problem that may exist in many districts, but for districts that don't suffer from the same problem, there is typically no flexibility to get dispensation from regulation. Providing mandatory solutions to problems that do not exist is burdensome and a waste of time and resources. Federal and state policy is a blunt instrument, and there is something to be said for a more targeted approach, which boards, with their ground-level insights and knowledge, are best positioned to inform. Just as public charter schools generally are exempt from certain regulatory requirements with the goal of providing room for innovation, public schools should be afforded flexibility while still being held accountable for ultimate outcomes.

UNIQUE SCHOOL BOARD POTENTIAL

School boards are structurally the best place to provide the governance oversight necessary to avoid initiative fatigue and drive innovation. Federal and state governments, with all their good intentions, do not have the capability to understand the complete picture within each district of what initiatives are being executed and the connectivity (or lack thereof) between the various initiatives in process. States need to show restraint in launching new initiatives, but when a new mandate is critical, it should come with adequate funding and the state should consider sunsetting an older initiative to ensure adequate institutional capacity.

It is at the district level that shortcomings can be pinpointed, and solutions can be tailored to meet specific needs. For example, if a district achieves outstanding outcomes in math but has subpar reading scores, the school board's focus can be on ELA. If a district's academic outcomes exceed expectations but schools face a mental health crisis, the school board may want to allocate resources to initiatives that address student stress, anxiety, and well-being.

It is not enough for boards to be granted more autonomy in overseeing initiatives. Success will be predicated on how well the board carries out this responsibility. The first challenge is to stay in the governance lane. Boards are responsible for setting district goals and priorities and ensuring accountability. They also oversee the resource allocation process and need to approve certain curriculum decisions. All these duties have a direct link to preventing initiative fatigue. At the same time, boards are not domain experts. They should harness idea flow from teachers, staff, administrators, students, and parents to understand priorities and develop solutions. They should rely on administrators for professional education advice and for the day-to-day execution of planned initiatives.

The second challenge is to employ good governance skills. I've come up with an acronym to help with this that board members can remember to combat initiative fatigue: "SIFT," as in sift through the clutter of initiatives to determine what matters the most for your district. Focus on four important factors when evaluating any potential initiative:

1. Systems
2. Implementation
3. Focus
4. Time

SYSTEMS

When contemplating the launch of a new initiative, administrators and school board members as the district leaders should ask a series of difficult but pertinent questions:

- Is the initiative addressing a problem the district is experiencing?
- How does the initiative integrate into the district's mission, strategy, and goals?
- Does the scope of the initiative match the magnitude of the problem?
- To avoid a superficial, piecemeal approach, do administrative leaders have a plan to integrate the initiative into the fabric (the systems and structure) of the district, including the other ongoing initiatives?

Let's use a real-world example of addressing high school stress and anxiety. A piecemeal approach might be an annual mandated curriculum module that addresses mental health. A more systemic approach would be to first measure the stress and anxiety problem, perhaps through a survey or focus group. Once the magnitude of the problem has been identified, the district may convene a task force of key stakeholders to consider a full range of systemic issues, such as school start times, scheduling, mental health/guidance support, testing, and homework policy. Students may need supplemental instruction in developing executive functioning skills or stress-reduction strategies. Addressing staff stress and anxiety is also critical: adults set an example, and their stress may rub off on the students. Parent workshops on the initiative can bridge the gap between school and home.

It is a lot of hard work for just one initiative, but thinking about the relevant structures and systems makes success more likely and durable. It's better to devote time, energy, and resources to a few successful initiatives than many half-hearted ones.

While a lot of this work will be led at the administrative level and involve constituents throughout the district community, the school board has a specific role as the governance body of the organization. Responsibilities include ensuring that there is ample institutional capacity for the initiative alongside the district's other priorities and applying systems thinking, focus, and a realistic timeframe.

An initiative should also have measurable outcomes. District leaders should determine in advance how they will know if an initiative is effective. Chapter 10 includes a more detailed discussion of how data can be harnessed to monitor initiatives.

IMPLEMENTATION

As described by a team of researchers led by implementation scientist Dean Fixsen, "Thoughtful and effective implementation strategies at multiple levels are essential to any systematic attempt to use the products of science to improve the lives of children" and "implementation is synonymous with coordinated change at system, organization, program, and practice levels."[24]

Strong implementation involves training, coaching, monitoring, and evaluation. Another important element to a smooth implementation process is clear communication. Consideration should also be given to funding and whether policies are in place to support the initiative. Some of the ways in which boards can ensure the smooth execution of an initiative include: (1) allocating adequate budgetary resources, (2) soliciting input from staff and community to achieve buy-in, (3) incorporating the initiative into district goals and monitoring progress, (4) including the initiative in the superintendent evaluation criteria, (5) negotiating any relevant terms into employee/bargaining unit contracts, and (6) determining any necessary changes to district policy.

FOCUS

Perhaps the most obvious but most difficult element of SIFT is to maintain focus. Greg McKeown's concept of essentialism states that it is important to repeatedly ask, "Am I investing in the right activities?" He argues that opportunities outweigh time and resources, so we must make wise choices, learn to "filter through all those options" and select "only those that are truly essential."[25]

Every organization, and every individual within an organization, has a finite amount of bandwidth. How we deploy that bandwidth will likely dictate what gets accomplished and what fails. Does the district have capacity to take on something new? Does an existing initiative—or more than one—need to be displaced to free up resources?

State regulators are not in the position to know how much organizational capacity exists at each district for new initiatives. In contrast, local school boards have the capability of assessing their own organizational strengths and weaknesses. This insight makes these boards uniquely suited to prioritize goals and initiatives.

A school board can steer the focus by setting district goals each year and holding the organization accountable for achieving those goals. A critical part of this process is to be bold but also ensure that there are sufficient resources and organizational capacity to achieve success. Potential initiatives must be weighed, and only the very best ones should be chosen.

Douglas Reeves, as outlined in his book *Finding Your Leadership Focus*, conducted an analysis of two thousand U.S. and Canadian schools and found that only one-half of 1 percent of schools achieved the highest "focus" score (defined as having "six or fewer claimed priorities"). Notably, one school recorded 246 initiatives![26]

Reeves attempted to explain the importance of focus to the schools and encouraged them to follow his "rule of six," which implies that focus is lost after exceeding six priorities. After year three, more than 10 percent met the definition of highly focused. These schools also showed the best gains in math, reading, science, and social studies.[27]

Reeves explains that when districts focus and take time to monitor and emphasize professional learning, assessment, and feedback, student achievement gains are over five times greater than schools that fail to focus.[28]

TIME

The final element to prevent initiative fatigue is time. In addition to assessing ample institutional bandwidth to take on a new initiative that we touched upon in the preceding section, it is important to set a realistic timeframe for achieving results. For too long, reformers have had unrealistic expectations to achieve quick results. Funding streams themselves often have short time horizons or are one-time in nature, making it challenging to take a long-term perspective. Examples of this short-term focus include federal funds in 2009 during Race to the Top and again during the pandemic.

All too often, we lose patience when an initiative doesn't quickly solve everything, and we jump to the next promising new idea prematurely. After experiencing the constant churn of initiatives, teachers and staff learn that they can outlast any initiative they don't like if they wait long enough.

If an initiative is high priority, the district should communicate a realistic timeframe upfront to set expectations. It is critical to maintain discipline and patience until there is enough evidence to suggest whether the current initiatives are working. Employing a strategy for sustainability of the initiative is also of critical importance.

The principles underlying SIFT can make a profound difference in avoiding initiative fatigue. As the former executive director of the Yale Center for Emotional Intelligence (YCEI), I witnessed real-world examples of why following SIFT is so critical. YCEI, led by Professor Marc Brackett, works with schools around the world on teaching the skills of emotional intelligence to foster well-being. YCEI's approach to emotional intelligence, RULER, has been associated with improved school climate and increased engagement, enhanced academic performance, stronger relationships, reduced bullying and aggressive behavior, and better management of stress and anxiety.[29] Having said that, it is next to impossible for any organization to accomplish all these aspirational goals at once.

We cautioned school leaders to take a measured and realistic approach in implementing RULER. Some schools were tempted to tackle too many problems at once, while other schools approached the work without specific goals and outcomes in mind.

Instead, it is best to ask a series of questions consistent with the SIFT principles. What specific problem is the school trying to solve? How can implementation be systemic instead of piecemeal? Is there ample institutional capacity given other ongoing initiatives? Is there a thoughtful implementation plan? Will there be patience to stick with the plan and measure results over a realistic implementation timeframe? Addressing these questions increases the chances of achieving a successful outcome.

In addition to avoiding fatigue, a school board that pursues initiatives thoughtfully also has the capability of driving innovation. Consider board best practices in driving innovation that have been compiled by Linda Hill and George Davis in the *Harvard Business Review*. While they were designed for corporate boards, I have adjusted them slightly to apply the concepts to school boards:

- Instead of delivering polished presentations to the board with "perfunctory questions," administrators should bring incomplete ideas and ask for help in the brainstorming process.
- Understand that the board can add value by engaging in dialogue and sharing thoughts; there does not always have to be deliberations that reach a definitive answer. Innovation comes from iterative dialogue.
- The board must have appetite to take calculated risks to achieve district innovation.
- The board must be willing to have a long-term view.
- Time needs to be carved out of the board's agenda from the mundane (but important and required) business of oversight to provide space for discussions regarding new ideas.
- Metrics must be put in place to measure progress if a new idea progresses to the execution stage.
- There must be space for some degree of conflict. Tough questions and genuine dialogue are prerequisites.
- The board and administration need to have a partnership mindset and maintain mutual respect for their specific roles.[30]

Hill and Davis observe that oftentimes board members are reluctant to bring some of the most pressing questions to a management team, fearing they will be viewed as micromanaging. School board members, like corporate board members, need to get comfortable asking what is on their minds, while always respecting the line between governance and day-to-day management.

Asking tough questions, however, is even more difficult for school board members since school board meetings take place in public. Having said that, paying the price of slightly awkward moments under the spotlight is well worth it in the end if mutual respect is maintained and positive innovation is achieved.

My own school district has a powerful example of successful innovation that originated in 1989, well before I became a board member. The board debated a key curricular decision, a proposal to develop an Authentic Science Research program (ASR). It was not a completely novel idea. In 1939, Edward Pendray, a Westinghouse executive, and Watson Davis, director of Science Service (now Society for Science) developed a national competition to encourage high school students to pursue scientific research. Over time, program sponsorship has transitioned from Westinghouse to Intel to Regeneron. It has awarded students who have gone on to become leaders in every discipline of scientific inquiry.[31]

Despite ASR's long and storied history and its popularity among magnet schools focused on science, it was unusual for a traditional suburban public school to consider adopting the program back in 1989. Though the New York State Regents eventually allowed it to become a three-credit course, the ASR program did not satisfy the core Regents requirements that count toward receiving an advanced high school diploma. The course's content did not directly prepare students for Regents exams, satisfy state curriculum mandates; nor did it directly cover content for the SAT, ACT, Advanced Placement exams, or Achievement Tests (the latter no longer exist but were popular at the time). It required extra budgetary funds and took up precious classroom time.

Additionally, the structure of the course broke from tradition. It lasted three years instead of the usual one or two semesters. Sophomores, juniors, and seniors were in class together, with older students providing guidance and mentorship.

Students could not be evaluated with conventional testing techniques. ASR programs often encouraged, or even required, students to seek mentoring outside of the school from university professors who had expertise in a particular topic. They also required summer work. Rather than memorization of facts regarding prescribed topics, students would conduct proprietary research in an area of their choosing.[32]

The board of my district weighed the merits and drawbacks of instituting the new program and ultimately approved it. It took courage and vision to move in a direction that did not fit into the state's formula for how to educate students.

The idea to institute this innovative initiative came from an interaction between a student and teacher. The student, who had taken every AP course offered, said, "I listened to what the teacher told me, then I memorized what the teacher told me, and then on the next exam I wrote down what the teacher told me. And I got an A. That is not what I want to do. I want to do science."[33] After listening to this student, a teacher provided space for proprietary research, and the idea of establishing an authentic experience where students could deeply explore scientific topics took shape.[34]

The Authentic Science Research program turned out to be a resounding success. ASR was ahead of its time. It encompasses all the buzzwords and concepts to which schools aspire in the twenty-first century. Students learn how to learn. No matter what field they pursue, they will understand what it takes to master a topic, identify gaps in the literature, and conduct proprietary research. They will hone their communications skills by writing a scientific paper and presenting their findings at competitions and conferences. They practice collaborative learning and receive mentorship from experts in the field. They can discover their passion. They develop perseverance, navigating the ups and downs of an intensive three-year journey. They master time management skills. The program also benefits American society by inspiring a future generation of scientists, and sometimes science research students make discoveries and significant contributions to their fields of study during their time in high school.

ASR expands the opportunity set for a wide array of students, including those with special needs and students who dislike traditional school. As reported in the *Journal of Secondary Gifted Education* by George Robinson, there was one special education student years ago who received Cs and Ds in traditional classes and had no interest in school but thrived in the program. Here is her success story as described by her teacher:

This student studied a topic in psychology. She had a mentor at a university, and she entered the Westinghouse Science Talent Search. In those days, the Westinghouse representative called up the students around Martin Luther King

[Jr.] Day. They called up this student and said she was a winner in the science competition. I get home and on my answering machine I hear a crying girl hysterical on the phone . . . "I was chosen as a finalist in the Westinghouse Science Talent Search."[35]

Initially, the special education student's classmates were skeptical of her success because of her track record in traditional classes, but they ultimately realized the magnitude of her accomplishment. She received a standing ovation from the entire school community and ultimately earned a PhD and became a psychologist.

The launch of the Authentic Science Research program in my district served as inspiration for the replication of the program in more than 170 school districts across New York State as well as districts in five other states.[36] It is an example of an innovative idea that can transform the student experience. It is also an example of how a successful outcome can be achieved when students, staff, administrators, and the school board focus on innovation and take calculated risks. Finally, it is an example of what is possible when an initiative locally designed and implemented to meet a local need sparks broader interest so that it has uptake in other districts with similar needs and interests.

8

DISTRICT CLIMATE

It was a sunny, warm morning in late August 2018. I stood at the microphone and looked out at the audience, detecting mixed emotions as we said goodbye to summer but also reunited with colleagues. Palpable were the excitement and enthusiasm over the possibilities that a new school year brings.

As the school board president, I welcomed the district faculty back from summer vacation with a short address. I started by commending them for their dedication to last year's priority, student mental health. We had asked ourselves how we could do more to address stress, anxiety, and depression, important topics in schools across America even prior to the COVID-19 pandemic.

But I quickly shifted gears. I knew that the macroenvironment, or what was being said and done at the federal and state levels, weighed heavily on our outstanding, dedicated faculty. They had experienced New York State's aggressive approach to Race to the Top, which included the fast-paced rollout of new curriculum standards and the linking of teacher evaluations to standardized test scores, all of which had negative unintended consequences. School security concerns persisted, with active shooter lockdown drills becoming routine. While our region was fortunate to have some of the finest public schools in the country, the property tax burden was among the highest in the nation, exacerbated by the repeal of the state and local tax (SALT) deduction under the 2017 Tax Cuts and Jobs Act, which made raising taxes for school funding more challenging. I got straight to the point:

Teacher, administrative, and staff wellness is a topic that does not get as much airtime in the national discourse. Yet a recent Yale study surveying five thousand teachers across America on their feelings toward work concluded that 70 percent of the emotions that teachers used to describe their school lives were negative, the top 3 being "frustrated," "overwhelmed," and "stressed."[1]

I have a question for you this morning. You are clearly committed to taking care of our students, but *who is taking care of you?*[2]

The answer to this question underscores the important role of district climate.

THE PROBLEM

School climate as a concept was first identified and discussed in education literature over a hundred years ago. There is no agreed-upon definition of "school climate" in the literature, but the National School Climate Center describes climate as "the quality and character of school life." It is "based on patterns of students', parents' and school personnel's experience of school life and reflects norms, goals, values, interpersonal relationships, teaching and learning practices, and organizational structures."[3] Climate also has been described as "the atmosphere in which all other school activities and initiatives are taking place . . . it is a part of everything, from how safe students feel attending school to how likely they are to focus, learn, and perform."[4] School climate can be thought of as the sum of all the relationships in the district.

Researchers recognize that school climate is multidimensional but debate the precise parameters. In a review of the school climate literature, researchers Ming-Te Wang and Jessica Degol of the University of Pittsburg emphasize the multidimensionality of climate and highlight four key domains: community, academic, safety, and institutional environment. An abbreviated explanation of this climate categorization is shown in table 8.1.[5]

Achieving a positive climate across a school district is neither easy nor a challenge unique to school districts. Maintaining a positive climate and

Table 8.1 Climate domains

Domains	Description
Community	Quality of relationships and connectedness throughout the district, respect for diversity, and partnership with parents
Academic	Leadership, teaching and learning, and professional development
Safety	Social/emotional, physical, and discipline/order
Institutional environment	Availability of resources, environmental (physical infrastructure and maintenance), and structural organization (e.g., class size)

keeping employees engaged are universally recognized as critical to the success of any organization. According to McKinsey & Company senior partner Scott Keller who authored the book *CEO Excellence*, strong corporate executives viewed "the soft stuff just like the hard stuff. And what they meant by that is they put equal rigor into how they handled topics like talent, topics like culture, topics like organization design."[6]

On that late August morning in 2018, I thought about the concept of district climate as I attempted to answer the question *"Who is taking care of you"* that I had posed to the faculty. I concluded my speech with the following passage: "We can take care of each other—and we can draw upon the unique school culture and climate that you all have created that is at the core of our district."[7] I pointed out that a key takeaway from the Yale teacher survey is that a school's underlying culture and climate is a predictor of whether a teacher is likely to report negative emotions. "The combination of negative climate and these negative teacher emotions," I said, "contributes to burnout and intentions to prematurely leave the profession."[8] I concluded with the following words:

The board is humbled and inspired by our district culture and climate.

- We are inspired when we see the board room full of families and colleagues showing support for each other.
- We are inspired when we hear that teachers have gone beyond the call of duty.
- And we are inspired when we see the spirit of collaboration and teamwork transforming traditional classroom structures.[9]

As I left the podium, I thought to myself how blessed I was to be a part of the district and how committed I was to do everything I could as a board member to maintain the district's strength. A key to carrying out this duty was to take care of our employees. After all, it is people that make a school district great.

My August 2018 speech draws upon lessons learned from my former colleagues at the Yale Center for Emotional Intelligence. It was there that I learned how important it is to focus on students *and* the adults who are teaching them. Let's focus on the student crisis first, and then we will turn to the adults.

I was originally drawn to YCEI after noticing that the push for higher academic standards did not focus enough on the looming student mental health crisis. At the time, federal and state-led school reform focused intensively on raising academic standards through test-based accountability. The goal of these reforms was laudable. Too many students were dropping out or graduating from high school with a lack of academic proficiency, and more recently, the COVID-19 pandemic set us further back.

America often performs poorly on academic achievement tests when compared to other nations around the world, and raising the bar on academics needs to be a priority. Our economic and geopolitical competitiveness and the well-being of our citizenry are at stake. At the same time, I was worried that reformers were addressing the problem too narrowly, ignoring the concept of district climate and the growing mental health crisis that existed.

Even prior to the pandemic, too many students were becoming stressed out, disconnected, and disenchanted. A research study asked 22,000 high school students across the United States, "How do you feel each day in school?" Seventy-seven percent of responses were negative, with the three most frequent being "tired," "stressed," and "bored."[10]

During COVID, the situation became more dire. Consider these statistics:

- In 2021, a CDC survey showed that 42 percent of high school students struggle with "persistent feelings of sadness or hopelessness" (for females and the LGBQ+ community, the numbers are even larger, at 57 percent and 69 percent respectively).[11]
- Sixty-nine percent of public schools reported an increase in the percentage of students seeking mental health services since COVID started.[12]

- In 2020, suicide was the second leading cause of death in ten- to fourteen-year-olds.[13] In 2021, 30 percent of female high school students seriously considered suicide in the twelve-month period prior to the survey.[14]

These problems plague all types of schools, from urban to rural, from high-performing to struggling. Anxiety, stress, and depression know no boundaries.

Challenge Success, an initiative affiliated with Stanford University, works primarily with high-achieving schools. Their survey of high school students found that 75 percent reported exhaustion, difficulty sleeping, and headaches related to stress, and only 40 percent felt like they were part of a school community.[15]

A 2012 *New York Times* article discussed how academic pressure and competition have led to student abuse of prescription stimulants. The article states that doctors and teens from more than fifteen high-performing school communities estimated that 15 to 40 percent of students take stimulants to help them study.[16]

There are many root causes of the rise in mental health challenges. The world has changed from when I graduated from high school in the 1990s. There is the impact of social media. The world has become more competitive, with college acceptance rates plummeting (according to data compiled by Spark Admissions, Stanford dropped from 19 percent in 1990 to 4 percent in 2019; the University of Chicago dropped from 45 percent to 6 percent during that same period).[17] In 1994, there were just under half a million AP tests administered. Now, there are over five million.[18] Poverty, lack of affordable healthcare, a drug epidemic, and malnutrition are all contributing factors. The fear of school shootings adds to stress and anxiety. I could go on and on.

As administrators, faculty, and staff grapple with these student mental health challenges, it is important that they are supported. After all, if they are stressed and disengaged, how can we expect engaged students? And should we be surprised that the United States is experiencing a teacher shortage? According to the National Center for Education Statistics, 86 percent of U.S. K-12 public schools experienced challenges hiring teachers in the 2023–2024 school year, and 45 percent reported that their school is understaffed.[19] The high level of educator turnover destabilizes schools and deprives the system of experienced teachers.

Achieving a positive district climate can help address student and faculty engagement. Matthew Kraft of Brown University and William Marinell and Darrick Shen-Wei Yee of Harvard University analyzed middle schools in New York City and ultimately found that when schools "strengthen the organizational contexts in which teachers work," teacher retention and student achievement on standardized tests improve at a faster rate.[20]

A literature review conducted by Jonathan Cohen and colleagues finds that a healthy climate is associated with lower levels of student absenteeism and suspension, enhanced teaching and learning, better educator retention, prevention of violence and risky behavior, and more connectedness (the extent to which students feel like there is at least one adult in the school that cares about them), which is a predictor of better health and academic outcomes.[21]

Despite the evidence that underscores the importance of climate, many districts continue to fall short in this area. In a Yale Center for Emotional Intelligence (YCEI) survey of district board members and superintendents in New York and Connecticut regarding district climate, 49 percent of respondents described their climate as "moderately/highly positive," while 51 percent chose "slightly positive," "neutral," "slightly negative," or "moderately negative."[22] In other words, according to the survey results, if you randomly enroll your child in a district, you will have a roughly fifty-fifty chance of district leaders viewing their climate as less than ideal.

Even more worrisome, when respondents were asked to come up with a word that best describes their district climate, some of the answers were deeply troubling. They included: anxious, mistrustful, overwhelming, stressful, restricting, and threatening.[23]

When YCEI asked teachers and administrators how they wanted to feel when they come to work, responses included excited, connected, and inspired. Employees want to work in districts that emphasize transparency, physical safety, strategic clarity, and supportive relationships between and among administrators, faculty, staff, students, and families. They want to work where everyone feels welcome, regardless of their race, gender, religion, or socioeconomic status.[24]

One clear shortfall identified in the YCEI school board and superintendent survey was the lack of focus on district adults. Eighty-eight percent of respondents gauged mental health, stress, and burnout as a "moderate/large/enormous challenge" for their students, while 89 percent of respondents said the same for their teachers. But while 53 percent were implementing a plan to address mental health and engagement issues in their student body, only 23 percent were implementing a plan aimed at their faculty.[25] If we are serious about improving student mental health, we must first ensure that adults working in schools are engaged and are managing their stress, since they interact with students daily.

One of the prerequisites to a positive climate is to ensure that employees feel they are being managed and evaluated fairly. If there is a perception that the system is rigged or unfair, resentment and bitterness will trump connectedness and belonging. New York State's rollout of Race to the Top serves as an example of how attempts by a centralized government to manage teachers led to negative unintended consequences.

In 2013, when New York State rolled out Race to the Top, an important component of the reform was to hold teachers more accountable since it was difficult and rare to fire ineffective tenured teachers. To accomplish this goal, New York instituted a new statewide teacher evaluation formula that linked teacher ratings to the year-over-year change in student test scores.

The state deployed lawyers, statisticians, and trainers to include a growth model into each district's Annual Professional Performance Review (APPR). State legislators passed legislation that designated this growth model as the single largest component of the evaluation. The model measured the growth of state test scores year-over-year for each teacher's students and attempted to isolate the impact of the teacher from other factors that might influence academic growth. Ultimately, student growth scores for teachers across the state were compared.

It was quite an undertaking. New York has more than two hundred thousand teachers statewide, which is equivalent to the entire population of Rochester.[26] Yet the state believed it could evaluate each individual teacher by using a designated statistical approach.

A study by researchers Raj Chetty, John Friedman, and Jonah Rockoff showed how a value-added model (VAM), a statistical analysis used to measure growth in student test scores from year-to-year, can also be used to identify the impact of teachers on the lives of their students. The research analyzed a large dataset encompassing 2.5 million children. The results of the study suggested that students with high value-added teachers (teachers who have a positive impact on student test scores) were more likely to attend college, earn better salaries, and save more for retirement.[27]

On the heels of establishing this research linking effective teaching to positive student outcomes, New York State attempted to use a value-added model to evaluate individual teachers by attempting to measure student test score growth in each class. VAMs try to estimate a teacher's contribution to student test score results, attempting to control for other variables.[28]

Around the time New York began to use this model for the purposes of identifying and firing underperforming teachers, the American Statistical Association (ASA) issued a statement in April 2014 warning about the limitations of using VAM to evaluate individual teachers. The ASA recognized that VAM is useful to evaluate programs and policies; however, "ranking teachers by their VAM scores can have unintended consequences that reduce quality." The report warns that the impact of VAM on the educational system is "unknown."[29]

Bruce Baker, a professor at the University of Miami, similarly warned that "just because teacher [value-added] scores in a massive dataset show variance does not mean that we can identify with any level of precision or accuracy which individual teachers (plucking single points from a massive scatter plot) are 'good' and which are 'bad.' Therein exists one of the major fallacies of moving from large-scale econometric analysis to micro-level human resource management."[30]

The ASA statement points out specific limitations of VAM for teacher evaluation, including: (1) VAMs are based on test scores and not on broader student outcomes (such as creativity or collaboration), (2) VAMs have "large standard errors . . . [which] make rankings unstable, even under the best scenarios for modeling," (3) VAMs measure correlation and not causation, (4) student placement in a particular class can influence growth models, and ideally class assignments would have to be randomized to avoid bias, (5) VAMs were limited to math and ELA test scores only which could narrow instruction, (6) VAMs fail to isolate help outside of the classroom (such as parents or tutors) and the impact of multiple teachers through subject bleed, and (7) statistical anomalies exist, such as in high-performing schools where students are consistently scoring well and teachers have a harder time demonstrating growth on state assessments.[31]

Furthermore, a typical VAM analysis suggests that teachers only account for 1 percent to 14 percent of the variability in test scores. Much of the variability is associated with other factors such as "student and family background, poverty, curriculum and unmeasured influences."[32] The degree of error in VAM that is tolerable in an academic study is greater than when VAM is linked to individual teacher rankings, compensation, and employment status.

This new statewide system that relied on VAM to evaluate teachers had the unintended consequence of encouraging teachers to narrow instruction and "teach to the test." There were reports of schools deemphasizing social studies, art, music, writing, and literature to double down on math and nonfiction reading drills. Exams with open-ended questions that made students think critically were replaced with multiple choice.[33]

Parents and teachers throughout New York State widely opposed this new system, and one teacher in Long Island, Sheri Lederman, sued the state. She worked in a high-performing district and had a history of receiving stellar reviews. Yet the growth model one particular year churned out an "ineffective" rating on a portion of her evaluation related to VAM. The court ruled that the teacher's rating was "indisputably arbitrary and capricious." Because her students performed so well on the state exams in both the prior and current year, she was penalized by a ceiling effect of students with very high prior scores.[34]

According to an interview in *The74*, the Long Island teacher's lawyer (who is also her husband), stated that they brought the case to court because they were troubled by how "insulting and dispiriting" the evaluation system was to teacher morale.[35] As reported by the New York State School Boards Association *OnBoard*, upon winning the case, Sheri Lederman stated, "Every teacher, every administrator, every child is impacted by this ridiculous notion that in order to do our best in the classroom, we have to be monitored by the State Education Department and the state Legislature."[36]

Employee evaluation is just one example of how federal or state micromanagement does not help create a healthy district climate. Local administrators must lead the effort to evaluate teachers, and it is the board that has oversight responsibility and must ensure a thoughtful evaluation system. Despite the state's intention to create a better evaluation mechanism, it was not possible to achieve that centrally.

In addition to evaluating individual employees, many of the important steps needed to foster a positive climate across all four climate domains—community, academic, safety, and institutional environment—fall into the realm of local governance. State government can take certain constructive actions to address district climate, such as mental health funding, making climate surveys available, providing informational resources and frameworks, benchmarking data, and supporting the teacher pipeline. That said, we must recognize the limits of centralized government and turn our attention to the capability of boards and superintendents to provide district climate leadership.

UNIQUE SCHOOL BOARD POTENTIAL

Revisiting the definition of climate as the sum total of all of the relationships in the district, how can leaders create an inspirational environment full of strong relationships? School boards have the power to do just that. Relationships cannot be legislated. Relationships cannot be mandated. Instead, relationships are forged through the interactions of individuals operating within an organization, in our case a school district. Unlike state politicians and regulators who are structurally *outside* of the district, boards and superintendents reside *inside* of the district. They are an integral part of the fabric of the district and have the unique potential to create a positive, or negative, district climate. It is the leaders on the ground within a school district who have the power to authentically set the organizational tone.

Additionally, it is worth noting that improving school climate is a local endeavor because each district is in a different spot. There is no statewide uniformity. Some districts have negative climates that need transformation, while others have positive climates that simply need to be maintained. Initiatives at the district level represent the best way to assess climate and put together a tailored action plan.

At first glance, it may seem like school climate has everything to do with employees and students who work and attend school in the district day-to-day and nothing to do with the governance board. A closer look at each domain reveals a critical board role.

The first step for a board to take when trying to create or sustain a positive climate is to incorporate climate into district goals. Boards can measure progress by reviewing data frequently and weaving climate into the superintendent evaluation process. Table 8.2 provides specific examples of the role a board can play in each of the four climate domains.

Table 8.2   School board actions to improve district climate

Domain	Role of the board
Academic	• Making a commitment to high standards and continuous improvement • Setting district goals for enhanced academic programs • Measuring outcomes and ensuring accountability • Allocating resources to professional development that supports pedagogical techniques to sustain classroom engagement
Community	• Modeling civil discourse and mutual respect • Setting the tone for collaboration through a healthy board—superintendent relationship • Holding superintendent accountable for building community • Setting policies and structures (such as committees or liaison positions) that facilitate broader community involvement • Analyzing survey data to measure progress • Supporting and prioritizing extracurricular activities to foster student belonging
Safety	• Ratifying code of conduct and discipline policies that strive for fairness and keep community members safe • Approving a comprehensive district safety and emergency response plan • Allocating resources to student counseling and mental health services • Analyzing safety data
Institutional environment	• Maintaining and upgrading physical plant to create collaborative learning environment • Ensuring accessibility • Setting policies regarding class size, structure of school day, and school start times

Next, taking a deeper dive into the community domain illustrates the specific role boards can play to set a positive tone.

MODELING BEHAVIOR

America is experiencing a K-12 mental health and bullying crisis. Prepandemic statistics paint a sobering picture. According to the U.S. Government Accountability Office, about 20 percent of students nationwide ages twelve to eighteen were bullied in the 2018–2019 school year. Of this group, about one in four students were bullied because of their race, religion, national origin, disability, gender, or sexual orientation.[37] The pandemic exacerbated the situation. According to the CDC's 2021 "Adolescent Behaviors and Experiences Survey," "about one in three high school students experienced poor mental health."[38]

One intervention schools deploy to address student mental health is to build social and emotional learning (SEL) skills that help students refine their relationship, self-management, and responsible decision-making skills. Schools globally spend over $3.6 billion on SEL interventions, and this number is projected to grow to over $10.3 billion by 2028.[39]

One of the central themes of SEL is the importance of adults modeling behavior for kids, which is precisely what makes bad behavior in the school boardroom particularly ironic. We spend billions of dollars teaching children how to manage their stress, anxiety, and relationships, but not a week goes by without another battle in the boardroom somewhere in America. Too many of these battles have anger and vitriol on display, overtaking any remaining trace of civil discourse.

Isn't it unrealistic to expect third graders to master SEL skills when boardrooms require a security presence to maintain order? Why can't the adults keep it together for the sake of the kids? How realistic is it for the adults in the room to expect better district outcomes when they cannot model appropriate behavior?

Boardroom behavior is on display for the entire school district and world to see, and this behavior has consequences. Boards can set a poor example for students. Yet at the same time, they have the unique potential to serve as an example by establishing a constructive organizational tone.

Spencer Stuart, a leading executive search firm, believes that boards have a culture defined by "the unwritten rules that influence directors' interactions and decisions. These include the mindsets, hidden assumptions, group norms, beliefs, values and artifacts (such as the board agenda) that influence the style of director discussions, the quality of engagement and trust among directors, and how the board makes decisions."[40] At every school board meeting, the board is constantly modeling behavior and emphasizing specific values on display for the entire district, and broader community, to observe.

While every board member has the right and obligation to express their opinion when they disagree, we must work harder to maintain a basic level of civility. After all, if there is a bully on the board, how can we expect not to have bullies on the playground? If the board chair becomes unhinged, how can we expect a fourth grader to regulate their emotions? If board meeting discourse is a constant expression of anxiety and worry about the future, how can we expect teachers to exude confidence and optimism in the classroom?

We must remind ourselves that the boardroom sets the tone for the entire district.

BOARD-SUPERINTENDENT RELATIONSHIP

The board-superintendent relationship is highly visible at the top of the organizational structure. Consequently, it presents a unique opportunity to influence the overall district climate by setting the tone for every other relationship in the system.

The board hires, manages, and fires the superintendent, who is the ultimate day-to-day leader of the organization and is the driver of district climate. Choosing the superintendent is arguably the single most important decision that a board makes. Will it be a leader who is collaborative or sharp-elbowed? Empowering or micromanaging? Supportive or unapproachable? Inspiring or soporific? Can the person handle a crisis while maintaining composure?

Once the hiring decision is made, the challenge of maintaining a constructive board-superintendent relationship is not easy. I have heard all too often from superintendents comments such as: "I'd like to build a deeper level of trust with my board"; "I'd like to figure out how I can address the fact that one of my board members is a bully."

That board-superintendent relationships can get complicated is a long-established fact. Perhaps one of the most outrageous examples of the relationship going awry was in Wellesley, Massachusetts, during the 1930s. The three-person school committee fired the long-time superintendent and appointed a new leader in his place. However, the incumbent superintendent challenged the procedure the board followed to let him go, including the lack of a public hearing, and he refused to vacate his position. His resistance was strengthened by the fact that he was a longtime, well-respected leader in the community who enjoyed support from the staff and public.

For a span of time, the Wellesley Public School District had two superintendents running it simultaneously. It took the Massachusetts Supreme Judicial Court to opine that the incumbent was fired based on unsubstantiated charges and without a proper hearing and that he needed to be reinstated. A settlement was eventually reached, but not before the district incurred costs and reputational damage. This episode resulted in the decision to enlarge the board from three to five members to introduce more checks and balances, thereby reducing the chance that a few individuals with concentrated power would make poor decisions.[41] True for past, present, and future district climates, working hard to establish a productive relationship between board and superintendent is well worth the investment of time and energy. If a superintendent has a strained relationship with the board, it may reduce their job satisfaction, leading to higher failure and resignation risk and putting additional pressure on the already sobering superintendent longevity statistics.

Most superintendents report high levels of stress, and superintendent turnover is on the rise. A research study by Rachel White at the University of Tennessee-Knoxville analyzed twelve thousand five hundred school districts and found that superintendent turnover increased from 14 percent between 2019–2020 and 2020–2021 to 17 percent between 2021–2022 and 2022–2023. White also estimates that approximately 80 percent of superintendents who left their district likely did not take another position as superintendent in their state.[42] The statistics are even worse in the largest five hundred districts, of which according to the ILO Group, an education consulting firm, approximately half replaced a superintendent at least once between March 2020 and September 2022, and 21 percent of these districts lost a superintendent in the 2022–2023 school year.[43] Increased turnover results in a school board having to make superintendent hiring decisions more frequently. It is no easy task.

Consider what happened in New Haven, Connecticut, on November 20, 2017. The New Haven Board of Education discussed and voted on hiring a new superintendent, Dr. Carol Birks. The exchange between board members was heated, ultimately resulting in a four to three vote in favor of appointing Birks. According to press reports, the contentious public meeting ended with the board chair arguing with another board member, followed by a member threatening to sue the chair and challenging him to a duel. In the end, police had to separate the two board members, all on display for a room full of community members. Birks became the new superintendent, but her tenure lasted only a year and a half.[44]

The same Yale Center for Emotional Intelligence survey mentioned in earlier in this chapter that asked about district climate also explored superintendent and board member perceptions. The survey uncovered an interesting set of responses that may illuminate why there are hurdles to building a strong board-superintendent relationship.

The survey asked a group of superintendents and board members in New York and Connecticut how much impact the superintendent and the school board have on the district. The results are in table 8.3.

Most respondents agree that superintendents have a large/enormous impact on the district, but there is a startling difference between how superintendents and board members viewed the impact of the school board. While 100 percent of superintendent respondents believe the

Table 8.3 Superintendent and board impact on district

	Superintendent respondents		Board respondents	
	Large/ Enormous	Moderate/ Slight	Large/ Enormous	Moderate/ Slight
Impact of school board	100%	0%	41%	59%
Impact of superintendent	83%	17%	93%	7%

board had a large/enormous impact, only 41 percent of board member respondents believe they have a large/enormous impact.[45]

Why? One plausible explanation is the differing organizational perspectives of the school board members and the superintendent. Board members are not day-to-day managers. They have a governing role, and one of the most difficult elements of board service is finding a balance between micromanaging and acting as a rubber stamp. Board members are not there every day. They swoop in and swoop out, while the superintendent is there all day, every day. When you swoop, it's more difficult to feel that you have a large impact.

Furthermore, board members are reliant on the superintendent for their information flow. If an issue arises in the organization that the superintendent doesn't share, the board may be left in the dark, and trust between the board and the superintendent erodes.

Even when board members are fully up to speed, they face a challenge when they disagree with the superintendent. They have a duty to express their view, but because discussions on most topics must be conducted in public, they run the risk of straining their relationship with the superintendent.

From a superintendent's perspective, it is more obvious that boards have ultimate authority. After all, the board collectively establishes district goals, sets meeting agendas, provides financial oversight, and has the right to request information. Boards hold the superintendent accountable, set superintendent compensation and benefits, and have authority to fire the superintendent.

There is no doubt that superintendents have a central day-to-day role in establishing and maintaining district climate. But it is the board's responsibility to monitor climate from a governance perspective, and if a superintendent fails to embody the qualities that a board desires, the board can and should hold them accountable.[46]

The relationship between a board and the superintendent is fragile. It takes thought and care to build trust and establish mutual credibility. Board members should be willing to support the superintendent by providing thoughtful feedback that identifies strengths and areas for continued growth. Superintendents should have an opportunity to give feedback to the board. A positive tone can be set for the organization if a productive and respectful relationship is forged and maintained.

OVERSEEING MANAGEMENT OF DISTRICT EMPLOYEES

A district is only as good as its people and managing them effectively is hard work. The first step is building hiring practices that help the district find the best possible employees. In districts that grant tenure, it is the board that often formally casts the deciding vote. Ensuring a rigorous and fair evaluation process for tenure is tantamount to building a great district, since once tenure is granted, it is very difficult to let go of under-performing employees.

The next step is to foster an environment in which employees feel valued and engaged, which takes intentional and effective management. The board does not manage employees day-to-day, but it sets organizational goals and policies that can either support or detract from building a highly engaged district. Furthermore, through its role in evaluating the superintendent, the board can emphasize the importance of employee engagement.

Board actions set the tone by establishing thoughtful employee-related policies, setting clear and reasonable goals, treating the workforce professionally, compensating employees adequately, maintaining fair and thorough evaluation processes, investing in professional development, and evaluating the superintendent's management skills. Creating a culture of continuous improvement, clear processes, and teacher autonomy are all ways in which boards and superintendents can help retain and motivate employees.

THE IMPORTANCE OF TRUST

As is evident in all the action steps already addressed, trust is requisite for a productive, supportive, healthy school district climate. The more it is deliberately cultivated, the more resilient a climate becomes. This is experienced in myriad ways throughout a district but is amplified when a district confronts a crisis.

We all have fears and doubts when we first serve on a board, and we guess at what challenges we will face. However, it is typically not possible to anticipate the big issues that will arise. Our tenure as school board members will be defined by unexpected events. The best we can do is follow the best practices of crisis preparedness.

Crisis preparedness is easier said than done. While there is a dearth of literature on school board crisis management, McKinsey and Company and the National Association of Corporate Directors (NACD) fortuitously published a study on corporate board crisis preparedness in 2019, just prior to the outbreak of COVID-19. The McKinsey/NACD study is another instance when corporate insight is applicable to school boards.

McKinsey and NACD found that some of the largest and most well-run corporations in America had boards that were not prepared to navigate a crisis. Most of these companies had emergency management plans that did not include the topic of board governance and decision-making. Only 8 percent of corporate directors participated in crisis-simulation exercises with management, and fewer than 25 percent of corporate directors had explicit discussions with management (during the twelve months prior) regarding the board's crisis roles and responsibilities.[47] Many school districts similarly have emergency management plans, but it is likely that most school boards do not spend significant time preparing for a crisis from a governance perspective.

McKinsey's definition of a crisis fits COVID-19 to a tee, but by no means is it limited to pandemics. Crises have a series of characteristics:

- "A low-probability, high-impact event";
- A need to make big decisions—across financial, legal, regulatory, safety and communications—in a compressed period of time in an atmosphere of ambiguity;
- Significant external community and media scrutiny, with the potential for external factors such as social media and community stress and anxiety to amplify tensions;
- Prior weaknesses in governance structure and previous conflicts that often get exacerbated, with relationships that get tested.[48]

If there is a lack of trust between the CEO and the board, or if shareholders don't trust the board and the CEO, a crisis will amplify these weaknesses.

The same applies for school boards. If a district goes into a crisis with a strong level of trust among the board, superintendent, staff, and the community, the chance of navigating the crisis successfully increases. If there is a lack of trust, you are unlikely to get through the crisis without severe institutional damage. Trust is an essential ingredient for the health of a school district, and boards must focus on building trust when times are good. It is hard work, particularly because we are living at a time when we have witnessed an erosion of trust in all institutions.

In this chapter, we have touched on the importance of relationships within the district. A board and superintendent focused on building strong relationships and trust will help create a positive district climate, which in turn will support the growth and success of administrators, teachers, staff, and students.

Next, we turn to another important relationship, between the district and its community.

9

ENGAGEMENT WITH THE COMMUNITY

"One mother shed tears when she read the superintendent's announcement. Another said it felt like a body blow." This description appeared in a November 2018 Associated Press article about a school district in a wealthy Connecticut suburb just north of New York City that garnered national attention. The article described a board decision that ended a district tradition of permitting elementary school parents to join their children at lunchtime in the school cafeteria. Administrators determined that the visiting parents were disruptive to the school day.[1]

While elementary school parents joining their children for school lunch is an extreme example of parent involvement, this story epitomizes the inextricable link between parents and public schools. Whether it is volunteering as class parent, serving as a PTA leader, chaperoning the school dance, attending an athletic event, or voicing concerns regarding curriculum, many parents want to be connected and have a say in the education of their children.

I can relate as a parent and a school board member. As a parent, it is tempting to intervene if I believe one of my kids is being treated unfairly or is not afforded the school-related opportunities that I think they deserve. My parental instinct tells me to fight on their behalf, and I restrain myself to limit intervention to only the most serious circumstances. It is natural for parents to do what they think is best for their child, and if that involves trying to change the system—or at the very least complaining about the system—so be it.

As a school board member, I know what it is like to be the recipient of parent feedback. Through the years, I have been approached by many parents who have advocated for changes based on the experience of their child. Sometimes these changes may be right for their individual child but not for the district as a whole or may be unaffordable, impractical, or against state regulation. Other times, the feedback sparks positive change by becoming the impetus for a much-needed adjustment to curriculum, extracurricular offerings, policy, or budget allocation.

THE PROBLEM

While parental involvement may seem like an intuitive, built-in part of the system, many scholars have expressed a much more nuanced and complex view of its importance and value.

Education reformers gravitated to viewing centralized control as the optimal path to accomplish the well-intentioned goals of closing the achievement gap and improving the nation's most underperforming schools. A byproduct of their effort was, at times, the marginalization of voices in local communities, including parents, administrators, teachers, and elected school board members.

The issue of parental engagement surfaced during Virginia's contentious 2021 gubernatorial race. Responding to Republican candidate Glenn Youngkin's support of a bill that would have allowed parents to opt out of their children learning material deemed "sexually explicit," Democratic opponent Terry McAuliffe responded with a line that would plague the rest of his campaign. He stated, "I don't think parents should be telling schools what they should teach."[2] COVID-19 school closures under outgoing Virginia Democratic governor Ralph Northam also became a campaign issue. Despite Joe Biden carrying Virginia by ten points just one year prior, Youngkin prevailed. While political scientists have identified multiple factors that helped Youngkin, including a typical Virginia backlash against the incumbent president in off-year elections, exit polls found that education was the second most important issue to voters, with only the economy scoring higher.[3]

The consequences of state government ignoring parents played out in New York State as well regarding a very different issue, high-stakes testing. The Empire State provides a prime example of what happens when parents disagree with centralized education policy and their voices are not heard.

In 2015, parents took drastic action by orchestrating an opt-out movement. That year, 20 percent of eligible students opted out of the state tests to express their opinion that an overreliance on testing and the linking of tests to teacher evaluations had negative unintended consequences on students and teachers alike.[4] This unprecedented display of defiance against state requirements was viewed cynically by some reformers who labeled parents as fringe white suburban pawns of the teachers' union since they perceived the nexus of power to be in suburban Long Island and Westchester. However, a close look at the data disproves this theory and supports the authenticity of the opt-out movement.[5]

There was nothing fringe about the opt-outs in New York. To put the astoundingly high participation rate into perspective, Governor Andrew Cuomo prevailed in the 2014 election by garnering 17.5 percent of the eligible vote (given the low turnout in the election), a lower threshold than the opt-out rate.[6] Furthermore, the opt-out rate outside of New York City was higher, reaching a staggering 30 percent. New York City brought the aggregate rate down for multiple reasons, including that high-stakes tests were also used for middle and high school placement purposes.[7]

Opt-outs were not exclusively in the domain of white suburban moms either. While it is true that students opting out were more likely to be white, less likely to be English language learners, and less likely to be economically disadvantaged, once again this was partially driven by New York City having a larger proportion of these groups. Outside New York City, high-need districts had an opt-out rate in the 20 percent range, and a look at individual districts highlights the diversity of the movement.[8] Blind Brook and Bronxville were both well-resourced districts near each other, but they had opt-out rates of 23 percent and 2 percent respectively. Bay Shore, a majority nonwhite district with 54 percent of its students classified as economically disadvantaged, had a 44 percent opt-out rate. Lackawanna, which has a student population that is majority white and 90 percent economically disadvantaged, experienced an opt-out rate of 46 percent.[9]

Though the teachers' union supported the 2015 opt-out movement, the effort started in 2013 with a grassroots network of fifty parent and education groups forming New York State Allies for Public Education (NYSAPE). They held 100 forums for parents across the state. There were thousands of parent petitions, numerous letter writing campaigns to politicians, and many forums. One thousand five hundred and fifty-five principals signed a letter opposing the reforms, and school boards in seventy-seven districts opted out of Race to the Top altogether and returned their allocation of federal funds to the state even though by law they were still required to comply with the rules.[10]

Despite all the protests, the state reacted by doubling down on the controversial reforms. It increased the standardized testing component of the teacher evaluation from 20 to 50 percent.[11] NYSAPE leader Eric Mihelbergel expressed frustration, quoted in the *New York Times* as stating, "We've written letters to legislators for years, until we were blue in the face, and they didn't listen."[12]

National civil and human rights organizations denounced those who were refusing the test, expressing concern that measurement is important and asking parents to be "stimulating worthy discussions about over-testing" instead of opting out.[13] However, New York State parents initially tried to engage in discussion, but state leaders did not listen.[14] As I explained in an *Education Next* article on opt-outs in 2016:

Historically there has been a clear path for parents to influence their children's schools: reach out to the principal, superintendent, or school board, or run for a spot on that board. However, Race to the Top reduced local control, and parents had difficulty navigating advocacy at the state level. The first hurdle was identifying the decision-makers. Was it the governor who had the authority? The legislature? The Board of Regents (appointed by the legislature)? The State Education Department (appointed by the appointees)?

Even leaders in Albany didn't seem to agree. A December 2014 letter from Cuomo's office to the Chancellor of the Board of Regents said, "The Governor has little power over education, which is governed by the Board of Regents." The Chancellor responded: "The questions and concerns outlined in the letter relate to issues of State Law, which are under direct control of the State Legislature and the Governor, not the Department or the Board of Regents."[15]

In January 2014, Arne Duncan, the secretary of education at the time, gave a speech to parent leaders. He said, "Please raise your voice for excellence—and against complacency. Organize other parents. . . . Ask the hard questions, even when it means shaking things up and challenging the status quo."[16] By 2015, parents in New York State followed Duncan's advice, but they did so for the purpose of fighting against Duncan's signature policies.

Many modern-day efforts aimed at large-scale, rapid school reform align with governors, state legislators, and federal officials who promise top-down change instead of engaging at the grassroots level. In doing so, local communities on the ground have at times viewed reformers negatively, as aligned with big business.

It hasn't always been this way. At the turn of the century, Phoebe Hearst thought differently. The wife of Senator George Hearst and the mother of media titan William Randolph Hearst, Ms. Hearst was a prominent philanthropist dedicated to improving the lives of children.

In 1895, Hearst met Alice Birney, a mother of three who lacked the resources and connections of the Hearst family but shared a similar passion for helping underprivileged youth. Birney had the novel idea to convene a new group she would call the National Congress of Mothers.[17]

Hearst's financial backing helped Birney's idea come to fruition. In February 1897, the first convocation took place in Washington, D.C. It garnered national press and drew two thousand people. A central tenet of this new organization was the "growing belief in the need for a close partnership between home and school. The foundation of such a partnership was likened to a three-legged stool—one that required the support of thoughtful mothers, fathers, and teachers."[18]

There were some interesting aspects of this new advocacy group. First, before women in America attained the right to vote, the movement championed women's equality and the importance of women's voice in matters related to the education of children. As reported in the *New York Times*, Helen Gardener of Boston addressed the 1897 National Congress of Mothers by stating:

Self-abnegation, subserviency to man, whether he be father, lover, or husband, is the most dangerous theory that can be taught to her whose character shall mold the next generation. . . . If a woman is not brave enough to demand and obtain personal liberty and entire control of her great and race-endowing function of maternity, she has no right to dare to stamp upon a child and to curse a race with the descendants of such a service, a dwarfed, a time-and-master-serving character. Subject mothers will never product a race of free, well-poised, justice-practicing children.[19]

The convention emphasized the inextricable link between mother and school and why mothers should have significant influence in how schools educate children. Another *Times* article about the conference stated:

"The first ten years of a man's life belong to his mother." . . . In a country in which the education of children is the care of the State and in which "school age" begins much before the age of graduation from the tutelage of mothers, the counsel of mothers upon the education of the young is of more value than the counsel of any number of pedagogical theorists of either sex.[20]

The National Congress of Mothers soon realized that regional and state branches of the organization were needed to ensure that parents maintain a direct link to their community's public schools. In 1897, New York was one of the first states to start a chapter. State chapters then encouraged local communities to form parents' clubs. In 1901, Charles Skinner, the New York State Superintendent of Public Instruction, addressed the national convention. He emphasized that "Home and School are the two great agencies in the education of the child; their aims are identical; neither can work effectively in ignorance of the other." He went on to describe how "certain problems arise in the school which teachers should not be obliged to decide. (Questions of social life, dancing, etc., for example.) Where Parent-Teacher Organizations (PTOs) exist, the responsibility is readily placed upon the parent." Last, he argued that when lobbying for school improvements, parents would have more sway than teachers with the Board of Education.[21]

In 1908, the organization rebranded itself as the National Congress of Mothers and Parent-Teacher Associations, and over time local and state PTA chapters proliferated across America.[22] Phoebe Hearst's philanthropic approach of empowering parents to improve education was nothing short of revolutionary and stands in stark contrast to the modern-day approach that many philanthropists choose to take.

Today, in the still early decades of the twenty-first century, the national PTA stands 2.5 million members strong.[23] The collective scope and impact of the PTA across all local chapters is incalculable. It is one of the vastest networks of volunteerism in America and its accomplishments during the past one hundred-plus years has resulted in transformational change. The PTA has advocated for a wide array of issues including desegregation, children's health and safety initiatives (from vaccines to fire escapes and sprinklers to bus safety), nutrition, sex education, tobacco and alcohol education, child labor laws, arts education, parental education, and volunteerism in schools.[24]

We must heed the lesson from Phoebe Hearst and Alice Birney. For too many decades, parents have been an afterthought of many well-intentioned policymakers and reformers. Including parents will lead to more enduring educational improvements. A Connecticut district may have been able to stop parents from visiting their children in the cafeteria during lunchtime, but if the COVID-19 pandemic taught us anything, it's that parents cannot be ignored. Holding classes online via Zoom and the rise in social media chat rooms have more closely connected parents to the classroom than ever before.

While technology may be the most recent parent connector, parents have long influenced public schools through many channels. In addition to serving on the PTA, they have been plaintiffs in court battles regarding desegregation, special education, and equitable funding. They have been written into legislation such as the Head Start program in 1964 that required parents to serve on advisory boards and participate in the classroom and the 1975 Education for All Handicapped Children Act (later changed to the Individuals with Disabilities Education Act) that mandated individual programs for students with special needs be developed by the school and parents together.[25]

Simply put, parents expect to be engaged and connected to public schools, which is difficult to achieve in a top-down system.

UNIQUE SCHOOL BOARD POTENTIAL

When it comes to governance, school boards are uniquely suited to be a forum for community engagement. On the one hand, federal and state officials are simply not well positioned structurally to play a similar role. School boards, on the other hand, provide a viable forum for direct interactions.

A FORUM FOR DIRECT CONNECTIVITY

An inherent advantage of school boards is the fact that they provide a direct outlet for community dissatisfaction and anger, without which we run the risk that frustration bottles up and is more likely to explode. School boards are a highly accessible lever of democracy because it is so easy for community members to show up at a board meeting to express their opinions.

School boards give community members the opportunity to face board members in person and express their opinions during the public comment period. And they can do this every time the school board meets. Good luck gaining the same level of access to a president, congressman, governor, or state representative. While federal and state legislators host town halls, meet with constituents, and deliberate publicly, these mechanisms for public input do not compare to the systematic and user-friendly process in place for community members to attend school board meetings in their own neighborhood so they can provide direct and personal feedback just before a vote.

Although voter turnout is often woefully low, those community members who exercise their right to vote for school board members are expressing their view and exerting influence on the singular issue of public education. Voting for a state or federal official requires prioritization of issues because no single candidate is likely to reflect all of a voter's policy stances. I might favor one candidate's education policy, but prioritize voting for another candidate's position on healthcare or fiscal policy.

School board members are also more likely to know their constituents given the local nature of who they represent. Within the confines of law and regulation, they can govern the district with their specific community in mind. Even if a state or national politician is genuinely trying to understand the perspectives of voters gathered to meet them, the diversity of each legislative district, state, and the country overall makes it difficult to design a one-size-fits-all approach.

The best way to reverse the erosion of trust discussed in part I is on a local, district-by-district basis. We have seen conspiracy theories arise regarding every level and facet of government, from local school boards to the CDC, but at the community level it is easier to debunk rumors and myths.

School board members reside in the local community. You can find your board's members at the grocery store, on the soccer field, or at church, which in turn increases the chance of discovering our common humanity and connectivity. Seeing each other in more informal, local settings creates opportunities to further explore differences and find common ground, or at least attempt to understand each other.

PARENTAL PREFERENCE FOR LOCAL CONTROL

Perhaps the most compelling reason school boards are best positioned to facilitate community engagement is because parents believe in local control and have more faith in their local district than in the broader system.

Jonathan Collins of Brown University published a 2021 study that underscores this point. Local governance structures were preferred by approximately 60 percent of respondents (with school boards at 31 percent and site councils at 27 percent), beating out mayoral control (8 percent), the state (16 percent) and the U.S. Department of Education (12 percent). Those who preferred mayoral control were more likely to have characteristics of political or bureaucratic insiders, such as school employees. Those who preferred the state take charge were more likely to be nonwhite and less likely to be a parent. After tabulating the initial survey results, Collins exposed participants to school boards where there is active stakeholder participation and public deliberation, which resulted in an increasing number of respondents choosing school boards. Post-exposure to these boards, support for school boards garnered 35 percent, versus only 13 percent for the state, 8 percent for the federal government, and 7 percent for mayoral control.[26]

A recent PDK Poll found that 56 percent of respondents believe that school boards should have "a great deal or good amount" of influence over what's taught in public schools, while only 33 percent felt the same way about the governor and state legislature.[27]

Polling data also has consistently suggested a higher level of satisfaction with a parent's local district than with their perceptions of U.S. education overall. According to the 2023 results, 76 percent of parents reported being "completely or somewhat satisfied" when asked how satisfied they are with the quality of education their oldest child is experiencing. When U.S. adults were asked about the quality of K-12 education in the United States overall, only 36 percent reported being "completely or somewhat satisfied."[28]

The reasons for these divergent results are likely multifaceted. We tend to gravitate to communities to which we feel an affinity, making us more likely to be positively predisposed to feel good about our local schools in the first place. We know that there is a well-understood mechanism to complain or provide suggestions to our local district. Last, we form a view of our local schools from lived experience, whereas our view of the U.S. education system overall is shaped by national media narratives, social media, and political stump speeches that often focus on outliers and brim with tales of failure, controversy, and underperformance.

There are concrete practices that school board members can engage in to facilitate parent feedback and maintain positive community relations. The overall goal should be to create a boardroom environment that engenders trust by maintaining transparency. Here are suggestions to foster strong community relations:

- If there is bad news, don't bury it. Be transparent and confront it head-on by admitting the problem and developing potential solutions.
- If there are parents who disagree with a policy or practice, listen intently to the feedback and ensure that there is a process in place to take concerns seriously.
- Find opportunities for board members to interact with the public outside of the formal boardroom setting, while still complying with open meeting laws.
- Appoint board liaisons to sit on the boards of key community groups, such as the PTA, town government, or local education foundation.
- Pay attention during public comment periods and provide a forum for concerns to be expressed in an even-handed manner.
- Form board committees or subcommittees that include community members, each with a clear purpose, particularly if there is a lack of board expertise in certain domains or if the goal is to achieve broader buy-in.
- Form site-based committees at each school to solicit input from community members regarding building-level issues, with findings reported back to the board.

- Administer surveys to gauge where the community stands.
- Take the time to explain the line between state, federal, and local control so that community members understand the limits of board power.

A persistent challenge that board members face is judging whether an opinion expressed during the public comment period represents a tiny (but vocal) community faction or is shared broadly. It is sometimes difficult to know what the majority believes on any given issue. While everyone deserves to be heard, sometimes the loudest voices may not be in lockstep with the broader district community. Board members must rely on analyzing data and maintaining close community relationships as they attempt to gauge whether the loudest voices are representative of the prevailing public view.

The same dynamic exists with public company boards that face activist shareholders. Consequently, there are many parallels between activist shareholder dynamics and vociferous community members pushing school board members for change. Examples are highlighted in table 9.1.

Corporate activists are driven by their own objectives, which sometimes can align with the long-term best interest of the firm and most shareholders. Other times, however, because the activist has bad judgment, a personal agenda, or plans to hold the stock for a short time horizon, their ideas may not sync with what is in the best interest of the corporation. It is up to board members to always listen but to act only when they think it is in the organization's best interest.

Deloitte Consulting published a report that highlights best practices for dealing with corporate activists. Suggestions are identifying and being ready to discuss key issues that activists might focus on, which include changes in strategy, governance, and significant events. Another suggestion is to always be transparent and ready to grant access to information.[29] "The Director's Guide to Shareholder Activism" posted by the Harvard Law School Forum on Corporate Governance provides additional suggestions that include taking an honest view of your company, engaging with and knowing your shareholders, and looking for consensus-building opportunities.[30] Building trust and transparency when possible is also crucial for managing more difficult moments of activism. All these practices are applicable to a board of education's community relations.

Table 9.1 Comparison of activist approach

Public companies	Public schools
The majority of activists are friendly and quietly approach the board, but they also can be aggressive and mount a public campaign.[a]	Community members often approach board members with issues in a friendly manner, but they also can speak out loudly and aggressively during public comment periods.
Activists are attracted to situations where they believe changes in corporate governance or financial management will improve outcomes (shareholder returns). Sometimes activists focus on environmental and social issues. Activism also happens when boards ignore shareholder concerns.[b]	Community members often push on issues related to budget, policy, or social/cultural related changes, and any perceived governance weakness can increase the intensity of the approach. Desired outcomes can be student- or taxpayer-related. Community members get especially agitated if ignored by the board of education.
Activists may or may not represent the majority shareholder view.[b]	The most vocal community members may or may not represent the majority of voters in the district.
Activists try to convince management, board members, and shareholders of their view, sometimes via the press and word of mouth.[c]	Dissenting community members will often express their views to administrators, the board, and the broader community through social media groups and word of mouth.
Shareholder activism leads to increased rates of director turnover.[c]	Though national data is not robust, there seems to be a rise in school board turnover since battles in the boardroom have grown in intensity.
Activists sometimes launch campaigns to secure a board seat.[b]	Disgruntled community members may decide to run for office in the next election.

[a] "Activist Shareholders: How Will You Respond?," Deloitte United States, accessed February 14, 2024, https://www2.deloitte.com/us/en/pages/finance/articles/cfo-insights-shareholder-investor-activism.html.

[b] Leah Malone, Maria Moats, and Paul DeNicola, "The Director's Guide to Shareholder Activism," Harvard Law School Forum on Corporate Governance, June 11, 2021, https://corpgov.law.harvard.edu/2021/06/11/the-directors-guide-to-shareholder-activism/.

[c] Ian Gow, Sa-Pyung Sean Shin, and Suraj Srinivasan, "Consequences to Directors of Shareholder Activism" (working paper, Harvard Business School, May 26, 2016).

Often an information asymmetry can exist between the school board and the community. Consider a hypothetical example of a beloved teacher who is let go by a district. The board ratifies the decision because it learns in executive session that an internal investigation revealed that the teacher sexually harassed a colleague. The public may loudly protest this decision by organizing petitions and speaking out during the public comment period, but the board is obligated to keep personnel disciplinary matters confidential. Confidentiality rules can make it difficult for a board to provide the information necessary to justify a seemingly controversial decision.

Trustees typically do not poll the public before every decision they make, nor should they be expected to do so. If they are doing their job, however, they stay close to their community and work to gauge public sentiment. Ultimately, they are elected to use their judgment as fiduciaries to make reasonable decisions in the best interest of the district overall, considering students, employees, and taxpayers. Their ability to do this ultimately depends on their ability to earn and be extended the faith of all district participants.

It is from this vantage point that we must recognize the importance of community voice as part of the decision-making process of public education. School boards are vital to ensuring that their local community's voice is properly elevated and that board members ultimately are accountable to those they serve. In chapter 10 we will explore ways to bolster district accountability.

10

ACCOUNTABILITY

The push to make our public education system more accountable has been the cornerstone of every significant reform initiative in recent decades, and in theory, an elaborate system has been put in place to ensure that districts are performing to a certain standard. In practice, because so many parts of the education governance ecosystem have a hand in how schools operate, accountability is hard to achieve.

Consider, for an example, Kernan Elementary School in Utica, New York, which was downgraded to "priority" status by the state in 2016 and required to implement a "Whole School Reform" model. The *Utica Observer-Dispatch* ran an editorial titled, "Our View: Put Blame for Failing Schools on State." The editorial asks whether "bureaucrats and politicians who write the education policies and approve the laws ever step inside a classroom? Do they ever visit the troubled schools they pass judgment on? They most certainly should. . . . They'll most likely see that the school's problems aren't due to the principal, teachers, or other educators involved in the process. But, hey, somebody has to be blamed, right? It certainly couldn't be the state's fault, could it?"[1]

That, in a nutshell, is the dilemma with our current system. When something goes wrong, there is finger-pointing. How did we get here? There is a long history of how we arrived at this point.

THE PROBLEM

Standardized tests have been administered since the mid-nineteenth century for the dual purpose of assessing individual student learning and holding schools and districts accountable. Early in American history, exams were first administered orally. The first reported use of a written exam occurred during Horace Mann's tenure as secretary of the Massachusetts Board of Education. As the U.S. public education system scaled significantly in the early twentieth century, assessments became a critical component of the push to ensure that children across vast geographies had similar opportunities and that educational services were provisioned efficiently.[2]

A key testing milestone occurred in 1926 with the first administration of the Scholastic Aptitude Test (SAT). Though we think of the SAT as a tool to compare students across secondary schools and to improve the objectivity and transparency of the college admissions process, it also was designed to raise the level of instruction in U.S. high schools and form the basis for a discussion regarding the contours of a college-ready curriculum. At the same time, the College Board, a nonprofit that develops standardized tests, wisely cautioned that tests have limitations and that institutions should not rely solely on the results.[3]

As technology advanced and administration of exams became more streamlined, testing proliferated and became an important component of assessing learning, sorting students, and measuring overall outcomes. At the same time, controversy endures concerning the purpose and limitations of standardized testing.

In the 1980s, the topic of accountability took on heightened urgency and received increased attention. After the 1983 *A Nation at Risk* report that called for elected officials across the nation to be held accountable for improving the quality of our educational system, Terrel Howard (T. H.) Bell, the secretary of the Department of Education under Ronald Reagan, used a "wall chart" to rank states by ACT and SAT scores. "We believe that the publication of the wall chart, with its acknowledged flaws, has helped validate state-by-state comparisons as a means of holding state and local school systems accountable for education," Bell stated.[4] Though it was a rudimentary attempt at measuring relative performance, it was nevertheless symbolic of the direction that federal education policy was headed.

Held just a few years later, the 1989 Education Summit in Charlottesville, Virginia, was a seminal moment in the accountability movement. President George H. W. Bush convened forty-nine of the nation's governors, supported by Governors Bill Clinton and Carroll Campbell who cochaired the National Governors Association education task force. The bipartisan conference helped shape the three decades of education policy that followed.[5]

In his summit address, President Bush expressed concern over how America was falling behind other nations academically and how the security and economic prosperity of the nation was at stake. He referenced recent National Assessment of Educational Progress (NAEP) results to prove his point:

Fewer than one in four of our high school juniors can write an adequate, persuasive letter. And only half can manage decimals, fractions, and percentages. And barely one in three can locate the Civil War in the correct half-century. No modern nation can long afford to allow so many of its sons and daughters to emerge into adulthood ignorant and unskilled. The status quo is a guarantee of mediocrity, social decay, and national decline.

Education is our most enduring legacy, vital to everything that we are and can become . . . will we be the children of the Enlightenment, or its orphans?

To be accountable, we need to know just how much progress we're making. . . . We must now evaluate ourselves on a tougher grading curve, one that includes the other major industrial nations. And accountability also means we must act on what we discover.[6]

The Charlottesville Summit set the tone for many initiatives that followed, including the 2001 landmark No Child Left Behind Act that served to enhance the federal role in holding schools accountable for outcomes by requiring every state to administer annual standardized tests to grades three to eight. In 2009, the launch of Race to the Top upped the ante with the Common Core curriculum and more aggressive measures that encouraged tying teacher evaluations to test scores. The 2015 Every Student Succeeds Act (ESSA) attempted to continue to emphasize accountability and measurement, albeit in a more flexible way.

Despite numerous federal and state efforts to strengthen accountability, these attempts have fallen short, in my view, because they lack a few essential prerequisites. First, there needs to be a consensus regarding what should be measured, and the mechanism of measurement must be viewed as high-quality and transparent to ensure trust in the ultimate results. Are basic reading and math exams sufficient, or does this approach incentivize schools to narrow the curriculum? Are we willing to embrace standards? Can important skills such as collaboration and creativity be measured in a standardized way? Are "cut scores" (the results required to fall into the various performance levels such as "proficient" or "below standard") set without political influence or interference, and are measures directly comparable year-over-year? The controversy regarding the role of standardized testing continues, and the complexities regarding these questions are deserving of a separate book.

A less commonly discussed condition necessary to achieving accountability relates to governance. To establish an accountability system with integrity, the entity being measured (in this case, the district) needs to have clear roles and responsibilities. Additionally, it needs to be granted enough autonomy and not be micromanaged. Under these conditions, it becomes possible to hold a district accountable for outcomes, because it also becomes impossible to place blame elsewhere if performance is subpar.

Governor Lamar Alexander in 1987 articulated a vision to hold districts accountable:

The kind of horse-trading we're talking about will change dramatically the way most American schools work. First, the Governors want to help establish clear goals and better report cards, ways to measure what students know and can do. Then, we're ready to give up a lot of state regulatory control—even to fight for changes in the law to make that happen—*if* schools and school districts will be accountable for the results. We invite educators to show us where less regulation makes the most sense. These changes will require more rewards for success and consequences for failure for teachers, school leaders, schools, and school districts.[7]

The system we have today is far from what is described in this passage. We have veered in the opposite direction of Alexander's vision. Instead of clear, high-level goals and less regulation, states have become more involved in dictating how districts operate. Laws have been passed across the country and layers of bureaucracy have been added attempting to micromanage accountability, yet when outcomes disappoint, the result is a lot of finger-pointing.

UNIQUE SCHOOL BOARD POTENTIAL

Our current accountability system is broken, and a sensible shift would be to provide districts more autonomy over day-to-day governance decisions without state micromanagement, with states focused on monitoring higher-level results to ensure that districts are achieving targeted outcomes. That will prevent districts from blaming state mandates if performance dips below expectations. Instead, districts would be held to account. Rather than spreading resources to micromanage all districts, states could direct those resources to more substantively assist districts that genuinely need more support. This would also allow a more effective allocation of state resources.

To be clear, I am not arguing for states to abandon their regulatory role, which includes holding school districts accountable. After all, states have the ultimate responsibility for the provision of educational services, and they are particularly well suited to measure results across districts and draw meaningful comparisons regarding whether quality standards are being upheld. States are best positioned to collect a repository of data to ensure adequate district performance, and local districts can benefit from using state benchmarking data to better understand their relative performance.

Furthermore, the shift in school funding underscores the need for the state to hold districts accountable. When each American public school district was funded almost entirely by its local taxpayers, citizens had a built-in accountability system by virtue of their right to vote in school board elections. Now that the largest component of school funding is derived from state income and sales taxes, taxpayers who foot a large portion of the bill for any specific school district may live well beyond the school district border. Without some type of imposed state accountability, income and sales taxpayers would have no way to assess the result of what tends to be the single largest state government expenditure. And in the instances where local governance proves ineffective or insufficient, it is only the state that has the means and the statutory authority to hold a manifestly dysfunctional district to account.

Determining what gets measured is always a source of controversy. There are some groups that have argued for the complete abandonment of high-stakes tests, such as the Massachusetts Teachers Association that advocated for the elimination of high-stakes components of the Massachusetts

Comprehensive Assessment System (MCAS). Some parent groups also voiced opposition to state testing regimes, and a 2024 ballot measure to decouple the MCAS from high school graduation requirements ultimately passed.[8]

Standardized testing can play a pivotal role as a component of a holistic and thoughtful accountability system, but in some cases, a reboot of the state testing apparatus would help restore credibility. Cut scores indicating student performance levels need to be calculated with consistency and transparency. Furthermore, test length and content need to be more stable so results can be comparable from year-to-year.

Some states take many months for results to be tabulated and distributed to schools and parents, rendering them outdated and contributing to increased public skepticism of value and reliability. Since these tests are generally multiple choice and we live in a modern era of automation, states must do better. Rapid turnaround of results would help guide instruction and boost confidence in the system. Test content transparency is also important, not only to make visible to the world the quality of the administered test, but also to give students greater opportunity to learn from their mistakes.

State-level accountability metrics beyond test scores also matter. Some potential data points include graduation rate (which of course depends on graduation requirements), the need for remedial coursework, and satisfaction surveys. Instead of trying to micromanage schools by measuring individual growth scores or imposing regulations dictating everything from the school calendar to detailed curriculum, it would be ideal for states to take a more macro view of accountability, giving districts latitude to set strategy, manage their workforce, and chart their own path. The state can play a role in ensuring that each district is proactively identifying their areas for development and using systematic quality improvement processes to address issues that arise.

It is important to note that each district faces a unique set of challenges. While there are universal goals we want to impose on all public schools, districts must measure progress on addressing their specific weaknesses. For example, one district may have an academic achievement issue that stems from absenteeism. Its leaders should put a plan in place to combat absenteeism and regularly monitor metrics related to this issue. Another district may have no issue with absenteeism but perhaps middle-school math results are below the state average. Board members and school administrators may want to make changes to the curriculum or add resources to the math department and measure whether these action steps lead to improved results.

In addition to high-level state accountability metrics and boards and administrative leaders monitoring the success of new initiatives and district outcomes, it is important to remember that there are a series of accountability mechanisms built into the education governance ecosystem. These mechanisms are different from those of general-purpose county, state, and federal government, where power is tempered by the checks and balances among multiple branches of government (executive, legislative, and judiciary).

School boards, in contrast, are single-purpose entities. They have an array of constituencies within the education governance ecosystem that help check school board power, in addition to federal and state oversight. As depicted in figure 10.1, these include: (1) the judiciary in which court

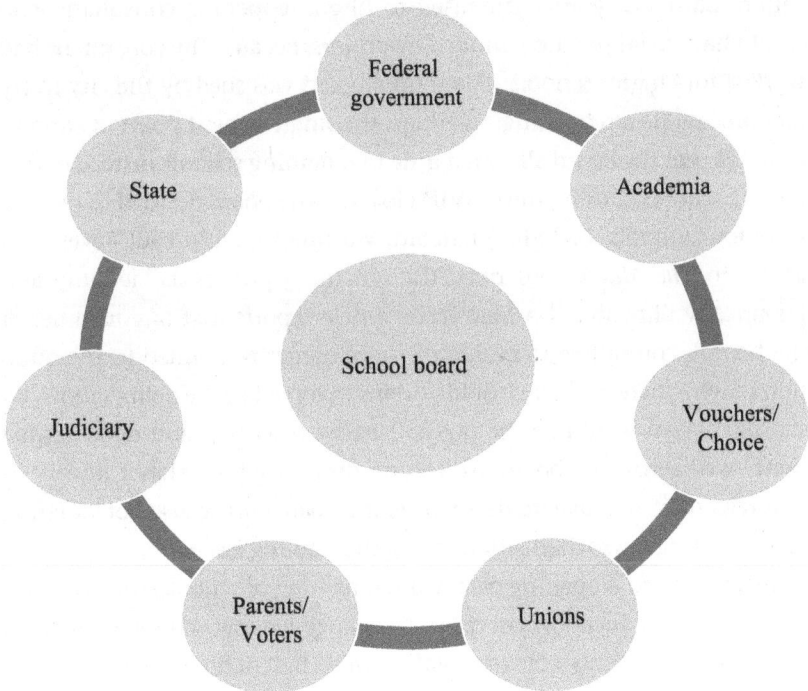

10.1 Ecosystem of accountability.

cases can challenge districts that infringe on the rights of stakeholders, (2) unions that maintain significant power over districts as they bargain for compensation, benefits, class size, and policies, (3) voters who have the ability to elect or recall board members, (4) the school choice movement that provides citizens with a mechanism to vote with their feet, and (5) academics who can use research and data to measure and shine light on successes and failures.

Let's explore two situations to better assess when these checks and balances work and when there is a need for more state intervention. First, San Francisco is an example of local accountability.

The more than fifty thousand students in San Francisco's public schools suffered from longer closures during the COVID-19 pandemic than students in other large American cities. Unfortunately, the San Francisco Board of Education had failed to orchestrate a reopening, and elementary schools were closed for a year, while middle and high schools were virtual until the fall of 2021.[9]

Parents grew increasingly angry at the San Francisco Board of Education, particularly after it refused to hire a reopening consultant who would have been privately funded by donors, because the consultant had worked for charter schools. The school board was sued by the city to try and precipitate a reopening.[10] Perhaps the single biggest point of contention was that the board allocated time to renaming schools instead of reopening schools. During the COVID closures, the board decided to rename forty-four schools, including Lincoln, Washington, and Paul Revere. An article in *The Atlantic* described the renaming process as "lengthy and historically illiterate."[11] A *New Yorker* article reports that one member of the board's committee to evaluate school names responded to the question of why there was a lack of historians involved in the deliberations by stating, "What would be the point? History is written and documented pretty well across the board. And so we don't need to belabor history in that regard."[12] To make matters worse, the board was accused of violating open meeting laws when adjudicating the naming issue.[13]

In addition to reopening delays and renaming of schools, the San Francisco Board of Education's decision to change magnet school admissions criteria proved highly controversial. Lowell High School generally relied on grades and test scores as the criteria for admissions, which resulted in a majority Asian and white student body. In their desire to increase the number of Black and Latino students, the board switched to a lottery system for admissions instead. This angered many Lowell alumni and parents, particularly in the Asian American community.[14] Adding fuel to the fire, the board's process came under scrutiny, and ultimately a superior court judge found that the board violated the law by inadequately noticing public hearings before changing Lowell admissions policy.[15]

As reported in *The Atlantic*, in 2016 the then vice president of the board authored a series of tweets that include: "Many [Asian Americans] believe they benefit from the 'model minority' BS. In fact, many Asian Americans [teachers, students, and parents] actively promote these myths. They use white supremacist thinking to assimilate and 'get ahead.' . . . Being a house n****r is still being a n****r. You're still considered 'the help.'"[16] Community members throughout San Francisco were irate.

A board of education recall effort was launched at the grassroots level and eventually attracted larger donations. The three board members who were eligible for recall were targeted.[17]

The grassroots coalition garnered enough signatures on the ballot to trigger the recall election, which was the first since 1983. Voters cast ballots in favor by a large margin.[18] To put the vote in context, traditional party lines did not matter. San Francisco is a very liberal city where 86 percent of residents voted for Joe Biden in 2020. Yet the recall prevailed, despite the teacher's union campaigning against it. The successful recall vote gave the mayor of San Francisco the power to appoint replacements until the next election cycle when the decision would go directly to the district's voters.[19]

All in all, San Francisco's recall illustrates how our current system has various checks and balances beyond state government that hold school boards accountable. But there are also cases, such as East Ramapo Central School District in New York, where local community members look to the state for assistance, ranging from additional financial support to governance intervention.

In the preface, I shared the story of East Ramapo during the time that I was a student in the district. Georgine Hyde, a well-known and respected school board president, served on the board for thirty-six years. Under her leadership, East Ramapo maintained extensive academic and extracurricular offerings and consistently produced impressive student outcomes.

In 2005, East Ramapo's shifting demographics led to Hyde's electoral defeat. While contested elections and incumbent losses are by no means unusual, the school board power dynamics in East Ramapo were unique, because candidates from a large and growing Haredi community that sends their kids to private schools eventually won control of the public school district board.[20]

When the Great Recession hit New York hard in 2008, the state reacted to the subsequent decline in tax revenue by reducing school funding across the board through a Gap Elimination Adjustment. While some communities were able to draw from reserves or raise local property taxes to make up for lost state funding, East Ramapo resorted to the elimination of 400 teaching positions and aggressively cut social workers, the music program, Advanced Placement courses, and extracurriculars.[21]

The boardroom became a tense place, with some community members accusing the board of being inadequate stewards of public schools by shifting resources to private school students. At the behest of many community members, including a coalition of clergy representing Christian and non-Haredi Jewish communities, the state eventually appointed a fiscal monitor in June 2014. Nevertheless, the board retained ultimate decision-making authority.[22]

It was around this time that the weekly public radio program *This American Life* broadcast a story on East Ramapo that raised the governance dilemma of the district to the national stage. The Haredi board members were elected in a democratic process and the Haredi community pays property taxes to fund public schools while simultaneously supporting their network of private yeshivas. These residents have a legitimate right to representation. At the same time, the district was in a state of financial disarray, there were allegations aimed at the board, and student outcomes fell far below state averages.[23]

In November 2014, the state-appointed fiscal monitor released a report about East Ramapo titled *A School District in Crisis*. The report cited "poor financial practices" and a lack of long-term planning, concluding that the district was "by any measure . . . fiscally impaired." According to the report, there were 9,000 students attending public school in the district.

Seventy-eight percent of these students qualified for free and reduced lunch, and 91 percent were Black and Latino. At the same time, there were 24,000 students within district boundaries attending private school, most of whom were in fifty-two yeshivas.[24]

Per New York State law, the district budget funds busing and special education services for all eligible students (public and private), and in East Ramapo, these spending categories were particularly large. The report noted that from the 2006–2007 school year to the 2013–2014 school year, the district experienced a 48 percent escalation in transportation costs and from the 2010–2011 school year to the 2013–2014 school year, special education tuition cost increased by 33 percent. Despite these growing expenditure categories, East Ramapo's budget, as of 2014, was defeated by voters in four of the previous five years and eight of the previous eleven years, representing the highest rejection rate in the state of New York.[25] Thus, it was impossible to raise revenue locally to support ballooning expenses.

By 2014, graduation rates and academic outcomes were lagging the region and state. Fifty-five percent of students scored "well below proficiency" in math, grades three to eight (compared to 31 percent statewide), and the graduation rate was eleven percentage points below the state average, at only 64 percent.[26]

Furthermore, according to the fiscal monitor's report, the district was subjected to a New York State Education Department enforcement action because it engaged in "patterns and practices inconsistent with Individuals with Disabilities Education Act and related laws," placing students in private schools when they could have received a "Free Appropriate Public Education."[27]

The fiscal monitor specifically leveled criticism at East Ramapo's school board, highlighting turnover in the board president role (five individuals in three years) and reporting that "board meetings degenerate into verbal brawls, with the board's attorneys berating students and parents." To top it all off, criminal charges were filed based on allegations that public school buildings were sold at below-market prices to the Haredi community. Transparency was also cited as an issue, with the board spending an estimated 60 to 70 percent (or more) of its meeting time in executive session and sustaining a practice that involved pushing public comments to the end of the meeting.[28]

In 2020, the U.S. District Court ruled in favor of an NAACP lawsuit seeking to switch East Ramapo to a ward-based school board election system rather than an at-large system to facilitate Black and Latino voices.[29] Despite this ruling, the Haredi community maintained a board majority.

While the state-appointed monitor brought attention to many of East Ramapo's issues, the fiscal and student outcome data continued to deteriorate. Given the concerning situation, in 2021, the New York State legislature and Governor Andrew Cuomo took the unusual and aggressive step of subverting a democratically elected school board by enacting legislation that allows for up to two East Ramapo state monitors that have the power to override school board decisions if they are not consistent with long-term strategic improvement plans, among other reasons. Monitors can approve or disapprove the appointment of a superintendent. The legislation also requires the board to adopt a conflict of interest policy and form a ten-person community advisory board that meets four times per year.[30] In addition to the fiscal monitor, an academic monitor was appointed in April 2022.[31]

Despite the increased state oversight, the district continues to struggle. A letter to the commissioner from the monitors regarding budget year 2024–2025 paints a bleak picture, stating that the district "faces its most dire circumstances since legislation first authorized the Commissioner to appoint monitors to the district." The report warns that with one-time state and federal cash infusions ending, there is a "structural imbalance," a liquidity issue, and a loss of access to the bond market. The report emphasizes "twin threats of fiscal calamity, both in the very near term and over the next several years."[32]

The report explains that "for the last decade, the district's voters have failed to adopt a budget that has contained tax levy increases. By holding the tax levy flat . . . the district effectively crippled itself." The report argues that even the draconian strategy the district developed to close the deficit—which includes eliminating art, music, the daily cleaning of schools, all extracurricular activities and athletics, and all nonmandated course offerings—would not be sufficient.[33]

Fiscal distress has resulted in poor academic outcomes and an inadequate physical plant. The district's four-year graduation rate as of August 2023 was 63 percent compared to the state average of 86 percent. In

2022–2023, only 22 percent of East Ramapo students were proficient in
ELA and 16 percent were proficient in math, compared to the state averages of 48 percent and 52 percent, respectively. Buildings have closed
because of asbestos, kitchen facilities were not up to code, the drinking
water contains lead, and district facilities were out of compliance with
the Americans with Disabilities Act. East Ramapo has tremendous student needs given "almost every student who attends the district's public
schools is economically disadvantaged, an English language learner, identified for special education services, or experiencing homelessness," yet
the proposed 2024–2025 budget was deemed "academically unsound."[34]

Various constituents have pushed for very different solutions. In the
spring of 2024, one bill introduced by a state lawmaker accelerates state
funding to help the district meet its obligations, conditioned on gaining
voter approval for a 1 percent property tax increase and agreeing to a new
community liaison position.[35]

Another bill was introduced in the New York State Assembly to install
a fiscal control board appointed by the state that would have broad
powers, including the ability to raise local property taxes, issue bonds,
establish benchmarks for revenues and expenditures, approve contracts,
mandate training, and conduct audits.[36] An organization called Agudath
Israel, advocating on issues affecting the Haredi community, opposed this
bill, labeling it "a misguided effort which would completely overturn the
will of the voters as reflected through their democratically elected school
board." Instead, they place blame on an "inequitable formula for distribution of state foundation aid" that is based on the public school (not
private school) student census.[37]

The situation reached a critical point in July 2024, when in response
to a parent's appeal, the NYS Commissioner of Education ordered the
East Ramapo board to adjust its tax levy for the current school year from
1 percent to 5.38 percent on the basis that the original budget was not
adequate. After a local judge rejected an effort to stay the commissioner's
order, the board members unanimously approved the tax increase out of
fear they would be removed from office, with the majority doing so under
duress.[38]

A spokesperson for Agudath Israel said, "Instead of appreciating parents who, at great personal sacrifice, self-fund their children's education,

saving the state nearly a half a billion dollars annually . . . the state has enacted punitive tax levies to compensate for a broken (state aid) formula." The New York State Education Department stated, "Equity has been, and continues to be, an issue at the local level."[39]

In the end, regardless of which side of the argument you are on, what is clear from the East Ramapo situation is that sometimes local control is not sufficient, and state action is required.

An *Education Next* piece by Vladimir Kogan argues that East Ramapo is an extreme example of the problems many communities face across the country when the board does not reflect the diversity of the student body attending the public schools.[40] While it is true that boards and those who exercise their right to vote in school board elections tend to be whiter and wealthier than the underlying student populations they serve, in East Ramapo, the majority of voters send their kids to private school, a highly unusual dynamic that makes East Ramapo an outlier.

In most districts across America, a smaller proportion of households send their kids to private school versus public school. As was discussed with respect to San Francisco, public-school-minded voters provide an element of accountability to hold school boards accountable for public school outcomes.

But for local governance and accountability to work, board members and community members must have access to meaningful data that tracks student, financial, and operating performance. This next section describes how data can be used to make informed governance decisions.

THE POWER OF SCHOOL GOVERNANCE DATA AND ANALYTICS

In my experience, most school boards have a thorough process to evaluate the superintendent each year and routinely conduct self-evaluations to measure board performance. Where school boards often fall short is utilizing data to measure district outcomes. In contrast, public company boards tend to regularly monitor progress and measure outcomes using concrete data and peer benchmarking. Business schools teach it, research analysts and investors demand it. KPIs (key performance indicators) are used by managers to run the business, by boards to hold management accountable, and by investors who evaluate and monitor the business.

According to KPI.org, KPIs are defined as "the critical (key) indicators of progress toward an intended result." They help an organization focus on what matters most by concretely and analytically measuring progress toward ultimate outcomes.[41]

Many school boards and administrators at the local level have generally fallen short of producing quantifiable metrics to measure progress. There are plausible reasons why many school boards do not embrace KPIs the same way that corporate boards do. First, the definition of a successful outcome is a hotly contested topic. While public stock investors can look to a company's stock price and financial results as indicators of value and success or failure, there is no such singular, universally accepted measure of public education.

States and the federal government have used standardized test scores as the key measure of success. Policymakers and economists gravitate to standardized tests because results are simple, quantifiable, and allow for comparison across districts. Many constituents, including teachers' unions and parents, have pushed back on standardized testing and instead argue for measures like performance assessments. While these alternative assessment avenues are worth exploring, they make it more difficult to benchmark performance across districts, which complicates accountability.

Another reason KPIs are underutilized among school boards is that the school board professional development universe has not always focused on them. Opportunities as a school board member to improve knowledge of school law, hire a superintendent, develop leadership skills, and contemplate the board's role in curriculum or mental health are easily accessible, but opportunities to learn about KPIs do not materialize as frequently.

Last, because of open meeting laws, most school board KPIs would need to be presented in public session. If the data shows deterioration in some or all the metrics, school boards and superintendents will owe an explanation to the public. While boards of private companies, nonprofits, and public companies face a similar challenge with the metrics they choose to disclose, they have discretion to keep certain KPIs for the board and management team only, without needing to disclose the metrics to investors, employees, or the public.

Despite these concerns, it is important for districts to consider how they can adopt KPIs to improve accountability. An advantage of developing district-level KPIs is that each district can tailor their metrics to match their unique goals and issues. While there are overlapping themes that cut across districts, KPIs should be expected to vary so that measures have utility and meaning. One effective use of KPIs is to measure and monitor a specific new initiative or change.

Using data to measure the impact of a new way of doing something can help administrative leaders and boards understand whether changes in any aspect of school life, from curriculum to discipline policy, has a positive or negative effect. For example, let's say a district decides to change the science pathway for middle school and high school students. The most common approach is to make the change and hope for the best. Instead, districts should closely measure and compare results of the new pathway to the old pathway. The optimal approach, though perhaps not always politically palatable and practical, would be to create a pilot group for the new pathway and a control group following the old pathway, and then to measure the difference in results of the two groups.

Another use of KPIs is to measure overall district progress and outcomes. One approach to doing this is the balanced scorecard set of measures developed by Robert Kaplan and David Norton for corporations. Their approach is designed to look at a constellation of important metrics that together paint a picture of overall performance and progress. Measures should incorporate outcomes and the performance drivers that lead to outcomes. Ideally, the balanced scorecard articulates the business strategy and aligns individuals to achieve organizational goals. The Kaplan and Norton model suggests including data from (1) the customer's perspective, (2) an internal business perspective, (3) an innovation and learning perspective, and (4) a financial perspective.[42]

Similarly, boards and senior administrative teams can think about their districts and develop a framework of KPIs that capture a holistic view of performance. In addition to student outcomes, metrics that monitor operations, financial health, and community relations should be included. Table 10.1 outlines a list of potential KPIs to consider.

Local districts can strengthen accountability by selecting measures meaningful to their circumstances and tracking results over time. School board meetings are the logical forum to review these measures with full transparency. Positive trends can be celebrated and reinforced. Plans can be discussed to address negative trends. Explanations can be provided

Table 10.1 Framework for district measurement

Category	Potential key performance indicators
Students	• Graduation rate • Standardized test scores • Number of students in advanced classes; AP scores • Participation in extracurriculars/athletics • Student engagement survey results • Disciplinary metrics • Attendance and graduation/job placement rate • College graduation rate • Utilization of resources (mental health, tutoring) • Academic outcomes by demographic subgroups
Community relations	• Community survey results • Number of events attended by board members • Number of opportunities for public to have informal dialogue with board members • Community member presence on committees
Finance and operations	• Per pupil expenditure (compared to peers) • Transportation efficiency • Metrics for liquidity, reserves, and liabilities • Budget versus actual results • Growth of expense base • Cybersecurity training/incidents • Quality of physical plant
Strategy and management	• Progress on annual goals • Results of pilot programs/new initiatives • Teacher engagement/satisfaction survey • Teacher and staff retention • Safety plan self-assessment results • Participation in professional development • Board time spent discussing innovation

when underlying one-time factors impact the data. The benefit of the work being done locally is that school boards and superintendents can develop metrics that are most relevant to their local circumstances rather than relying solely on centralized, uniform metrics.

The state can serve as a repository for data collection that can be used by local districts to facilitate benchmarking. Simultaneously, it can monitor high-level outcomes to ensure that each district is satisfactory and intervene as appropriate when targets are not met.

Care must be taken when districts and the state use benchmarking data. Context needs to be applied, as factors such as the level of resources a district has or the proportion of English language learners may not make all data comparable. Additionally, what if one district posts better test scores than its closest peers but does so because it encourages struggling students to drop out of school? It is critical to ensure that data analysis uncovers the full story and that data does not drive districts to act without careful consideration.

In the end, accountability can be accomplished on two levels. First, centralized government must continue its role of defining and measuring high-level accountability standards but should avoid micromanaging. Second, school districts need to embrace the concept of using metrics to govern and monitor progress.

One common problem when organizations manage themselves using metrics is a tendency to focus on the short term. But ultimately, school boards and administrators bear responsibility to be fiduciaries of the district with a focus on the long term.

11

SHORT-TERMISM

Short-termism, or prioritizing short-term results while ignoring long-term risks, is a problem for all types of organizations. Short-termism is another example of a phenomenon that is discussed regularly in corporate management and investor circles and has been written about extensively in the business literature.

Public companies are required by the Securities and Exchange Commission to conduct a quarterly earnings call, and it can be easier for management teams facing investors with such frequency to make decisions that result in immediate positive momentum rather than something that sacrifices short-term results for long-term gain. Experiencing weak near-term quarterly performance can put pressure on a stock price, which can increase vulnerability to an activist shareholder or an unsolicited takeover and negatively impact employee morale.

Roger Martin, former dean of the Rotman School of Business at the University of Toronto, explained in a 2015 *Harvard Business Review* article that consequences of short-termism are hard to measure since there is no control group and data is contradictory, but in his view, if "decisions are made with little regard for the long term, it is fair to expect that long-term performance of [the] business will suffer."[1] Those of us who have worked closely with CEOs can attest to the fact that they feel pressure to manage quarterly earnings. John Graham, Campbell Harvey, and Shiva Rajgopal surveyed more than four hundred executives and found that a majority of managers would not begin a positive NPV (net present value) project if it prevented them from achieving their quarterly consensus earnings estimate. Three-fourths would sacrifice economic value for smooth earnings.[2] The CFA Institute and Fund Governance Analytics studied the impact of short-termism over a twenty-two-year period and estimated foregone earnings of $1.7 trillion.[3]

School boards and administrators can relate to the corporate quarterly earnings call. They are under constant public scrutiny as they must conduct their business transparently in front of the public at every school board meeting.

THE PROBLEM

While it is important for all organizations to resist short-termism, it is especially critical for school districts. In contrast to the merger and acquisition activity that defines corporate America, school district mergers are few and far between. The public school district you attended as a student was likely there for the preceding generation and will likely be there for generations to come.

The fact that most districts serve not just current but also future generations of K-12 students should weigh heavily on school boards. There is no shortage of challenges looming on the horizon:

- School district debt continues to rise. According to the U.S. Census, debt per pupil in 2006 was $6,671, rising to $11,711 in 2022.[4]
- School infrastructure is rapidly aging. Physical plant expanded in the 1950s and 1960s to accommodate increased enrollment of the baby boomer generation. Sixty-plus years later, facilities continue to age. According to the National Center for Education Statistics, the main buildings for U.S. public schools are on average forty-nine years old, and 31 percent of schools have at least one portable building in use on campus.[5] Our collective school infrastructure has been graded D+ by the American Society of Civil Engineers.[6]
- In some cases, looming unfunded long-term liabilities present an even more serious threat than debt to long-term financial stability. Many districts have defined benefit pension plans and postretirement

healthcare benefits that were structured during a time of shorter life expectancy and more modest healthcare inflation.

- Ironically, declining public school enrollment in many parts of the country, driven by demographics and school choice, can exacerbate financial challenges. Since state aid is often linked (at least in part) to enrollment, a shrinking student body reduces revenue. At the same time, it may be difficult to reduce a district's fixed cost base, which leads to diseconomies of scale. The fixed cost base consists not only of obvious components such as infrastructure and administrative expenses but also may include postretirement benefits (from when a district may have had a bigger staff) and debt service associated with past projects.
- In addition to financial challenges, employee turnover, a lack of leadership succession planning, and teacher and staffing shortages leave districts vulnerable.

Though the shift in education funding from local property taxes to state income and sales taxes has enhanced equity, it also makes district revenue more cyclical and unpredictable. Income and sales tax tend to fluctuate with economic cycles and could also be impacted by migration patterns of wealthy individuals who pay a disproportionate share of state taxes. With our modern-day funding model, we should fully expect a greater degree of revenue volatility.

Furthermore, while forty-nine states are required to balance their annual budget, according to the nonprofit Truth in Accounting Project, many states have significant levels of unfunded pension and postemployment benefits liabilities that are not always transparent. According to their calculations, twenty-eight states did not have enough money to pay all their bills.[7]

If a district faces a fiscal crisis, there are several possible ways the state could help. Some states provide a bridge loan to schools that have trouble issuing debt or agree to accelerate the timing of their state aid payments, providing temporary liquidity. Some states require distressed districts to provide additional disclosure or even get state approval before ratifying the budget.[8]

It is precarious for school districts to ignore long-term financial risks with the hope of a state government bailout. For that to happen, there needs to be state budget capacity and political will at the time the bailout is needed.

Betting on a federal government bailout is even more risky. First, not all districts and states have equivalent debt loads, and the prospect of a retired educator in a state without generous benefits paying federal taxes to bail out a state that gave generous benefits to their retirees is hard to imagine being popular politically. Furthermore, the federal debt load, and its enormous interest-expense burden, calls into question the certainty of future federal education-spending levels.

In the direst circumstances, some districts believe that bankruptcy can be an option to wipe out their obligations, but the bankruptcy process is not the same as it is for a for-profit entity. Depending on state law, bankruptcy is not always a viable option. There were only six districts that went bankrupt between 1954 and 2014. Provisions vary significantly by state, with some permitting districts to file for bankruptcy under Chapter 9, while others do not. Idaho, for example, has provisions to allow districts to renegotiate union contracts in a financial emergency. Twenty-nine states have the authority to take over a distressed district.[9]

Not only should districts avoid counting on states and the federal government to bail them out, but they should be equally hesitant to rely on them for preventive solutions. State and federal policy can serve to compound short-termism since newly elected presidents, governors, and legislative majorities may change the direction of education policy rather than stick to a long-term plan.

There are also a series of federal and state policies and practices that exacerbate short-termism. For example, many grants provided to school districts come with "use it or lose it" spending deadlines, sometimes incentivizing districts to spend money suboptimally.

Furthermore, some statutory requirements divert school board attention away from larger issues. For example, in Pennsylvania, the full board needs to approve contracts of any kind that exceed a $100 threshold.[10] While this requirement has the good intentions of ensuring a fair bidding process and protecting taxpayer funds, in practice it can mean losing the forest for the trees. While the board is busy approving a $200 purchase of pencils to meet statutory requirements, there is less time to devote to the material issues that can render a district insolvent.

Some states have material restrictions on the types of reserve accounts that can be established and limitations on the size of unused fund balances and permitted carryovers, making it difficult to save for future obligations. To be fair, school districts must be cautious when taxing residents today to build cash for potential liabilities down the road. Voters whose kids are in the district today may or may not care about the future of the district depending on their plans and circumstances. In a few years, their kids may be graduating. While they have a vested interest in keeping property values high, they may be renters or homeowners with near-term plans to move.

Perhaps the most typical reaction when education policymakers or district leaders confront risks down the road is that they are too busy putting out fires today and too constrained to deploy extra resources toward future investment. Maybe it's a current-year budget deficit, or an ongoing superintendent search, an emergency infrastructure issue, or a curriculum controversy that has erupted in the community. There is almost always some urgent situation that requires resources and diverts attention away from thinking strategically. Understandably, the priority is to hold things together year-to-year.

UNIQUE SCHOOL BOARD POTENTIAL

In addition to ensuring districts are meeting the needs of students currently enrolled, board members should be aware that they are merely temporary stewards in the very long expected life of a district. Do our actions as board members enhance long-term strength and stability or push problems down the road? When boards fail to ask and answer this question, they succumb to short-termism.

It is important to note that each district has a unique set of risk factors, and the board is best positioned to identify them with help from administrative staff and advisors. Some districts face an unmanageable debt load. Others may have little debt but significant postretirement obligations. Still others may be on solid financial footing but face significant enrollment swings, the result of which can mean fluctuations in state aid and the need for additional space. I know of one district that lost one-third of its revenue overnight upon closure of a power plant. Rural districts often face debilitating teacher shortages and lack a pipeline of future administrators. As we've seen in previous chapters, one-size-fits-all policies don't meet the needs of highly diverse districts. The same lack of uniformity across districts also applies to how individual boards should think about long-term risks.

One critical area of focus for boards should be long-term fiscal stability. At the end of the day, districts are organizations, and part of being an organization is to manage the financial obligations of the entity over time. Doing so begins with addressing issues when you have institutional runway, when it is easier, and before any of them become a crisis. This is always preferable to waiting until the last minute when the only way to solve the problem is by dramatically raising taxes, drastically cutting the budget, or begging the state.

A study conducted by EY-Parthenon, the strategy consulting arm of Ernst & Young, provides hope that school boards can proactively address anticipated financial issues. The findings suggest that there are specific district-level factors that are predictive of future economic distress. The study also helps identify specific steps that can be taken, if enough runway exists, to avert disaster. The series of factors they identified are as follows:

- Size of unassigned general fund balance and change in balance (which is indicative of a surplus or deficit position in operations);
- Three-year growth in revenues versus expenses, which provides evidence of whether a district is running at an annual surplus or deficit;
- Three-year enrollment trends, since declining enrollment often means less state and federal funding but the continued burden of a large fixed- (and semi-fixed-) cost base;
- Funded ratio of pension, which is a key indicator of future obligations.[11]

While this is by no means an exhaustive list of what a district should monitor, EY-Parthenon found these variables to matter. Forty percent of districts in the study were deemed financially healthy, 40 percent showed early warning signs of problems to come, and 20 percent were already facing moderate to high financial risk. Districts with over 75 percent of students receiving free or reduced lunch were two times more likely to fall into the moderate to high-risk category.

All in all, 60 percent of districts in the sample needed long-term financial planning to avoid a crisis down the road. Just as in the private sector, distress most typically happens when risk factors build over time and leaders fail to address issues when they first appear. Long-term financial modeling and planning can make all the difference. Distress typically happens slowly with advanced warning, and some of the most critical levers to improve the financial health of a district often have significant lag times.[12]

Based on case study analysis, EY-Parthenon finds that districts should take early steps to address financial issues. The long-term approach correlated with better financial outcomes. Districts that conducted advanced planning and identified heightened risk of a looming crisis took corrective steps. They limited wage growth, reduced staff and services, increased the tax levy, or developed new revenue sources. In these cases, districts crafted a multiyear strategy to improve financial results rather than triggering a massive one-time cut that severely impacts student outcomes. The prognosis for the districts that failed to engage in advanced planning was negative.[13] Because most district spending is embedded in multiyear contracts and because it is difficult to dramatically increase the tax rate in one given year, waiting until the last minute is disastrous. It is also avoidable by following a series of best practices.

ENTERPRISE RISK MANAGEMENT

Many well-run boards in corporate America have long been focused on a concept called enterprise risk management (ERM). While definitions of ERM vary, the concept is to manage risks across the organization with a coordinated approach rather than in silos.[14] Researchers Paul Sobel and Kurt Reding define it as "a structured and disciplined approach to help management understand and manage uncertainties" that "encompasses all business risks using an integrated and holistic approach."[15] Practicing ERM facilitates mitigation steps that can be taken to at least prepare as much as possible for risks on the horizon.

School boards and administrators would benefit from following a similar practice. ERM may identify classic compliance risks such as inadequate financial controls, but the scope extends more broadly to all aspects of the organization. Here are some examples of enterprise risks a school district may face:

- A recession that triggers a loss in funding;
- A state funding formula change;
- Substantial projected enrollment fluctuations;
- A looming labor shortage;
- Cybersecurity or physical security threats;
- Long-term liabilities;
- Erosion of the property tax base;
- Inadequate succession planning.

The idea behind ERM is to encourage boards and administrators to have discussions about these risks on a routine basis so that adequate attention is given to taking steps to mitigate them whenever possible.

For example, if enrollment is projected to decline, the board can spend a couple of years studying fixed and variable costs to determine how to reduce the cost structure without impacting the student experience. If cybersecurity is a concern, as it should be for every district, dedicating budget dollars to purchase software and train employees can pay dividends.

TIME ALLOCATION

On the surface, ratifying the budget may seem like the most significant financial decision a school board makes. School districts typically have lengthy debates about budget allocation, and in many states, districts also propose an annual tax levy to ensure adequate funding. The process is highly transparent and not rushed, with ample opportunity to incorporate public input. Sometimes you can find boards deliberating over relatively small items, such as a modest capital improvement or the hiring of a consultant. Other times, there could be more meaningful debates that move the needle, such as class size, staffing levels, or large capital projects.

But in unionized districts, by the time you get to the budget hearings, the largest financial decisions have already been made. Most of the budget is personnel-related expenses, and economic terms get locked in by negotiating multiyear contracts separate from the budget process. These contracts go far beyond salaries. They spell out benefits for active and retired employees and often include limitations on hours worked per day and class size. With a stroke of a pen, and with little or no flexibility to change, a district binds itself to significant obligations. After a labor contract has been executed, if the district faces a deteriorating macroeconomic environment, there are fewer levers to reduce the district's cost base. Far beyond the current year budget, these multiyear contracts have significant long-term financial ramifications.

While there are requirements in many states that spell out how many budget hearings a board needs to conduct, there are typically no such requirements for time devoted to deliberation of labor contracts (other than certain state deadlines). The board can meet in executive session, outside of the public spotlight, as many times as necessary to discuss terms and negotiating strategy. It is imperative that boards realize the importance of contract negotiations and allocate adequate time to ensuring a productive outcome.

Every contract negotiation should involve several analytical exercises. The first is benchmarking, comparing salary and benefits offerings to peer districts to ensure employees are being treated fairly and that the district can attract talented employees. Benchmarking must consider all key provisions of the contract, including salary scale, healthcare benefits, and any embedded operational restrictions (e.g., how many periods a day a high school teacher is required to teach).

Any proposal needs to be modeled to reflect the financial impact on the district. This is complex and time consuming. Each variable can have an impact not only during the life of the contract but also for many years beyond. Let's say a district is committed to providing more value to its employees and has an incremental $3 million to spend on either incremental salary or more subsidized healthcare benefits. How should a district think about the relative long-term financial trade-off of increasing salary versus benefits?

Salary increases in any organization are very hard to reverse, so each incremental dollar not only will raise the cost of labor during the term of the contract, but it will likely be carried forward to the next contract, which will provide further increases off a higher base, ultimately having a compounding effect.

On the benefits side, if decreasing the employee healthcare contribution by 1 percentage point costs the district $3 million today, the analysis would not be complete without projecting the impact into the future.

Healthcare inflation typically runs higher than overall inflation. From
1945 to 2023, the rate of healthcare inflation was 5.0 percent, while the
rate of overall inflation was 3.7 percent.[16] This differential in rate implies
that a $1,000 healthcare expenditure in 1945 equates to approximately
$47,000 in 2023, while a $1,000 nonhealthcare expenditure in 1945
equates to approximately $17,000 in 2023.[17] Furthermore, except during
the pandemic, life expectancy typically increases over time. The board
should be analyzing long-term financial impact considering underlying
assumptions of healthcare inflation and longer life expectancy.

Each contract negotiation has financial, actuarial, and labor relations
components. Allocating the necessary time to consider all components is
also a function of the help extended to school boards. Do district business
officials and outside experts provide the board with analytics to understand the trade-offs of each decision? Has the board considered the long-
term impact even beyond the contract term? Employees deserve to be
compensated fairly, while board members must balance fiscal sustainability and taxpayer responsibility. Given the long-term consequences of
the decisions being reached, boards need to allocate appropriate time and
resources to their consideration.

PAY AS MUCH ATTENTION TO THE STATEMENT OF NET POSITION AS THE BUDGET

Districts spend time debating small fluctuations in annual budget each
year but do not always have a dialogue regarding the massive looming
liabilities that are sitting on the statement of net position.

Ask a board member the size of their district's annual budget, and
it is highly likely they will know the answer. But ask a board member
about the district's total liabilities or aggregate reserves, and they may or
may not be able to respond. While boards tend to focus on revenue and
expense projections, understanding assets and liabilities is critical when
determining the fiscal health of the district and when making financial
decisions. Board members should ask key questions, including:

- Does the district have ample liquidity and a sound cash management
  policy?
- Does the district have adequate reserves to meet potential future
  obligations?

- Is the level of indebtedness manageable? Is there a need to raise additional debt, and if so, is there adequate debt capacity? What is the district's credit rating, and does the district have access to the bond market?
- What additional long-term liabilities does the district have and do any steps need to be taken to ensure that the district can meet its future obligations without compromising educational quality for the next generation of students?
- Are there any other variables (e.g., enrollment trends) that impact the ability of the district to meet its obligations?

Sometimes looming issues are easy to identify and understand, while others are highly complex, such as other post-employment benefits (OPEB). OPEB liabilities result from promising employees their healthcare benefits in retirement. Per government accounting rules, actuaries calculate how much cash will be required for the district to pay for this benefit over time. Eligible retirement age varies across states. In states where employees are eligible for retirement at age fifty-five and where generous healthcare plans are offered to retirees, the costs of post-employment benefits can reach staggering levels.

There are some big differences between pension and OPEB obligations. Pensions are typically guaranteed and protected by state constitutions, whereas retirement healthcare benefits are not. Therefore, while a district often lacks authority to amend pension terms, it retains the right to determine the level of retiree healthcare benefits, subject to collective bargaining.[18]

Furthermore, employers set aside funds for pension obligations. These funds are invested by a pension manager and typically earn a return over time that helps fund the future liability. In many states, there is no mechanism to do the same thing for future healthcare obligations. Therefore, the size of the OPEB liability continues to grow, but no pool of invested capital exists to offset this liability.[19]

The Reason Foundation found after reviewing 30,000 audited financial statements for states, municipalities, and school districts, that in addition to pension obligations, state and local governments, as of the end of fiscal year 2019, have $1.2 trillion of net OPEB liabilities, the largest component of which is postemployment healthcare. After municipal bonds and net pension liabilities, this is the third largest source of indebtedness for subnational governmental bodies. Perhaps more astoundingly, fifteen governmental entities make up half of the total, including my home state of New York.[20]

Some New York districts have OPEB liabilities that run twice their annual revenue, with several districts' liabilities totaling more than 3.5 times their revenue. Astoundingly, New York's collective OPEB liability is $16,137 per capita. Said another way, New York has accumulated over $313 billion state and local OPEB liabilities, an amount that exceeds the annual New York State budget. California, New Jersey, Texas, and Illinois also have sizable OPEB liabilities. The OPEB liability is driven by the projected number of employees and their average life expectancy, benefits packages offered, the discount rate utilized to determine the present value of the liability, and an assumption for healthcare inflation. Specifically, the liability represents the projected healthcare insurance premiums the districts will pay for retirees until they reach Medicare eligibility age, but often it will also include Medicare supplemental insurance.[21]

If a district chooses to provide healthcare benefits to retirees, it needs to ensure that it has the financial resources to meet its obligations. As tempting as it may be, it's not acceptable to pass the problem onto a future board when their only option may be to take draconian steps such as cutting other parts of the budget, levying additional taxes, or reducing benefits for current employees.

To the extent that board members want to provide retirees with healthcare, reserving funds can be the answer, particularly if the district is shrinking and the proportion of retirees to students increases. However, not all states permit a district to set up an OPEB reserve fund. To the extent that board members do not believe the benefit at the current level is sustainable, they must work collectively with labor to develop a prudent long-term plan. Another option is to advocate for more reserve flexibility through state legislation. Not discussing it or putting it off until some future date when it becomes a crisis is not fair to future students and taxpayers.

COMPLETE A FIVE-YEAR FORECAST

Just as the board spends substantial time conducting due diligence on next year's budget, five-year forecasting is an equally important practice. Many variables such as enrollment trends, labor costs, and capital projects typically can be forecasted with reasonable accuracy.

Economic cycles, major adjustments to state and federal funding formulas, and unexpected events (such as the pandemic) are more difficult to predict. To factor in volatility, a district can run an expected ("base case") forecast and then can run sensitivities that incorporate possible upsides and downsides in projected revenue and expenses. The benefit of running sensitivities is learning to anticipate what can go wrong and determining whether the district has the strength to withstand potential downside scenarios. Anticipating potential financial shortfalls, for example, the district can identify cost-savings opportunities or raise revenue. If a district is fortunate and experiences a positive revenue scenario, determining how to best deploy a surplus is also important.

FOCUS ON SUCCESSION PLANNING

A school district's most important asset is its people, and special attention should be paid to ensuring a long-term strategy that builds a pipeline of future district leaders. While there are times when hiring leaders from outside the district is the most sensible option, boards should budget time at least annually to consider the robustness of its internal pool of future leaders. If the pipeline is insufficient, perhaps it's time to consider encouraging (and incentivizing) promising employees to attain their administrative certifications. Or perhaps potential future leaders need specific training, coaching, mentoring, or experiences that will better prepare them for a promotion. They might benefit from more exposure to the school board well before the next superintendent search takes place. Thinking about these issues early and often typically requires modest investments in time and resources but can pay off when it's time to fill the next critical position.

School board succession planning is also important and very different from how it works in the corporate and not-for-profit sectors. Board members have no control over who runs (and who wins), but districts can certainly take steps to disseminate information on upcoming elections and be clear regarding the steps required to get on the ballot.

PLANNING AND GOAL SETTING

When I first became a school board member, I heard a story about a district that spent a year developing an extensive five-year plan, only for it to collect dust in the district office. The usefulness of any plan reflects the thought that went into creating it, and the willingness to follow it. While a long-term plan may be useful for some districts, a clear and thoughtful set of annual goals may be a better planning mechanism for others.

The most important aspect of setting annual goals and engaging in long-term strategic planning is to pick a methodology that works for your district. Measure progress being made and ensure that resources are aligned with goals and priorities. Also ensure that district goals, administrative goals, and building-level goals are in sync.

Regardless of whether or not you have a five-year strategic plan, it is critical when setting goals to think about the long-term trajectory of the district from a human resource, financial, and risk perspective.

Chapters 7–11 have outlined the potential that school boards have to solve problems and the specific steps board members can take to strengthen districts. Chapter 12 will address several shortcomings of school boards and how a collaborative effort can maximize board effectiveness.

III

OUR SHARED RESPONSIBILITY

12

STRENGTHENING SCHOOL BOARDS

It was during the COVID-19 pandemic when I detected a disconnect. The public and the media were paying far more attention to school boards than were scholars and policymakers. School boards have historically received little attention and are not well understood. Even students at the nation's finest graduate schools of education are not taught much about them. There are few offerings in course catalogs with "school boards" or "board of education" in the description, and there haven't been many research studies conducted on boards of education. Because district-level data is highly fragmented, compiling school board election statistics or any type of information regarding board composition or board action is an arduous task. Foundations fund very few initiatives related to school boards, and state policymakers, sometimes intentionally and sometimes unintentionally, have continually taken steps to erode board power.

Yet the pandemic taught us that school boards matter. Whether it was setting COVID prevention protocols or deciding whether to institute DEI training, battle after battle took place in boardrooms across the country. Even when it was a topic on which the school board had no control, that did not stop the community from venting their frustrations during public comment periods.

The impact of a school board extends far beyond adjudicating the contentious issues of the day. When a recession hits that requires cuts to the

budget, school boards matter. When it's time to hire or fire a superintendent, school boards matter. If there is a union contract to negotiate, school
boards matter. If a policy needs to be adopted on a highly controversial
topic, school boards matter.

Even when all is quiet, school boards still matter. They can be forward-
thinking about succession planning or have no pipeline of future leaders.
They can make prudent financial decisions, or little by little, drive a district
into a financial abyss. And as outlined in part II, boards have the capability of tackling many of public education's greatest challenges, which
include avoiding initiative fatigue, establishing a positive climate, facilitating community engagement, ensuring accountability, and engaging in
long-term planning.

Boards have the potential to improve our education system, but reaching their full potential requires a collective effort. My hope is that all of us
will play our respective roles in challenging assumptions, asking questions,
and conducting research necessary to fill the gaps in our understanding
of how to make board governance stronger. Boards have shortcomings,
and it will take a concerted effort to help them realize their full potential.

In these pages, I have made the case that the pendulum of state involvement in public education has swung too far. States have become more
activist, inserting themselves into every facet of district affairs, which in
turn has reduced school board power. We should strive for a better balance by avoiding state-level micromanagement while maintaining state
oversight. Moving in this direction will require a stepped-up investment
in boards of education across multiple fronts.

The first involves conducting additional research to help address the
perceived shortfalls and lingering questions regarding school board governance. The second is to realize that a healthy, productive school board
depends on a collective effort. From researchers to administrators to policymakers to school board members themselves, all of us have a critical
role to play in establishing and maintaining a healthy education governance system.

VOTER TURNOUT AND UNCONTESTED RACES

Perhaps the most frequently discussed problem of school board governance is disappointing voter turnout. Low turnout elections narrow constituent voices and risk amplifying the influence of special interests. The scope of the problem has attracted scholarly research, but more is needed.

According to a National School Boards Association estimate, school board election turnout can be often as low as 5 to 10 percent, far below the U.S. presidential elections (over 60 percent) and midterm elections (over 45 percent), but much closer to the less than 15 percent turnout typically seen in municipal elections.[1] An issue brief authored by political scientist Michael Hartney includes an estimate that two-thirds of elected school board members experience races with a 10 to 15 percent voter turnout.[2]

Recent research conducted by Brian Jacob at the University of Michigan suggests that more voters turned out during COVID when tensions were high and key decisions needed to be made. Among the sample of districts analyzed, turnout was 80 percent higher early in the pandemic, and through the end of 2022 was 27 percent higher when compared to pre-pandemic levels. The increase was more pronounced in districts with a higher proportion of college graduates and Republicans, while it was less pronounced in districts with more economically disadvantaged students.[3]

In situations where turnout is low, there is concern that it's easier for any special interest group to exert influence. Some tactics are obvious, such as endorsing candidates and donating money. More subtle approaches deployed include attempting to mobilize certain types of voters that may be sympathetic to their cause.

And they achieve results. Michael Hartney recently conducted a large study of four thousand teachers' union endorsements of school board candidates. He found that in California and Florida, union-endorsed candidates were elected at a 71 percent and 63 percent rate, respectively. Hartney's results mirror research by Terry Moe in the early 2000s finding that favored candidates of the California teachers' unions were elected 76 percent of the time.[4]

Another factor that contributes to union influence is the disproportionate number of school board members who come from the field of education. Hartney reviews several surveys conducted since 2001 and finds that 22 percent of school board members are current or former educators, compared to 6 percent of the overall population, implying a 400 percent overrepresentation.[5]

The fact that many school board members come from the education sector is not particularly surprising. Individuals who have dedicated their lives to educating children likely have a genuine interest in schools, and their experience in education can provide a useful foundation of knowledge. Furthermore, just because a board member is an educator by training or an active union member, does not automatically imply that they will be partial to union positions when negotiating contracts and setting policy. I have known many education professionals on school boards who act as earnest fiduciaries when conducting board business. Furthermore, education sector candidates may be particularly well-versed in addressing the electorate on school-related issues.

Having said that, survey data suggests that candidates affiliated with unions tend to support union-friendly policy positions at higher rates. For example, a 2009 NSBA survey found that 22 percent of board members who are teachers support performance pay concepts, versus 44 percent of nonteacher board members. Forty-four percent of teacher board members said that across-the-board pay raises were "very" or "extremely important" compared to 25 percent of nonteacher board members.[6]

Another study by Moe published in 2006 provides potential evidence of self-interest underlying teachers' involvement in school board politics. Teachers living outside of the district in which they work were found to be no more likely to vote than the general public, while those living within district boundaries were two to seven times more likely to vote.[7]

Some scholars believe that state politics is harder for unions to influence than local school boards. They argue that local communities often lack other organized voices, while at the state level there can be a better balance between unions and other special interest groups. Having said that, unions have a strong voice in many state capitals. In fact, state laws often legitimize and empower unions by recognizing them as the exclusive representative of all employees and requiring districts to grant certain powers to unions that facilitate recruiting and mobilization, including the provision of district space, the sharing of data, embedding dues directly as a payroll deduction, and the use of district communication channels.[8] Empirically, teachers are more likely to be active in elections with state-level races.[9] Teachers' unions influence state policy by contributing to PACs and lobbying for specific legislation and regulation. In the end, strong unions have the power to influence any part of government that plays a role in shaping public education. In Chicago, a teachers' union organizer recently became mayor.

One way to balance the influence of any type of special interest group is to increase voter turnout. More effort is needed to educate the community on the importance of school board elections and to encourage citizens to vote. There are a range of steps that can be taken to accomplish this, including school board awareness campaigns, making the registration process clear and easy, making polling locations accessible, disseminating information about the election, and involving community organizations. Districts should use their communications channels and partner with parent advocacy groups (such as the PTA) to encourage members of the community to vote. High turnout ensures that all voices are heard and that any one voice does not control the outcome.

Researchers can also explore why some districts have higher turnout rates than others. One important question is optimal election timing. Some states have school board elections coincide with November general elections, while others conduct elections off cycle.

As expected, November elections, particularly in presidential election years, drive participation higher. Michael Hartney argues that states should move away from the Progressive Era off-cycle tradition and move local elections to an even-year November timeframe based on the latest empirical research.[10] Arguments against on-cycle contests include risk of further politicization of school board races and a reduced window for new board members to get up to speed before budget season. In some states that have voters approve the tax levy increase, like New York, November timing would be awkward with the timing of the budget cycle, and holding elections every other year only (to coincide with on-cycle federal elections) would not work with the annual budget vote requirement. An election every other year would also disturb the staggard term structure that many boards employ.

Others have questioned whether the incremental voters in a November election access candidate and district information to make informed decisions or find difficulty in a sea of election information on other local, state, and federal races. In jurisdictions that require school board members to run as Republicans or Democrats, how much voting is straight ticket, where the voter chooses candidates from one political party only for every contest on the ballot? More research related to election mechanics will continue to help policy makers determine the best possible system.

Another question deserving of further analysis is whether elections are effective at holding board members accountable. On the one hand, a study in Ohio by Vladimir Kogan, Stephane Lavertu, and Zachary Peskowitz found that publicly available measures of district performance had little impact on school board turnover.[11] On the other hand, in these same school districts, failed federal Adequate Yearly Progress designations under NCLB were found not to be particularly good measures of district performance yet increased the probability of the school district levy not passing.[12] More studies need to be conducted to parse through these nuanced and important questions of local accountability.

A study conducted by Julia Payson who analyzed a panel of California data (from 2003–2012) suggests that incumbents are more likely to win elections when their district's test scores improve only in presidential election years, when voter turnout is highest.[13] Another analysis by Valdimir Kogan and colleagues reviewed 10,000 school tax referenda across four states. The study found that turnout is highest in presidential elections, lower in midterms, even lower in off-cycle elections, and particularly low for special elections and primaries (turnout was under 30 percent in all four states during special elections). Yet the study found that election timing influences voter composition such as interest groups and partisanship but only has a modest effect on election outcome. While low-turnout elections had an increased share of education employees, the difference was small, and they were still a modest proportion of voters. Timing was found to have the most significant impact on voter age. Seniors represent a larger share of the electorate in special elections (accounting for about half), the effect of which varies across states.[14]

Despite the need for more research, there are some clear steps we can take to help increase the quality of school board elections. First, more effort should be made to educate citizens on the role of the board versus district administration and the board versus state government. Many candidates run on issues that the board has no legal authority to impact.

Second, local districts and the state should do everything possible to clearly disseminate performance data to inform voters.

In addition to turnout, another school board election issue is the large number of uncontested seats, which according to Ballotpedia data ranges between 24 and 40 percent.[15] It is difficult to discern whether uncontested elections stem from contentment with incumbents, apathy, or lack of awareness.

Some communities have taken concrete steps to improve the pipeline of potential candidates by creating independent nominating committees that throw their weight behind a specific slate of candidates, though there are drawbacks to this approach as it puts power in the hands of a small number of people. Another approach is to view other community organizations, such as the PTA or the local education foundation, as fertile ground to find a pipeline of potential future school board candidates with district leadership experience. PTAs and foundations typically stop short of candidate endorsement, since they are nonpartisan organizations restricted by their charter and tax-exempt status, but they can be a source of potential candidates and can drive election turnout.

Undoubtedly, more research needs to be conducted to determine optimal election timing, methods for getting citizens out to vote, and steps to ensure a robust pipeline of election candidates. We need studies that not only measure what variables correlate with more turnout, but also whether voters have access to candidate information and are in the position to make informed choices.

SCHOOL BOARD MEMBER DIVERSITY

Boards are often criticized for their lack of diversity and for not reflecting the diversity of their community. Too often overlooked is the fact that school boards have achieved better gender diversity than other levels of elected government. According to a 2018 survey of school board members compiled by the NSBA, 50 percent were female.[16] Ballotpedia calculates that school board members are 43 percent female and 52 percent male, with no information available for the remaining 5 percent.[17] Both estimates compare favorably to the significantly lower percentage of women in other government leadership roles during the same time period, including 25 percent of state legislators and 20 percent of Congress members.[18]

The fact that women make up between 40 and 50 percent of school board members has positive implications for gender representation in government beyond the boardroom. School board service has been shown empirically to be a steppingstone to the state legislature, suggesting that school boards serve as a positive factor in achieving better representation of women in governing bodies beyond education. While that is worth celebrating, there is more progress to be made on other demographic metrics.

A breakdown of board member racial composition suggests under-representation. Table 12.1 illustrates school board members and public school students by race, though it should be noted that these statistics are not directly comparable. The left-hand column of the table reflects all U.S. public school students during the 2017–2018 school year, while the right-hand column shows a sample of just over one thousand school board members from a 2018 NSBA survey, which may or may not be representative of districts generally. It should also be noted that bigger city districts generally have a larger share of minority students. Therefore, even if school boards reflect the diversity of their communities, white school board members would be overrepresented in an aggregate sample. While the percentage of white school board members in the sample, at 78 percent, is far from reflecting the nation's underlying population, state legislatures had an even higher percentage of white representatives, at 82 percent as of 2020.[19]

Numerous academic studies have identified the benefits of boards better reflecting their underlying population of students and citizens, but more research is needed to gain a deeper understanding of the drivers and

Table 12.1   Racial composition of public school boards

	Public school students	School board members
Black	15%	10%
Hispanic	27%	3%
White	48%	78%
Other	10%	9% (7% preferred not to answer)

impact of board diversity. Some argue that compensating board members will increase board service accessibility and broaden the pool of potential board candidates. The NSBA survey suggests an estimated 61 percent of board members receive no salary and 28 percent receive less than $5,000 per year. Seventy-three percent received no per-meeting stipend, while 16 percent received less than $100. Many other types of elected officials receive salaries and benefits, but for most school board members, service is a labor of love.[20]

There are drawbacks to implementing more widespread school board member compensation. At the height of the pandemic, when public trust in school board members was tested, the fact that board members receive no compensation was helpful in restoring board credibility. Providing compensation to school board members may undermine public trust during the times it is most needed.

Alternatively, perhaps a compromise would be to give school board members the option of reimbursement for reasonable expenses directly associated with school board service, such as meals on nights of meetings, transportation, and babysitting services for board members' children, which could make it easier for economically disadvantaged members of the community to serve while avoiding increased public skepticism of school board member intent.

Another commonly cited solution to help diversify boards is to establish ward-based instead of at-large elections. A ward-based system provides more opportunity for each neighborhood to separately attain direct representation, which in some communities may result in a more racially diverse board. As discussed in chapter 10, a court ordered East Ramapo to switch to a ward-based system for this very reason. Progressive Era reformers pushed to eliminate ward-based systems, concerned that they might facilitate cronyism, pit one community against another, and make it more difficult to attract the very best individuals to board service by shrinking the potential pool of candidates for any one seat.

The research on ward-based versus at-large elections is nuanced and sometimes conflicting. In *Besieged*, edited by William Howell, Melissa Marschall finds that African Americans won more seats in ward-based elections, though for Hispanics the findings were trivial.[21] Kenneth Meier and Eric Juenke find that in Hispanic minority districts, ward-based systems lead to "descriptive and substantive gains" for Hispanics, but in Hispanic majority districts, ward-based systems "slightly restrain both the quantity and quality of representation" perhaps because other minority groups use ward-based elections to make it more difficult to achieve policies that the Hispanic community supports.[22]

Even with at-large elections, there is always a concern that school board members will make decisions that benefit their specific neighborhood. Recent research conducted in North Carolina found that there was a correlation between non-Democratic party winners of school board elections and the performance of neighborhood schools in which they lived. The study showed an improvement in performance specific to the neighborhood of the non-Democratic board members, suggesting the possibility that they may have influenced decision-making to benefit their neighborhood. On larger boards, the seemingly self-interested behavior was less pronounced. The authors argue not only for expanding board size but also for ward-based systems that would give representation to diverse neighborhoods.[23]

Further research is needed, however. A ward-based system could incentivize elected members to make decisions that benefit their specific group of constituents, even at the expense of the district overall since they do not have to answer to all constituents. The potential downsides of a ward-based system seem too great to deploy them universally, but for certain communities that struggle with neighborhood representation, they can be a useful and legitimate tool.

THE POLITICIZATION OF SCHOOL BOARDS

In a *Wall Street Journal* editorial about Governor Ron DeSantis endorsing Florida school board candidates, William McGurn called school boards "among the most politicized institutions in modern America." He went on to say that most school boards are "dominated by or are in cahoots with the teachers unions" and that DeSantis's endorsements serve to recognize "the reality" and puts it "out in the open where voters can decide."[24]

The magnitude and consequences of school board politicization is a subject that requires continued research. School boards undoubtedly can be political, but when compared to other types of elected office they have elements that provide some buffer against the most partisan tendencies. One of the most polarizing forces in contemporary American politics has been the gerrymandering of legislative districts.

It has been well documented in political science literature that Republican and Democratic gerrymandering has further politicized our country. School districts follow specific geographic boundaries that remain static, except in the rare circumstance that a district merger occurs. While districts may experience self-selection of who chooses to live in each community, school board elections follow the generally static contours of district lines.

Because of gerrymandering, politicians worried about winning the primary can end up being pushed far left or right of center. Americans in the more centrist-moderate part of the political spectrum may be unaffiliated with a political party and unable to vote in primaries, depending on state election laws. This dynamic can sometimes result in general elections that lack candidates with middle-of-the-road views despite the large portion of the electorate being middle-of-the-road. This dynamic, however, doesn't play out in choosing school board members in many parts of the country. Although there is variation by state, most either do not have primaries for school board elections or hold primaries only when there is more than twice the number of candidates as open seats. A full ideological spectrum of candidates can run, including moderates.

If we further shift school governance power toward state or federal control, we risk further politicization of education. According to political scientist Eric Oliver at the University of Chicago, "The primary difference between national and local elections is that while the former are highly ideological, the latter are managerial in character."[25]

Another criticism of school boards is the broad-brush painting of members as ideologically skewed toward the progressive end of the political spectrum. The 2018 NSBA survey confirms that the largest group of school boards members, at 44 percent, are progressive/lean progressive. Yet the survey data also suggests 36 percent are conservative/lean conservative.[26]

While recently there has been an uptick of reports about significant amounts of money funneling into school board campaigns, the same NSBA survey suggests that most school board contests were not influenced by big spending, with less than $1,000 spent by 75 percent of school board members.[27]

During the Progressive Era, reforms were put in place to try and separate school boards from partisan politics. The majority of states either mandate or allow for off-cycle elections.[28] Furthermore, forty-one states require candidates to run unaffiliated with political parties. Only Alabama, Connecticut, Louisiana, and Pennsylvania require party labels on the ballots. Rhode Island, Tennessee, North Carolina, South Carolina, and Georgia provide the option to show party affiliation.[29] Supporters of affiliation argue that it makes the process more transparent by putting political beliefs on full display, while advocates to keep candidates unaffiliated argue that it insulates school board races from partisan bickering. Additional empirical research conducted on this question of party affiliation would help inform states as they consider changes to their current election framework.

Researcher Evan Crawford studied two states that vary on whether board members are elected on nonpartisan or partisan labels. Crawford found evidence that partisan-elected board members tend to be more influenced by party cues, but he also discovered a partisan gap in policy support among the nonpartisan control group. Additional research on this topic is required to understand the impact of ballot design.[30]

From a personal perspective, I have seen the benefits of the system we have in New York, where candidates are unaffiliated with political parties and elections take place off-cycle. When I last ran for school board, I expressed to my community that society is polarized and politicized, but our schools should not be—we should teach kids how to think, not what to think.

BOARD MEMBER EXPERTISE

Another common criticism of school boards is that members generally lack the skills and knowledge to govern districts. The extent to which this is true and the consequences of board members with wide-ranging backgrounds remains largely unstudied, however.

While many board members do not have backgrounds in education law, finance, or curriculum, the 2018 NSBA survey finds that board members are on average older, better educated, and more experienced than critics would like to admit. The median age of a board member in the survey was fifty-nine. Seventy-seven percent have a college degree, with another 19 percent having attended some college or postsecondary training.[31]

In addition, school boards are a single-purpose government entity, which allows board members to focus all their time and attention on education, in contrast to mayors, city councilmembers, or county and state legislators who must gain mastery of wide-ranging issues from healthcare to crime.

Boards also typically provide more underlying stability and continuity to a district than mayoral control. When a mayor loses an election or reaches their term limit, it is not unusual for their replacement to dramatically change school district strategic direction. This lack of continuity can happen over and over to a school district as the political tides turn. Conversely, school boards typically have staggered elections, where only a minority of board seats are up for election in any given year, making it unusual for a majority to turnover at once. Furthermore, length of school board service varies, with the average board tenure at 8.6 years.[32]

Long-serving members can contribute to continuity, stability, and institutional memory. There is also a built-in mentoring system whereby experienced board members can help educate newer board members on the more technical matters of board governance. Additional research into the mix of board member experience and optimal term length would be illuminating.

While corporate and nonprofit boards almost always have members with substantive finance and accounting experience, it is conceivable that some elected school boards may lack this expertise. While it's relatively straightforward to understand how to balance an annual budget, the oversight of long-term financial planning and asset and liability management is inherently more complex.

There are a couple of ways boards can make up for a lack of financial expertise. John Fullerton in *Education Next* argues that board members should expect that superintendents prioritize financial management along with instruction and supervise the business office adequately.[33] Board professional development can also help build financial literacy. Board members do not need to be financial experts, but to perform their fiduciary duty they must be in the position to identify risks and ask the right questions. Last, boards can include community members with financial expertise on various committees, such as audit and finance. While these volunteers will not have decision-making authority, they can draw on their knowledge to advise the board.

Identifying what we know as a matter of research and areas that call out for more data and attention is only one step. Another is turning to and in some cases tasking institutions, organizations, and individuals to help improve the system. All of us can play an integral role in making school boards better. From foundations to academic institutions to community members, our collective effort matters.

ACADEMIA

There are three ways in which our nation's universities that have degree programs in education can support school board governance. First, the topic of board governance should be woven into the curriculum to ensure that graduates understand the role of school boards and how they can work with boards productively. Regardless of what path students with education degrees choose to take after graduation, if they are in the public school universe, chances are that school boards will have direct relevance. Perhaps they may become school board members themselves. Second, school board–related research should be prioritized to develop a deeper analytical understanding of how to optimize school board elections, structure, and function. And third, professional development opportunities should be provided to school board members and superintendents.

SCHOOL BOARDS ASSOCIATIONS

Associations provide an invaluable opportunity for board members to network, compare experiences, and create learning opportunities. There is power in sharing best practices and soliciting advice from peers. Furthermore, associations are the single best source of professional development opportunities, providing board members with seminars on topics ranging from leadership to school law to school security. Associations often have substantial policy and education law expertise that can be valuable for member districts to tap. They also work to find consensus to support an advocacy agenda. Doing so allows school boards associations to bring a powerful collective voice to their respective state capitals.

Another role of associations that is often overlooked is their unique ability to disseminate information to the fragmented school board landscape. Researchers with findings that are relevant to districts can reach thousands of school board members through the association channel.

COMMUNITY MEMBERS

It all starts and ends with community members. If more community members meaningfully participate in the election process, we will have a healthier and more representative system. Higher turnout serves to mitigate the influence of any one special interest group. Turnout can be encouraged through awareness campaigns and by enlisting community organizations like the PTA to encourage citizens to exercise their right to vote.

Community members should not be shy about expressing their views to board members directly or participating in public comment periods. Having said that, some issues are better directed initially to a particular teacher, department head, or principal. It is helpful to follow the chain of command and to be mindful of which issues fall in the domain of the board versus central administration versus building administration. Ultimately, if a matter is not resolved at the administrative level to the satisfaction of the community member, or if a matter relates directly to board business (such as a district goal or policy or a budget allocation decision), it makes sense to directly approach board members.

Although community members have the freedom to advocate for any "hot button" issue of their choosing, a more comprehensive and collaborative partnership between the board and the community could be more impactful. Instead of narrowly focusing on a particular controversy of the day, a broader lens around instruction, fiscal responsibility, and student outcomes will help the district in the long run.

Additionally, a healthy relationship is predicated on the public having a better appreciation of the scope of board power. State and local leaders need to educate communities on where responsibilities lie. As discussed earlier in the book, there are two lines that often get confused—the line that delineates administrative versus board responsibility and the line between board power and the state. Complaining to the board about an issue that falls squarely outside of the board's responsibilities is not productive. Similarly, a candidate running for a board seat who makes campaign promises that are outside of the scope of board power may alienate administrative leaders. Candidates make promises that cannot be kept because of state versus board power, leading to frustration down the road.

Community members may face impediments to participation such as childcare and language accessibility, but there are multiple ways to elevate your voice. For example, if attending a meeting is logistically difficult, community members can email school board members. If language is an impediment, perhaps another community member can help translate.

Another way to incorporate community input is to have community members sit on certain committees. While these committees would not have fiduciary responsibility, they can advise the board. Reasons for including community members on committees are multifaceted. It is a way to channel community feedback and insight directly into the process. Additionally, if the board itself is lacking a particular skill, a committee can be formed to tap into the expertise of community members. It is important to have individuals at the table who have specific domain knowledge and know what questions to ask.

FOUNDATIONS

Historically, the largest American foundations that fund public education initiatives have focused on almost every aspect of education—from state policy to administration to teaching—but there has been little grant activity directly related to school boards.

There are many opportunities for foundations to support board-related research endeavors and professional development. If foundations are trying to improve school district performance, investing in board governance is a powerful mechanism that should not be overlooked.

MUNICIPAL GOVERNMENT, LOCAL AGENCIES, AND COMMUNITY PARTNERS

Some problems are well beyond the scope of what school districts can solve alone, and there is an opportunity for school boards and administrators to develop thoughtful partnerships with local government, community organizations, and agencies. For example, boards can work with municipal and county governments to bolster school security. Municipal government can also be a partner to leverage athletic facilities and after-school and summer programs. Outside agencies can help support student mental health, housing, healthcare, and food availability. Local hospitals can support public health initiatives.

The local business community can be a source of funding for specific projects and a source of volunteers. Business leaders can provide unique and practical insight into curriculum priorities to ensure that students graduate with the skills they need to attain gainful employment.

PTAS, LOCAL EDUCATION FOUNDATIONS, AND OTHER COMMUNITY EDUCATION-RELATED ORGANIZATIONS

The school board should maintain close relationships with important community organizations that focus on supporting public education and local schools. Liaison roles can be created for board members to interact with these groups and attend their meetings. There is a virtuous circle created when bridges of communication and mutual understanding are built between boards of education and key constituencies within the broader district community. The board benefits from staying abreast of what's happening across the district as it shapes district goals and makes important decisions. The community gains exposure to board members in settings that lend themselves to meaningful dialogue, a very different dynamic from the formality of the public comment period. These groups can encourage community members to vote on election day and serve as a source for future board candidates.

SUPERINTENDENTS

Superintendents are under tremendous pressure and have many competing priorities, but it is critical that they prioritize and invest in their relationship with the board. This relationship should be built on a foundation of mutual trust and full transparency.

Superintendents need to resist the temptation to share only good news with the school board. It is equally important to bring problems swiftly to board members' attention. At the same time, the board needs to refrain from taking rash action and instead should be deliberate and constructive when receiving negative news. The goal is to form a partnership, engaging in thoughtful, spirited, direct discussion to develop solutions that move the district forward, always mindful of the line between board and administrative roles and responsibilities.

EMPLOYEES AND STUDENTS

District administrators, teachers, staff, and students should not be overlooked as critically important sources of input as governance decisions are made. There are many ways to incorporate employee and student voice into the process. Some examples include employee/student surveys, invitations to present to the school board on certain topics, or participation on committees and advisory groups. Montgomery County, Maryland allows their student member of the board to vote on matters such as the budget, school closings and boundaries, and collective bargaining agreements. Each district should have the flexibility to determine the approach to engaging with employees and students that they find most appropriate.[34]

If employees or students have complaints or ideas, they should determine whether it falls within the realm of district administrative leadership and if so, approach them first. If the issue is not resolved and ultimately falls within the purview of the board, they should feel welcome to send a communication to the board president or participate in the public comment period at the next school board meeting. The board can also dedicate time to celebrate employee and student successes. Ultimately, building a respectful relationship between the board and district employees and students is tantamount to building a positive district climate.

STATE AND FEDERAL GOVERNMENT

As I've emphasized throughout this book, I believe state and federal policymakers should resist the temptation to encroach on local authority by instituting a one-size-fits-all approach to school district concerns. Avoid legislating curriculum, for example, which amplifies the risk of politicization and contributes to initiative fatigue. And be mindful of the ways in which local school boards can better tackle some of our most pressing education issues.

At the same time, there is an appropriate and important role for state and federal governments to play. This includes gathering and sharing reportable and quantifiable measures of achievement. Centralized government is charged with holding districts to account. Expectations for a minimum level of achievement should be established, while allowing districts flexibility to chart their own course on how to get there. If a school board fails to achieve expected outcomes, the state ultimately has the obligation to step in with additional support and oversight.

SCHOOL BOARD MEMBERS

This book makes the case for why school boards matter and how they can help improve our education system. But school boards can only be as good as their members.

Board members must put their personal agendas aside and act as fiduciaries, making decisions that are in the best interest of their districts. Members need to be willing to invest time in professional development to sharpen the wide-ranging skill set required to serve. Important focus areas include governance, finance, curriculum, school law, legislative advocacy, and leadership. While members do not need to be experts in all categories, they need ample insight to ask thoughtful questions and make reasoned judgments.

Part II of this book describes how board members can take steps to enhance their districts. These include combatting initiative fatigue, establishing a positive district climate, engaging with the community, maintaining accountability, and avoiding short-termism. This is by no means an exhaustive list, but it's a good start.

If school board members take their role seriously and serve with integrity and mutual respect, their impact is not limited to strengthening their district. They also have unique opportunities to strengthen American democracy.

13

BEYOND EDUCATION

There are few things that elicit as much passion and raw emotion as how our kids are being educated, and there are few things as important. As discussed in part I of this book, recent trends of polarization, social media, the demise of traditional local news outlets, outside money, and the blurry line between state and local control have made school board governance more difficult. At the same time, these very same trends underscore why boards are so essential. The best way I know of to counterbalance these problematic forces is to double down on local governance, and in doing so remind ourselves that our children deserve better.

Part II makes the case that school boards are well positioned to address some of the biggest challenges facing public education. Because school boards sit *inside* the district, they are well suited to address problems such as initiative fatigue, district climate, engagement with the community, accountability, and short-termism.

But the benefits of school boards extend far beyond the district to the very fabric of our democracy. America has become more polarized and divisive. Our polarization has strained how Republicans view Democrats and how Democrats view Republicans. Political differences have even led to families fighting at the Thanksgiving table and a reluctance to marry someone associated with a different political party.

We have lost something in America that is as precious as our liberty. We have lost our ability to productively air our differences and find common ground. We see evidence of this loss not only in our politics but in our society more broadly, even on college campuses that struggle to facilitate civil discourse.

School boards can help us fight pernicious polarization. We all are part of the fabric of our local communities, and school board meetings provide a forum and framework to address some of the most contentious cultural issues of our time. Because individuals with diverse and opposing views come together in the same room and can look each other in the eye, school boards have the potential to bridge differences and build trust.

I believe that in the school boardroom we can find what we've lost. We can rediscover what unites us. This is no naive hope. As messy and difficult as it is to watch contentious school board meetings, they are forums designed to air our differences. They force us to listen to our neighbors who don't always think like we do. They require us to make tough decisions with full transparency. Nothing festers, and nothing is left unsaid or unheard. School boards put everything on the table. Though individuals with very different viewpoints may populate a boardroom, the boardroom itself is a unifying force.

School boards have been dragged through the mud of state and national politics to a greater degree than in the past. Just as this shift can serve to weaken and taint school boards, the reverse is possible as well. Perhaps school boards can help strengthen the rest of our political system.

For this to happen, however, we must understand and get beyond the forces that are dividing school boards and communities more broadly. And we must invest in research and professional development to help school board members become exemplars of local governance.

Much of this effort begins by addressing the one question that I was asked over and over when I embarked on writing a book about school boards: *"What side are you on?"*

Despite the steps many states have taken to insulate school board governance from politics, including off-cycle election timing and ballots without party labels, partisanship has seeped into the boardroom as battles are forged over a wide array of contentious issues.

We naturally assume we know how each side thinks. Conservatives are associated with parental rights and the curtailment of lessons that focus on gender, sexuality, and race. During the pandemic, those on the political right were generally against mask and vaccine mandates. They tend to have a negative view of teachers' unions and are often suspicious of districts trying to instill progressive values in students.

Progressives, on the other hand, are associated with a social justice agenda. They tend to be supportive of diversity, equity, and inclusion programs and policies, and they often embrace sexual identity and race instruction. During the pandemic, those on the left were likely to support mask and vaccine mandates. They are typically teachers' union allies.

We have also seen school board politics and national politics collide. To be clear, national polling still shows that voters prioritize the economy, immigration, and poverty over education when ranking important national issues.[1] Nevertheless, astute politicians at the state and federal levels realize that controversial education issues activate parents, and activated parents translate into motivated voters. Democrats and Republicans have deployed this strategy across the country, particularly in suburban swing districts.

As discussed earlier in the book, education piqued the interest of political operatives after the Virginia 2021 gubernatorial election. Though political scientists debate the relative weight of education versus other factors on Glenn Youngkin's victory, as reported in the *New York Times*, Republicans believed that "capitalizing on the frustrations of suburban parents still reeling from the devastating fallout of pandemic-era schooling" provides "a highly effective political strategy" and an ability to unite a "diverse group of voters."[2]

On the heels of success in Virginia, Republicans across the country made education a focus for the 2022 midterm elections, targeting the pivotal group of suburban moderates across the country. Education also played into federal politics. In March 2023, House Republicans led by Speaker Kevin McCarthy passed a Parents' Bill of Rights Act.[3]

Republicans and Democrats increasingly have been endorsing their preferred local school board candidates, even in states where school board candidates run unaffiliated with a political party. In the 2023 election cycle, the *Loudoun Times-Mirror* reported that the Loudoun County Democratic and Republican committees endorsed a slate of school board candidates, despite Virginia's nonpartisan school board elections.[4] In Iowa, the *Des Moines Register* reported that the state's tradition of nonpartisan school board elections did not stop conservative and progressive political groups from endorsing school board candidates, some for the first time. State senators in Iowa also promoted school board candidates.[5]

Florida's Governor DeSantis routinely endorses school board candidates across his state and tapped into education issues, including parental rights, during his 2024 presidential primary campaign. Just prior to that year's Florida primary, it was reported that DeSantis had endorsed twenty-three school board candidates.[6]

A progressive group called the Campaign for Our Shared Future said that nineteen of its twenty-three endorsed school board candidates across Pennsylvania, Ohio, and Virginia had prevailed, while Moms for Liberty reported that it had a 44 percent success rate in the 2023 election cycle.[7] The founder of No Left Turn in Education quickly grew the effort from a handful of parents in her suburban Philadelphia living room to appearing on national TV as a voice for conservative activism aimed at school districts and amassing more than one million visitors to her Facebook page.[8]

While there is a clear trend toward the politicization of school boards, not every issue fits neatly into ideological boxes. In fact, viewing school-related issues through a lens of conservative versus progressive ideals oversimplifies the landscape.

Take book banning, for example. While conservatives historically have believed in hands-off government, they have been an active force in pushing districts to ban specific titles. The American Library Association list of commonly banned books includes *The Hate U Give* (about a police shooting) and *Gender Queer* (a memoir about gender identity), two examples of books to which some conservatives object. However, it would be a mistake to attribute book banning to conservatives only. Progressives have engaged in campaigns to ban books as well, focused on different titles such as *Of Mice and Men, Adventures of Huckleberry Finn*, and several titles by Dr. Seuss.[9]

There are other hotly contested education issues that, despite being debated in partisan policy circles, have achieved clear consensus among the public according to polls. One example is the question of whether parents should be notified by school administrators if their child decides to change their gender identity in school. Some states such as Florida, Alabama, and Virginia have passed state laws or issued guidance that prevent schools from withholding gender identity information from parents, while other states such as California, New Jersey, and Maryland have passed laws or issued guidance placing restrictions on parent notification.[10] Yet, according to an August 2023 Monmouth Poll conducted in New Jersey (a solid blue state), 77 percent of respondents and 81 percent of respondents who were parents of minors believe that middle schools and high schools should notify parents if students want to be identified as a different gender from their school registration.[11]

As highlighted in this book, throughout history there have been deeply divisive education issues that elicit strong emotion. Examples include religious instruction, busing, vaccinations, and curriculum. Again and again, Americans have expressed strong opinions about how their children are educated. Sometimes these divisive contests seem destructive and can temporarily suck up all the oxygen. Over the years, however, we also see that each contest subsides, giving way to new, different concerns. By focusing on that long view, we can also remind ourselves that finger-pointing over contentious issues misses the point. There is a more salient question than which side of a particular issue is right or wrong, which is: *Where should these contentious education issues be adjudicated?*

Instinctually, we may jump to the conclusion that even this question divides us along ideological lines. Republicans are thought of as champions of local control and hands-off centralized government, while Democrats are associated with more state and federal government activism.

But this is hardly the case. Lately, many blue, purple, *and* red states have become more activist, using legislation and administration as mechanisms to push their very different ideological agendas. It is not uncommon for one state to ban what another state imposes as a mandate. In both cases, states use centralized power to achieve their disparate goals.

Parental rights may be a term more frequently associated with the Republican Party, but liberal parents want rights just as much as conservatives. Many conservative parents may feel it their right to want instruction related to gender and sexuality banned from the classroom, while many liberal parents feel it their right to require that these very same lessons be taught. Both groups want their voices heard. In the end, despite our deep cultural and ideological differences, we are unified in our desire for schools to reflect our values as parents and as human beings.

In addition to Republicans, astute Democratic politicians have latched onto the universality of the desire for parents to have a say and have taken concrete steps to embrace the concept. Michigan Governor Gretchen Whitmer formed a "parents' council" to advise the state on education policy. Governor Josh Shapiro in Pennsylvania has expressed support for the concept of a certain school voucher initiative that gives parents more control. Whether or not you believe in vouchers as a policy prescription, the point is that leaders on both sides of the aisle are reckoning with the fact that parents are invested in how their children get educated.[12]

As the ultimate forum for parents to speak and be heard, school boards can play a pivotal role in bridging differences by celebrating what makes us uniquely American and reminding us that universal values unite us. It is time to put school boards at the forefront for the sake of our democracy.

Though public comment periods can sometimes include harmful, even hateful messages, they serve as a clarion call to remind us that we must do better to air our opinions with a greater degree of civility. The incivility of a few cannot prevent us from appropriately celebrating the role that school boards play.

The boardroom provides the space for community voice and open discussion. What would happen if we eliminated board governance and transitioned to a system of centralized control? Parent frustration and anger would not disappear. Social media would not go dark. Special interests would not stop trying to influence outcomes. Outside money would not stop flowing. Without school boards, anger and frustration would likely fester until it boils over. It's not hard to imagine that more parents who can afford it would opt out of the public education system by pursuing private, parochial, or homeschool options.

The recent battles in the boardroom affirm the original purpose of school boards that can be traced to colonial times: the facilitation of community input. The boardroom is a useful outlet for the expression of public opinion and should be celebrated as a hallmark of our democracy. It provides a forum to reach consensus on the most complex and contentious aspects of education policy.

School boards go a step further than corporate boards to ensure checks and balances, transparency, and accountability. All deliberations are on full display for stakeholders, including parents, students, staff members, and taxpayers to watch. Board members are determined by free and fair elections, and community members have an open invitation each time the board meets to express their opinion before any decision is made. Whether we subscribe to a conservative, moderate, or liberal view of the world, we can celebrate the process by which boards incorporate community voice and transparency as they deliberate weighty decisions.

The most effective place to start building bridges across our differences is at the local level. Once issues migrate up to the state or national level, discourse becomes more impersonal. Many of us get our news from an echo chamber, and our positions tend to harden the more we listen to like-minded people. Civil discourse with our neighbors, however, provides us with an opportunity to gain mutual understanding for the fact that we can be well meaning but have different policy prescriptions on a controversial topic. The boardroom brings us together in person and gives us the best chance of recognizing our common humanity, of recognizing that we all want what's best for our children. There is a benefit to looking into each other's eyes instead of communicating via social media.

On November 30, 2023, the *New York Times* reported on a story about the political climate in Silverton, Colorado. After a highly contentious 2020 mayoral race decided by ten votes, a controversy over the recitation of the Pledge of Allegiance at town council meetings roiled the small community. Once it became national news, the town hall and visitors center had to close for security reasons. The mayor left town after being told that there were credible death threats and a lack of resources to properly protect him.[13]

Ultimately, an organization called Community Builders conducted very small group meetings with residents. In these intimate settings, they encouraged discussion and dialogue. They fostered a culture of listening. Through these in-person meetings, Silverton residents reconciled differences and built bridges of mutual understanding.[14] The story is an example of how our problems can be solved at a local level.

Another reason why school boards can strengthen our democracy is because it is the body that citizens trust to oversee our schools. While the reputation of school boards has taken a beating during the past few years, they still fare much better and maintain more public confidence than state or federal government and other American institutions.

Let's harness the relative comfort level citizens have with school boards to create a foundation from which we can combat the erosion of trust in all institutions that has plagued our nation. When it comes to governing schools, let's take fuller advantage of the accessibility and accountability of local boards.

Without school boards as a natural outlet for contests over education to be fought, anger will not go away. It will fester and eventually bubble up in ways that are unpredictable and counterproductive. By placing greater authority in state and federal-level governance we may save ourselves from some local spectacles, but we will lose something precious. We must recognize that these spectacles lower the temperature by providing citizens a forum to be heard.

One of the most striking concepts that I stumbled across when writing this book was "island" school districts, defined as a district in a red state that is blue or in a blue state that is red. A liberal community in Texas and a conservative community in Illinois are examples of island communities. The more the state weighs into education matters, the more island districts would feel more isolated and threatened. In a survey of education leaders, island districts were more likely to report incidents of verbal and written threats against educators or school board members.[15]

As states grow increasingly more red or blue, it is not uncommon to hear someone say, "I would never move to that state because of politics." Therefore, it is not a stretch to think that in a scenario where states continue to wield more educational power over local districts, island communities will shrink and become rarer.

While the political party in power may not be particularly troubled by a flight of people in the opposite political party moving out of their state, I firmly believe that the shrinking of these islands would be unhealthy for our democracy. Unless we want to become a nation sorted neatly by political party, ideological diversity among communities in proximity to each other can be enriching. Together, communities that represent a diversity of voices can feed into state politics, which in turn leads to better, more deliberative decision-making and unity.

We lament the fact that in one-party-rule states, maps get gerrymandered, policies become more extreme, and differences between states grow, tugging on the fabric of American cohesion. Islands are a healthy part of trying to keep us knit together as a country. They help us recognize differences across our local geographies. School board governance can help empower island communities to remain intact.

In addition, school boards can model civil discourse for students in their district. And ideally, students can take those cumulative lessons with them when they leave high school and home for college, the job market, parenting, and their role as citizens. Together, our collective voices are the very essence of our democracy.

Finally, a word to everyone who has, or hopes to, become a school board member.

Being a board member is not always easy. The role involves knowledge on wide-ranging matters such as finance, school law, governance best practices, communications, collaboration, and curriculum. Board members often invest time in professional development opportunities and build networks in other districts to share best practices and troubleshoot challenges.

Board members have a fiduciary duty to their district. They are obligated to do their due diligence, act with prudence, and make decisions in line with the district's best interest. They must always remember that board power resides in the group, not the individual, and their effectiveness is correlated with their ability to collaborate with other board members and district administrative leaders. In the end, their actions do not have to follow public opinion, but voters appropriately are the final arbiters of whether a board member gets reelected.

Corporate board members typically receive restricted stock or options as compensation. According to the leading search firm Spencer Stuart, the average corporate board member of an S&P 500 company is paid $327,096 per year.[16] Over ten years, assuming a 3 percent inflation rate, that would amount to in excess of $3.7 million of total compensation.

Serving on a school board is just as time consuming and can be publicly more taxing than serving behind closed doors on a corporate board. Yet most school board members receive no remuneration.

Serving on a school board is a labor of love. Social scientists have long pointed to education as the key ingredient that allows our society to function and to flourish. Education is the engine of social mobility. Researchers have found a correlation between education and higher wages, healthier behaviors, and longer life expectancy. Perhaps most awe inspiring is how education is often the key to a more purposeful, meaningful life where students can follow their dreams.

If you are a school board member, you will not receive any stock options or dividends. But you will be enriched every time a student in your district graduates and follows their hopes and dreams. Assuming an average U.S. district that has 3,700 students, a board member serving ten years will influence conditions that impact over six thousand matriculated students. By engaging in long-term planning, sound fiscal decision-making, thoughtful policies and practices, smart administrative hiring practices, and succession planning, board members can have an impact far into the future after they have stepped down.

A few years ago, I underwent heart valve repair surgery. Thanks to an amazing team of medical professionals, the procedure was successful, and I have made a full recovery. But I will never forget the feeling of being wheeled into a holding area as they prepped the operating room. In the hectic pace of everyday life, we lose sight of high priorities. We navigate day-to-day fire drills, get sidetracked by setbacks, and obsess over stresses. But in these final moments before surgery, my mind raced to filter out all this extraneousness, and with sharp focus and heightened clarity, I couldn't help but reflect on the important aspects of my life. I thought about what I most cherish. First, my family and friends. They are my greatest joy and my highest priority. Then, the pursuits in which I find meaning and purpose, and at the top of the list is my pursuit of school board service.[17]

School board service is a calling. I am proud to serve and privileged to dedicate my time to develop the leaders and citizens of tomorrow. I believe that school boards offer our best hope of ensuring that we maintain a public education system that supports our democracy and builds confidence that the future of our nation is bright.

ACKNOWLEDGMENTS

I want to start at the genesis of the idea for this book by thanking Ed Glaeser. Ed was my thesis advisor thirty years ago and has become a lifelong mentor and friend. After many discussions about school boards, Ed encouraged me to dig deeper and write a book. Harvard University is fortunate to have such a wise economics professor and former department chair who cares deeply about students (even former students from the 1990s).

Eric Lupfer at United Talent Agency was instrumental in helping me navigate the process of finding a publisher. A friend from my *Harvard Lampoon* days, Eric Rayman, and his law firm partner, David Korzenik, also provided advice on how to interface with the publishing world. I also received thoughtful guidance from Ted Dintersmith, who similarly has applied his private-sector insights to public education, championing school innovation.

MIT Press has been outstanding. They were supportive of my goal to develop a manuscript about a politically charged topic in a balanced way. The MIT team, led by Susan Buckley, provided insight every step of the way and understood my desire to gear the book toward practitioners. Kathleen Caruso and Julia Collins were thoughtful and meticulous editors, and their suggestions improved the manuscript. Special thanks to Thomas LeBien and Amanda Moon at Moon & Company for their editorial expertise. Their thoughtful advice helped me write in a clear voice and strengthen my arguments.

I would like to express appreciation to the Byram Hills Central School District community for affording me the opportunity to serve as a school board member in such an outstanding district. Working with my fellow board members (former and current), the administration, faculty, staff, and the entire community has been a collaborative, rewarding, and enriching experience. A special thanks to Jen Lamia. Not only is she an admired superintendent, but she was also an excellent English teacher, which shone through in her constructive edits to my book. A dear friend and community member, Danielle Fox, was an instrumental thought partner. She provided invaluable feedback on early outlines and drafts.

I have benefited from a strong network of superintendents and board members throughout my region. A special note of gratitude to Karen Belanger and Marjorie Schiff from the Westchester Putnam School Boards Association (WPSBA), experienced leaders with deep expertise. It has been a pleasure to work with the entire WPSBA board and with Stacy Agona, whose excellence keeps the organization running smoothly. I sincerely appreciate receiving constructive feedback from John Spatz, executive director of the Nebraska School Boards Association. I also want to thank executive director Bob Schneider and deputy executive director and general counsel Jay Worona of the New York State School Boards Association, along with members of their team, for reviewing the draft and providing helpful commentary.

I want to thank the team at the Yale Center for Emotional Intelligence. They exposed me to different perspectives and to school leaders across the country and world. Marc Brackett and Robin Stern, also authors themselves, were instrumental in providing step-by-step advice and encouragement. Thanks to Marc and Jessica Hoffmann for providing helpful feedback on the manuscript. Charley Ellis, a storied business leader, philanthropist, lecturer, and writer, has been a source of inspiration and sage advice.

I leaned on a group of thoughtful and talented faculty at Harvard. Thank you to Tom Kane for hosting me at the Center for Education Policy Research and for challenging me and broadening my thinking. Marty West, academic dean of the Harvard Graduate School of Education, is a strategic thinker and true thought partner with a mastery of education policy who understands the important role that school boards play. Thanks also to Danoff Dean of Harvard College Rakesh Khurana, a true intellectual who challenges me with his deep expertise in leadership and governance.

Finally, to my family, you truly are the light of my life. My dad Michael taught me ethical leadership, the value of hard work, and the importance of family and friends. His journey as an author helped give me the courage to write a book. My mom Lorraine's thirty-five years as a kindergarten teacher was a calling that has positively impacted many lives. She is selfless and kind, and the timing of her retirement coincided with becoming a grandmother. My brother Todd has dedicated his life to pediatric rehabilitation, and he is an expert practitioner and scholar. His instructive feedback on the draft made it stronger and made me laugh. I am grateful for my loyal dog Tucker, whose unconditional love and companionship enriched my writing journey.

To my children, I could not be prouder of the individuals you have become. Sydney, your kindness, humility, and determination shine through. Not only are you an outstanding scientist, but your edits to my book, which you managed to complete despite your insanely heavy workload, were extremely helpful. Andrew, you are a true intellectual with an incredibly diverse set of interests. Your bravery and devotion to serving others is inspiring. Jack, you are thoughtful, clever, and independent. You build strong relationships with your magnetic personality and sense of humor. I hope that each one of you follows your hopes and dreams, and please know how much I love you.

In closing, I turn to Cynthia, the love of my life. You are a true partner— including in this book, as your corporate governance experience provided a helpful perspective. I'm grateful to you for helping me pursue my dream of serving my community. Watching you become successful in a male-dominated industry is a testament to your expertise, tenacity, judgment, and independent thinking. I am grateful we are a team. The best decision I ever made was to ask you to marry me.

NOTES

PREFACE

1. Michael Powell, "A School Board That Overlooks Its Obligation to Students," *New York Times*, April 8, 2014, sec. New York, https://www.nytimes.com/2014/04/08/nyregion/a-school-board-that-overlooks-its-obligation-to-students.html; Merryl H. Tisch and David G. Sciarra, "Opinion | When a School Board Victimizes Kids," *New York Times*, June 3, 2015, sec. Opinion, https://www.nytimes.com/2015/06/03/opinion/when-a-school-board-victimizes-kids.html.

2. Vladimir Kogan, "Locally Elected School Boards Are Failing," *Education Next* 22, no. 3 (May 3, 2022), https://www.educationnext.org/locally-elected-school-boards-failing-pandemic-stress-tested-school-governance/.

3. Cheryl Platzman Weinstock, "If You're Thinking of Living in Pomona, N.Y.," *New York Times*, March 2, 1997, Late Edition, Sec. 9.

4. Weinstock, "If You're Thinking."

5. "Obituary: Georgine Hyde (January 20, 1925–August 28, 2015)," Dignity Memorial, accessed January 31, 2024, https://www.dignitymemorial.com/obituaries/suffern-ny/georgine-hyde-6573929.

6. "Letter: Georgine Hyde, a Woman of Peace and Advocacy," *Journal News*, September 3, 2015, https://www.lohud.com/story/opinion/readers/2015/08/31/letter-georgine-hyde-holocaust-survivor-east-ramapo-advocate/71478492/.

7. "Past Winners of the Everett R. Dyer Award for Distinguished School Board Service," New York State School Boards Association, accessed February 5, 2024, https://www.nyssba.org/distinguishedschoolboardserviceaward/past-winners-of-the-everett-r.-dyer-award-for-distinguished-school-board-service/.

8. "Obituary: Georgine Hyde."

9. John Hyde, phone conversation, April 15, 2024.

10. "Georgine Hyde (1927–2015)," *Historical Society of Rockland County*, accessed January 15, 2025, https://director74.wixsite.com/website/georgine-hyde-1925-2015?fbcli d=IwZXh0bgNhZW0CMTAAAR01A7LQfmgrI63ye-W7rTl1CxjMRJERna5StWUSN7P7 aQDCzmdbsab4iIM_aem_5rtupfuVFJvkMr0poSrAcQ.

11. *Jewish Survivor Georgine Hyde*, USC Shoah Foundation, 3:40:14 length, recorded on August 23, 1998, posted to YouTube on April 9, 2012, https://www.youtube.com /watch?v=ZTqhQzma5hI.

12. "Auschwitz," *Holocaust Encyclopedia*, United States Holocaust Memorial Museum, accessed January 31, 2024, https://encyclopedia.ushmm.org/content/en/article /auschwitz.

13. *Jewish Survivor Georgine Hyde*, 3:03:24.

14. Hyde, phone conversation.

INTRODUCTION

1. Mark Keierleber, "Free Speech vs. Violent Threats: Partisan Feud Pits Members' Safety against Parents' First Amendment Rights," *The74*, October 27, 2021, https:// www.the74million.org/article/free-speech-vs-violent-threats-partisan-feud-pits -school-board-members-safety-against-parents-first-amendment-rights/.

2. Anya Kamenetz, "What It's Like to Be on the Front Lines of the School Board Culture War," NPR, October 21, 2021, sec. Education, https://www.npr.org/2021/10 /21/1047334766/school-board-threats-race-masks-vaccines-protests-harassment.

3. Julie Wootton-Greener, "School Board Leader Tells of Death Threats after Vaccine Mandate Vote," *Las Vegas Review-Journal*, September 8, 2021, https://www .reviewjournal.com/local/education/school-board-leader-tells-of-death-threats-after -vaccine-mandate-vote-2435629/.

4. Jerry DeMarco, "Death Threats: Troubling Images Sent to Hackensack School Board Members NOT Up for Re-Election," *Hackensack Daily Voice*, September 30, 2021, https://dailyvoice.com/new-jersey/hackensack/news/death-threats-troubling-images -sent-to-hackensack-school-board-members-not-up-for-re-election/817320/.

5. "Glastonbury BOE Reaffirms Decision to Abandon Tomahawk Mascot After Violent Fight Derails Meeting," Fox61, December 20, 2021, https://www.fox61.com /article/news/local/glastonbury-boe-reaffirms-decision-discontinue-mascot-violent -fight/520-306ed753-b468-4ab3-9576-8062c693759d.

6. Drew Wilder et al., "'The Meeting Has Degenerated': 1 Arrest, 1 Injury at Loudoun Schools Meeting on Equity," *NBC News4 Washington*, June 22, 2021, https:// www.nbcwashington.com/news/local/northern-virginia/loudoun-school-board -transgender-student-policy-race-equity/2708185/.

7. Caitlin O'Kane, "11 People Charged for Interrupting School Board Meeting to Protest Utah Mask Policy," *CBS News*, July 7, 2021, https://www.cbsnews.com/news /mask-policy-protest-utah-school-board/.

8. Associated Press, "As School Board Meetings Get Hostile, Some Members Are Calling It Quits," NPR, August 30, 2021, sec. The Coronavirus Crisis, https://www.npr.org/sections/back-to-school-live-updates/2021/08/30/1032417970/school-board-members-hostile-meetings-mask-mandates-politicized.

9. "School Board Recalls," Ballotpedia, accessed February 1, 2024, https://ballotpedia.org/School_board_recalls.

10. Adapted from "School Board Election Statistics, 2018–2023," Ballotpedia, accessed February 1, 2024, https://ballotpedia.org/School_board_elections,_2023.

11. Henry Robert, *Robert's Rules of Order*, 12th ed. (New York: Public Affairs, 2020).

12. Clara Hendrickson, "Local Journalism in Crisis: Why America Must Revive Its Local Newsrooms" Brookings, November 12, 2019, https://www.brookings.edu/wp-content/uploads/2019/11/Local-Journalism-in-Crisis.pdf.

13. Michael Hartney, "Revitalizing Local Democracy: The Case for On-Cycle Local Elections," *Manhattan Institute: Issue Brief*, October 2021, https://manhattan.institute/article/revitalizing-local-democracy-the-case-for-on-cycle-local-elections; Rachel White, guest blogger, "Low School Board Election Voter Turnout? Increase the Pool of Eligible Voters," *Rick Hess Straight Up* (blog), *Education Week*, August 15, 2017, sec. Education, https://www.edweek.org/education/opinion-low-school-board-election-voter-turnout-increase-the-pool-of-eligible-voters/2017/08.

14. Jinghong Cai, "The Public's Voice: Uncontested Candidates and Low Voter Turnout Are Concerns in Board Elections," NSBA.org, April 1, 2020, https://nsba.org:443/ASBJ/2020/April/the-publics-voice.

15. William G. Howell, ed., *Besieged: School Boards and the Future of Education Politics* (Washington, DC: Brookings Institution Press, 2005), 14.

16. ERIC Database Search for 2024 Articles with the Following Identifiers: ("school board*" OR "board* of education") pubyear:2024, accessed January 23, 2025, https://eric.ed.gov/?advanced.

17. Diane Ravitch, *Reign of Error: The Hoax of the Privatization Movement and the Danger to America's Public Schools* (New York: Alfred A. Knopf, 2013), 19.

18. Lisa Dragoset et al., "Race to the Top: Implementation and Relationship to Student Outcomes," IES, NCEE, U.S. Department of Education, October 2016, https://ies.ed.gov/ncee/pubs/20174001/pdf/20174000.pdf.

19. "NY Wins Nearly $700 Million in Race to the Top Competition," press release, New York State Education Department, August 24, 2010, https://www.nysed.gov/news/2017/new-york-wins-nearly-700-million-race-top-competition.

20. Anthony Ciaccio et al., "Tying Teacher Evaluation to Student Test Performance in New York State," Scholarly Commons at Hofstra Law, Maurice A. Deane School of Law at Hofstra University, 2017, https://scholarlycommons.law.hofstra.edu/cgi/viewcontent.cgi?article=1010&context=hofstra_law_student_works.

21. Scott Levy, "Opt-Out Reflects the Genuine Concerns of Parents," *Education Next* 16, no. 4 (Fall 2016), https://www.educationnext.org/opt-out-reflects-genuine-concerns-of-parents-forum-testing/.

22. Levy, "Opt-Out Reflects the Genuine Concerns of Parents."

23. Melanie Hanson, "U.S. Public Education Spending Statistics," EducationData
.org, February 8, 2025, https://educationdata.org/public-education-spending-statistics;
Jacob Fabina, Erik L Hernandez, and Kevin McElrath, "School Enrollment in the United
States: 2021," U.S. Census Bureau, June 2023, https://www.census.gov/content/dam
/Census/library/publications/2023/acs/acs-55.pdf; "Analysis of School District and
Board Member Characteristics, 2022," Ballotpedia, accessed February 1, 2024, https://
ballotpedia.org/Analysis_of_school_district_and_board_member_characteristics,_2022;
"Digest of Education Statistics," Table 214.10, 2023 Tables and Figures, National Center
for Education Statistics, accessed January 19, 2025, https://nces.ed.gov/programs/digest
/d23/tables/dt23_214.10.asp.

CHAPTER 1

1. "Women Arrayed against Vaccine," *Morning Oregonian*, January 6, 1912.

2. Fred V. Hein, "A History of Health Education in the United States," *JAMA* 182, no.
11 (December 15, 1962): 1139, https://jamanetwork.com/journals/jama/fullarticle
/1388500.

3. "History of Vaccine Requirements and Vaccine Research Highlights," Mayo
Clinic, accessed February 1, 2024, https://www.mayoclinic.org/coronavirus-covid-19
/history-disease-outbreaks-vaccine-timeline/requirements-research.

4. "Must Vaccinate: School Board Issues an Order to School Children," *Arkansas
Gazette*, October 29, 1899.

5. "Clovis, CA," Niche, accessed February 1, 2024, https://www.niche.com/places-to
-live/clovis-fresno-ca/.

6. "CUSD Snapshot: Demographics," Clovis Unified School District, accessed March
5, 2024, https://www.cusd.com/Demographics.aspx.

7. "Foundation History," Foundation for Clovis Schools, accessed February 1, 2024,
https://www.foundationforclovisschools.com/.

8. "Clovis Unified School District Governing Board Meeting Agenda," Clovis
Unified School District, August 25, 2021, https://clovisschools.novusagenda.com
/AgendaPublic/.

9. Nancy Price, "Being Called Nazis Doesn't Faze Clovis School Trustees. But They
Don't Like It Either," GV Wire, September 1, 2021, https://gvwire.com/2021/09/01
/being-called-nazis-doesnt-faze-clovis-school-trustees-but-they-dont-like-it-either/.

10. C. R. Staff, "Masks, Tension, Nazi Germany, and CUSD," *Clovis Roundup*, August
27, 2021, https://www.clovisroundup.com/masks-tension-nazi-germany-and-cusd/.

11. Price, "Being Called Nazis Doesn't Faze Clovis School Trustees."

12. Staff, "Masks, Tension, Nazi Germany, and CUSD."

13. *8-24-2021 WCSD Regular Meeting of the Board of Trustees*, video, 2021, 3:30:03,
https://www.youtube.com/watch?v=9SWcSHbBw70.

14. *8-24-2021 WCSD Regular Meeting of the Board of Trustees*, 2:35:00 and 2:40:50.

15. Jeri Chadwell, "Public Commenters Continue to Spout Conspiracy Theories at School Board Meetings," *This Is Reno*, August 25, 2021, https://thisisreno.com/2021 /08/public-commenters-continue-to-spout-conspiracy-theories-at-school-board -meetings/.

16. Margaret A. Honein, Lisa C. Barrios, and John T. Brooks, "Data and Policy to Guide Opening Schools Safely to Limit the Spread of SARS-CoV-2 Infection," *JAMA* 325, no. 9 (March 2, 2021): 823, https://doi.org/10.1001/jama.2021.0374.

17. Juliana Menasce Horowitz, "More Americans Now Say Academic Concerns Should Be a Top Factor in Deciding to Reopen K-12 Schools," Pew Research Center, February 24, 2021, https://www.pewresearch.org/short-reads/2021/02/24/more -americans-now-say-academic-concerns-should-be-a-top-factor-in-deciding-to -reopen-k-12-schools/.

18. Doree Lewak, "Parents Are Spending $70,000 for Their Kids to Learn in 'Pods,'" *New York Post*, August 20, 2020, https://nypost.com/2020/08/20/parents-are-spending -70000-for-their-kids-to-learn-in-pods/.

19. Reema Amin, Alex Zimmerman, and Christina Veiga, "Thousands of NYC Students Won't Have Access to Computers before Remote Learning Starts Next Week," *Chalkbeat*, March 19, 2020, https://www.chalkbeat.org/newyork/2020/3/19/21196077 /thousands-of-nyc-students-won-t-have-access-to-computers-before-remote-learning -starts-next-week/.

20. Horowitz, "More Americans Now Say Academic Concerns Should Be a Top Factor."

21. "District-Level Learning Loss Data Evaluated," Harvard Graduate School of Education, October 28, 2022, https://www.gse.harvard.edu/ideas/news/22/10/new -research-provides-first-clear-picture-learning-loss-local-level.

22. Emma Dorn et al., "COVID-19 and Education: The Lingering Effects of Unfinished Learning," McKinsey & Company, July 27, 2021, https://www.mckinsey.com /industries/education/our-insights/covid-19-and-education-the-lingering-effects-of -unfinished-learning.

23. Dorn et al., "COVID-19 and Education."

24. Tali Raviv et al., "Caregiver Perceptions of Children's Psychological Well-Being During the COVID-19 Pandemic," *JAMA Network Open* 4, no. 4 (April 29, 2021): e2111103, https://doi.org/10.1001/jamanetworkopen.2021.11103.

25. Dorn et al., "COVID-19 and Education."

26. Honein, Barrios, and Brooks, "Data and Policy," 823–824.

27. Emily Oster et al., "Disparities in Learning Mode Access Among K–12 Students During the COVID-19 Pandemic, by Race/Ethnicity, Geography, and Grade Level—United States, September 2020–April 2021," *MMWR. Morbidity and Mortality Weekly Report* 70, no. 26 (July 2, 2021), https://www.cdc.gov/mmwr/volumes/70/wr /mm7026e2.htm.

28. Elizabeth Rosner and Tamar Lapin, "Teachers Bring Coffins, Guillotine While Protesting NYC Schools Reopening Plan," *New York Post*, August 4, 2020, sec. Metro, https://nypost.com/2020/08/03/teachers-get-creative-while-protesting-nyc-schools -reopening-plan/; Betsy Ladyzhets, "Reopening Schools—Safely: 5 Communities That Did It Right," *The74*, August 31, 2021, https://www.the74million.org/article /reopening-schools-safely-5-communities-that-did-it-right/.

29. Mike Antonucci, "Analysis: Amid Growing Parent Backlash, Teachers Unions Keep Trying to Rewrite School Reopening History," *The74*, November 9, 2021, https://www.the74million.org/article/analysis-amid-growing-parent-backlash -teachers-unions-keep-trying-to-rewrite-school-reopening-history/.

30. Antonucci, "Analysis."

31. Stacey Decker, "Which States Banned Mask Mandates in Schools, and Which Required Masks?," *Education Week*, August 20, 2021, https://www.edweek.org/policy -politics/which-states-ban-mask-mandates-in-schools-and-which-require-masks /2021/08.

32. Michael T. Hartney and Leslie K. Finger, *Politics, Markets, and Pandemics: Public Education's Response to COVID-19*, Annenberg Institute at Brown University, EdWorkingPaper No. 20-304 (October 2020), https://doi.org/10.26300/8FF8-3945.

33. Vladimir Kogan, "What's Behind Racial Differences in Attitudes Toward School Reopening (and What to Do About Them)," American Enterprise Institute, April 2021, https://www.aei.org/research-products/report/whats-behind-racial-differences -in-attitudes-toward-school-reopening-and-what-to-do-about-them/.

34. "Most Parents Don't Want Their Schools to Require COVID-19 Vaccination, But Most Favor Requiring Masks for Unvaccinated Children and Staff," KFF, August 11, 2021, https://www.kff.org/coronavirus-covid-19/press-release/most-parents-dont-want -their-schools-to-require-covid-19-vaccination-but-most-favor-requiring-masks-for -unvaccinated-children-and-staff/.

35. "Annual Report of the School Committee of the Town of Gloucester," *Gloucester Telegraph*, March 4, 1844.

36. "Annual Report of the School Committee of the Town of Portsmouth Presented March 25, 1833," *Portsmouth Journal of Literature and Politics Published as the Portsmouth Journal and Rockingham Gazette*, April 6, 1833.

37. Amanda Beyer-Purvis, "The Philadelphia Bible Riots of 1844: Contest Over the Rights of Citizens," *Pennsylvania History: A Journal of Mid-Atlantic Studies* 83, no. 3 (Summer 2016): 376.

38. Vincent Lannie and Bernard Diethorn, "For the Honor and Glory of God: The Philadelphia Bible Riots of 1840," *History of Education Quarterly* 8, no. 1 (Spring 1968): 56–57.

39. Lannie and Diethorn, "For the Honor and Glory of God," 65, 104.

40. Stephanie Ruhle, "Former Education Secy. Says Critical Race Theory Sends a 'False Message About What's Happening,'" MSNBC, November 4, 2021, https://www.msnbc .com/stephanie-ruhle/watch/former-education-secy-says-critical-race-theory-sends-a -false-message-about-what-s-happening-125371973777.

41. Fox News Staff, "Ingraham: Schools Want 'Complete and Total Control' with American Taxpayer-Funded 'Fiefdoms of Radicalism,'" Fox News, May 21, 2021, https://www.foxnews.com/media/ingraham-schools-want-complete-and-total-control-with-american-taxpayer-funded-fiefdoms-of-radicalism.

42. Peter Greene, "The Conversation About Critical Race Theory in Schools Is Over," *Forbes*, November 5, 2021, https://www.forbes.com/sites/petergreene/2021/11/05/the-conversation-about-critical-race-theory-in-schools-is-over/?sh=6b7b64ce6f04.

43. Helen Raleigh, "Woke Math Education Reform Is Too Dangerous to Ignore," *Newsweek*, December 8, 2021, https://www.newsweek.com/woke-math-education-reform-too-dangerous-ignore-opinion-1656527.

44. Brandon Wright, "Gifted Education Done Right Benefits Black and Hispanic Children. It's Not Inherently Racist," Thomas B. Fordham Institute, October 29, 2020, https://fordhaminstitute.org/national/commentary/gifted-education-done-right-benefits-black-and-hispanic-children-its-not.

45. "The Best High Schools in America, Ranked," accessed April 17, 2024, https://www.usnews.com/education/best-high-schools/national-rankings.

46. Edwin Rios, "Race-Neutral Admissions Are Next in Line of Fire After Affirmative Action Ruling," *Guardian*, August 23, 2023, sec. US News, https://www.theguardian.com/us-news/2023/aug/23/school-race-neutral-admissions-affirmative-action.

47. Rios, "Race-Neutral Admissions Are Next."

48. Robby Soave, "In the Name of Equity, California Will Discourage Students Who Are Gifted at Math," *Reason*, May 4, 2021, https://reason.com/2021/05/04/california-math-framework-woke-equity-calculus/.

49. Sonia Michelle Cintron, Dani Wadlington, and Andre ChenFeng, *A Pathway to Equitable Math Instruction: Dismantling Racism in Mathematics Instruction* (Equitablemath.org, May 2021), https://equitablemath.org/wp-content/uploads/sites/2/2020/11/1_STRIDE1.pdf.

50. Cintron, Wadlington, and ChenFeng.

51. Robert Pondiscio, "What Do School Boards Think About the 1619 Project Curriculum?," Thomas B. Fordham Institute, August 5, 2020, https://fordhaminstitute.org/national/commentary/what-do-school-boards-think-about-1619-project-curriculum.

52. Victoria Bynum et al., letter to the editor, "We Respond to the Historians Who Critiqued the 1619 Project," *New York Times Magazine*, last updated January 19, 2021, https://www.nytimes.com/2019/12/20/magazine/we-respond-to-the-historians-who-critiqued-the-1619-project.html.

53. Conor Friedersdorf, "What Happens When a Slogan Becomes the Curriculum," *The Atlantic*, March 14, 2021, https://www.theatlantic.com/ideas/archive/2021/03/should-black-lives-matter-agenda-be-taught-school/618277/.

54. Chelsea Connery, "The Prevalence and the Price of Police in Schools," *UConn Center for Education Policy Analysis* (blog), October 27, 2020, https://education.uconn.edu/2020/10/27/the-prevalence-and-the-price-of-police-in-schools/.

55. Lodi et al., "Use of Restorative Justice and Restorative Practices at School: A Systemic Literature Review," *International Journal of Environmental Research and Public Health* 19, no. 96 (December 23, 2021), https://pmc.ncbi.nlm.nih.gov/articles/PMC8751228/pdf/ijerph-19-00096.pdf.

CHAPTER 2

1. "Extremists and Contentious Language at School Board Meetings: What You Can Do," Anti-Defamation League, December 26, 2021, https://www.adl.org/resources/blog/extremists-and-contentious-language-school-board-meetings-what-you-can-do.

2. "Entire School Board Resigns After Members Caught Disparaging Parents," *TODAY*, February 20, 2021, https://www.youtube.com/watch?v=5FgJ4fONHoo.

3. "Extremists and Contentious Language at School Board Meetings."

4. Jeffrey R. Henig, Rebecca Jacobsen, and Sarah Reckhow, *Outside Money in School Board Elections: The Nationalization of Education Politics*, Education Politics and Policy Series (Cambridge, MA: Harvard Education Press, 2019).

5. Jennifer McCoy and Benjamin Press, "What Happens When Democracies Become Perniciously Polarized?," Carnegie Endowment for International Peace, January 18, 2022, https://carnegieendowment.org/2022/01/18/what-happens-when-democracies-become-perniciously-polarized-pub-86190.

6. Yascha Mounk, "The Doom Spiral of Pernicious Polarization," *The Atlantic*, May 21, 2022, https://www.theatlantic.com/ideas/archive/2022/05/us-democrat-republican-partisan-polarization/629925/.

7. Michael Dimock and Richard Wike, "America Is Exceptional in the Nature of Its Political Divide," Pew Research Center, November 13, 2020, https://www.pewresearch.org/short-reads/2020/11/13/america-is-exceptional-in-the-nature-of-its-political-divide/.

8. J. Miles Coleman, "The Shocking Decline of Senate Ticket-Splitting—Sabato's Crystal Ball," UVA Center for Politics, February 2, 2023, https://centerforpolitics.org/crystalball/articles/the-decline-of-senate-ticket-splitting/.

9. Mounk, "The Doom Spiral of Pernicious Polarization."

10. Shanto Iyengar, Gaurav Sood, and Yphtach Lelkes, "Affect, Not Ideology: A Social Identity Perspective on Polarization," *Public Opinion Quarterly* 76, no. 3 (Fall 2012): 405–431.

11. Dimock and Wike, "America Is Exceptional in the Nature of Its Political Divide."

12. Mounk, "The Doom Spiral of Pernicious Polarization."

13. Lydia Saad, "Americans' Satisfaction with K-12 Education on Low Side," Gallup, September 1, 2022, https://news.gallup.com/poll/399731/americans-satisfaction-education-low-side.aspx.

14. "Race, Ethics, and Culture: New National Survey of US Adults," Advanced Studies in Culture Foundation, Institute for Advanced Studies in Culture at the University of Virginia; Heart and Mind Strategies, January 14, 2021, https://www.heartandmind

.us/wp-content/uploads/2021/03/HeartMind-Pulse-2021-Pulse-Omnibus-ADVANCED
-STUDIES-IN-CULTURE-FOUNDATION.pdf.

15. Jeffrey Jones, "Confidence in U.S. Institutions Down; Average at New Low,"
Gallup, July 5, 2022, https://news.gallup.com/poll/394283/confidence-institutions
-down-average-new-low.aspx; Lydia Saad, "Confidence in Public Schools Turns More
Partisan," Gallup, July 14, 2022, https://news.gallup.com/poll/394784/confidence
-public-schools-turns-partisan.aspx.

16. "PDK Poll of the Public's Attitudes Toward the Public Schools: The 54th Annual
PDK Poll," 2022, accessed February 6, 2024, https://pdkpoll.org/2022-pdk-poll-results/.

17. "Grosse Pointe Teacher Roasts Board of Education in Intense Resignation
Speech," *Click on Detroit*, Local 4 WDIV, April 28, 2021, accessed April 18, 2024,
https://www.youtube.com/watch?v=mJBlgIA3K24.

18. "All Hell Breaks Loose at School Board Meeting When GOP Lawmaker Slams
Trans-Inclusive Bathroom Rules," *Forbes Breaking News*, January 13, 2023, accessed
April 18, 2024, https://www.youtube.com/watch?v=dNAg-7nSJOc.

19. "Entire School Board Resigns After Members Caught Disparaging Parents,"
TODAY.

20. "Amazing Speech Delivered by a Parent at the Cabarrus County Schools Board
Meeting This Week," Facebook.com, accessed April 18, 2024, https://www.facebook
.com/watch/?v=517842066343782.

21. "Georgia School Board Shuts Down Mom Reading Explicit Lines from School
Library's Book," Fox News, March 26, 2022, accessed April 18, 2024, https://www
.youtube.com/watch?v=wAWZyRkhL7w.

22. "Georgia School Board Shuts Down Mom Reading Explicit Lines."

23. Eric Randall, "What Board Members Need to Know About Their 'Personal' Social
Media," New York State School Boards Association, *On Board Online*, November 6,
2023, https://www.nyssba.org/news/2023/11/03/on-board-online-november-6-2023
/what-board-members-need-to-know-about-their-personal-social-media/.

24. O'Connor-Ratcliff v. Garnier No. 22-324, Supreme Court Slip Opinion, March
15, 2024, https://www.supremecourt.gov/opinions/23pdf/22-324_09m1.pdf.

25. Judge Amy Coney Barrett, Lindke v. Freed, No. 22-611 (Supreme Court of the
United States, March 15, 2024).

26. Wake County Board of Education Meeting, January 18, 2022, 51:50, https://
www.youtube.com/watch?v=2n4XVyftJxE.

27. Elmhurst Community Unit School District 205 Board of Education Meeting,
February 8, 2022, 2:34:00, https://www.youtube.com/watch?v=CsARDU6oWWc.

28. Jake Burns, "Why a Group of Chesterfield Parents Is Upset with the School
District," *CBS 6 News Richmond*, VA, February 9, 2022, https://www.wtvr.com/news
/local-news/why-a-group-of-chesterfield-parents-is-upset-with-the-school-district.

29. Ankeny Board of Education Meeting, February 15, 2022, 3:50, https://www
.youtube.com/watch?v=LKQLPZbtrxI.

30. "Questions and Answers: What Is a Surety Bond?," Bonds for the Win, accessed February 2, 2024, https://bondsforthewin.com/q-a/.

31. "Step By Step Guide," Bonds for the Win, accessed February 2, 2024, https://bondsforthewin.com/filing-claims/.

32. Tyler Kingkade and Ben Collins, "'Paper Terrorism': Parents against Mask Mandates Bombard School Districts with Sham Legal Claims," *NBC News*, February 21, 2022, https://www.nbcnews.com/news/us-news/parents-mask-schools-surety-bonds-rcna16872.

33. "School Board Watchlist: About Us," School Board Watchlist, accessed April 18, 2024, https://schoolboardwatchlist.org/aboutus/.

34. "Most Radical School Board Members," School Board Watchlist, accessed February 2, 2024, https://schoolboardwatchlist.org/mostradicalboardmembers/.

35. "School Boards 101—No Left Turn," No Left Turn in Education, accessed February 6, 2024, https://www.noleftturn.us/school-boards-101/.

36. "Who We Are," Moms for Liberty, accessed February 2, 2024, https://www.momsforliberty.org/about/.

37. Tyler Kingkade, "Liberal Parents Are Joining the School Culture Wars—but Conservatives Are Way Ahead," *NBC News*, October 22, 2022, https://www.nbcnews.com/politics/politics-news/democrats-republicans-school-board-elections-parents-rcna52698.

38. "Toolkit: Combatting Critical Race Theory in Your Community," Citizens for Renewing America, accessed February 2, 2024, https://citizensrenewingamerica.com/issues/combatting-critical-race-theory-in-your-community/.

39. "About Us: Who We Are" Parents Defending Education, accessed April 18, 2024, https://defendinged.org/about/.

40. Danielle Kurtzleben, "Progressives Take a Leaf out of the Conservative Playbook to Target School Boards," NPR, May 31, 2022, sec. Politics, https://www.npr.org/2022/05/31/1101399058/progressives-take-a-leaf-out-of-the-conservative-playbook-to-target-school-board.

41. Kingkade, "Liberal Parents Are Joining the School Culture Wars."

42. Kingkade, "Liberal Parents Are Joining the School Culture Wars."

43. Sarah Naseer and Christopher St. Aubin, "Newspapers Fact Sheet," Pew Research Center's Journalism Project, November 10, 2023, accessed February 2, 2024, https://www.pewresearch.org/journalism/fact-sheet/newspapers/.

44. Mason Walker, "U.S. Newsroom Employment Has Fallen 26% since 2008," Pew Research Center, July 13, 2021, accessed February 6, 2024, https://www.pewresearch.org/short-reads/2021/07/13/u-s-newsroom-employment-has-fallen-26-since-2008/.

45. "Local News: Revitalizing Local News to Better Inform Communities and Strengthen American Democracy," MacArthur Foundation, Big Bets Program on Local News strategy, accessed February 3, 2024, https://www.macfound.org/programs/bigbets/local-news/strategy.

46. Meghan E. Rubado and Jay T. Jennings, "Political Consequences of the Endangered Local Watchdog: Newspaper Decline and Mayoral Elections in the United States," *Urban Affairs Review* 56, no. 5 (September 2020): 1327–1356, https://doi.org/10.1177/1078087419838058.

47. Joshua P. Darr, Matthew P. Hitt, and Johanna L. Dunaway, "Newspaper Closures Polarize Voting Behavior," *Journal of Communication* 68, no. 6 (December 1, 2018): 1007–1028, https://doi.org/10.1093/joc/jqy051.

48. Hendrickson, "Local Journalism in Crisis."

49. Lee Shaker, "Dead Newspapers and Citizens' Civic Engagement," *Political Communication* 31, no. 1 (January 30, 2014): 131–148, https://doi.org/10.1080/10584609.2012.762817.

50. Pengjie Gao, Chang Lee, and Dermot Murphy, "Financing Dies in Darkness? The Impact of Newspaper Closures on Public Finance," Hutchins Center Working Paper #44, September 24, 2018, https://www.brookings.edu/articles/financing-dies-in-darkness-the-impact-of-newspaper-closures-on-public-finance/.

51. Henig, Jacobsen, and Reckhow, *Outside Money in School Board Elections*, 40.

52. Darr, Hitt, and Dunaway, "Newspaper Closures Polarize Voting Behavior."

53. "Stanford Cable TV News Analyzer," Stanford Cable TV News Analyzer, accessed February 7, 2024, https://tvnews.stanford.edu/.

54. Hendrickson, "Local Journalism in Crisis."

55. Brad Cooper, "1776 Project PAC Fundraising Almost Doubles, Report Shows," *Sunflower State Journal*, October 15, 2021, sec. Elections/Voting, https://sunflowerstatejournal.com/1776-project-pac-fundraising-almost-doubles-report-shows/.

56. "Priorities," 1776 Project PAC, accessed April 19, 2024, https://1776projectpac.com/priorities/.

57. 1776 Project PAC [@1776ProjectPac], "From November 2021 to November 2022, the 1776 Project PAC Has Flipped 100 School Board Seats across the Country. The Parents Revolution Is Winning across the Country," Tweet, Twitter, November 9, 2022, https://twitter.com/1776ProjectPac/status/1590210743345246208.

58. Mike Hixenbaugh, "How a Far-Right, Christian Cellphone Company 'Took Over' Four Texas School Boards," *NBC News*, August 25, 2022, https://www.nbcnews.com/news/us-news/-christian-cell-company-patriot-mobile-took-four-texas-school-boards-rcna44583.

59. Henig, Jacobsen, and Reckhow, *Outside Money in School Board Elections*, 21, 45.

60. Henig, Jacobsen, and Reckhow, 2, 50.

61. Henig, Jacobsen, and Reckhow, 91–92.

62. Henig, Jacobsen, and Reckhow, 92.

63. Henig, Jacobsen, and Reckhow, 1–5.

CHAPTER 3

1. "Fishbowl Definition & Meaning—Merriam-Webster," accessed February 3, 2024, https://www.merriam-webster.com/dictionary/fishbowl.

2. Linda Hill and George Davis, "The Board's New Innovation Imperative," *HBR's 10 Must Reads: On Boards* (Boston: Harvard Business Review Press, 2020), 123–124.

3. "Is There a Right to Participate in Public Meetings?," Reporters Committee for Freedom of the Press, n.d., https://www.rcfp.org/open-government-sections/a-is-there-a-right-to-participate-in-public-meetings/.

4. "First Amendment at Board Meetings," *American School Board Journal*, October 1, 2019, https://www.nsba.org:443/ASBJ/2019/October/First-Amendment.

5. Frank LoMonte, "Legal Analysis: Can School Boards Restrict Public Comments?," Student Press Law Center Report, February 21, 2017, https://splc.org/2017/02/legal-analysis-can-school-boards-restrict-public-comments/.

6. "Asked & Answered: What Are Limits on Speech During Public Comment at Board Meetings?," *New Jersey School Boards Association School Board Notes* 43, no. 27 (February 11, 2020), https://www.njsba.org/news-publications/school-board-notes/february-11-2020-vol-xliii-no-27/asked-answered-what-are-limits-on-speech-during-public-comment-at-board-meetings/.

7. Tim Hains, "Viral School Board Speech: It Is My Constitutional Right to Critique Your Fascism," RealClear Politics, June 23, 2021, https://www.realclearpolitics.com/video/2021/06/23/viral_school_board_speech_it_is_my_constitutional_right_to_critique_your_fascism.html.

8. The New York Times Company, Petitioner, v. L. B. Sullivan. Ralph D. Abernathy et al., Petitioners, v. L. B. Sullivan, No. 84 S.Ct. 710 (U.S. Supreme Court, March 9, 1964).

9. John F. O'Connor and Michael J. Baratz, "Some Assembly Required: The Application of State Open Meeting Laws to Email Correspondence," *George Mason Law Review* 12, no. 3 (2004): 719–774.

10. Alex Aichinger, "Open Meeting Laws and Freedom of Speech," Free Speech Center at Middle Tennessee State University, July 2, 2024, https://firstamendment.mtsu.edu/article/open-meeting-laws-and-freedom-of-speech/.

11. O'Connor and Baratz, "Some Assembly Required," 727.

12. O'Connor and Baratz, 730–732.

13. "NJ Dad Wants "Whole School Board Gone" After Daughter Dies by Suicide," CBS New York, February 10, 2023, https://www.youtube.com/watch?v=udqWYck9b3U.

14. Sarah Hammond, "Emotions Run High as Parents, Teachers Address Newport News School Board," *13NewsNow*, January 17, 2023, https://www.13newsnow.com/article/news/local/mycity/newport-news/parents-teachers-address-newport-news-school-board/291-d26fa6c6-292a-46d1-ae6a-04599f999f69.

15. "Emotions Flare at Uvalde School Board Meeting before Police Chief's Firing," KENS 5, August 24, 2022, https://www.youtube.com/watch?v=gHnozg2s2Tg.

16. Richard Briffault, "The Local School District in American Law," in *Besieged: School Boards and the Future of Education Politics*, ed. William G. Howell (Washington, DC: Brookings Institution Press, 2005), 26.

17. Briffault, "The Local School District in American Law," 25, 45–46.

18. "Analysis of School District and Board Member Characteristics, 2022," Ballotpedia, accessed February 1, 2024, https://ballotpedia.org/Analysis_of_school_district_and_board_member_characteristics,_2022; "Rules Governing Party Labels in School Board Elections," Ballotpedia, accessed January 18, 2025, https://ballotpedia.org/Rules_governing_party_labels_in_school_board_elections.

19. "Today's School Boards & Their Priorities for Tomorrow," 2018 Survey, National School Boards Association & K12 Insight.

CHAPTER 4

1. Richard Briffault, "The Local School District in American Law," in *Besieged: School Boards and the Future of Education Politics*, ed. William G. Howell (Washington, DC: Brookings Institution Press, 2005), 31.

2. Jon Wiles and Joseph Bondi, *The School Board Primer* (Newton, MA: Allyn and Bacon, Inc, 1985), 71–72, 81.

3. Brandi Snowden, "Moving with Kids—National Association of Realtors," National Association of Realtors Research Group, 2019, https://www.nar.realtor/sites/default/files/documents/2019-moving-with-kids-08-12-2019.pdf.

4. Jonathan Rothwell, "Housing Costs, Zoning, and Access to High-Scoring Schools," Research, Brookings, April 19, 2012, https://www.brookings.edu/articles/housing-costs-zoning-and-access-to-high-scoring-schools/.

5. Nadav Shoked, "An American Oddity: The Law, History, and the Toll of the School District," *Northwestern University Law Review* 111, no. 4 (2017): 946.

6. "K-12 Governance: Chief State School Officer: How Is the Chief State School Officer Selected, and Are There Term Limits/Lengths?," 50-State Comparison, Education Commission of the States, November 2020, https://reports.ecs.org/comparisons/k-12-governance-chief-state-school-officer-03.

7. Monaghan v. School District No. 1, 211 Or. 360, Thomson Reuters casetext, September 25, 1957, accessed February 3, 2024, https://casetext.com/case/monaghan-v-school-district-no.

8. Briffault, "The Local School District in American Law," 27–29.

9. City of Montpelier v. Barnett, 49 A.3d 120, Thomson Reuters casetext, May 11, 2012, accessed February 7, 2024, https://casetext.com/case/city-of-montpelier-v-barnett.

10. Briffault, "The Local School District in American Law," 29.

11. Briffault, 27.

12. Shoked, "An American Oddity," 963–965.

13. Shoked, 965–967.

14. Shoked, 970–971.

15. Gene Maeroff, *School Boards in America: A Flawed Exercise in Democracy* (New York: Palgrave MacMillan, 2010), 4; Shoked, "An American Oddity," 969.

16. Matt Miller, "First, Kill All the School Boards," *The Atlantic*, February 2008, https://www.theatlantic.com/magazine/archive/2008/01/first-kill-all-the-school-boards/306579/.

17. Shoked, "An American Oddity," 969.

18. "Acts and Resolves of Massachusetts 1788–89" (1788), https://www.gctrust.org/wp-content/uploads/2021/03/Massachusetts-Acts-and-Resolves-of-1789-excerpts.pdf.

19. Shoked, "An American Oddity," 965–974.

20. Shoked, 974.

21. Maeroff, *School Boards in America*, 5.

22. Jeffrey R. Henig, *The End of Exceptionalism in American Education* (Cambridge, MA: Harvard Education Press, 2013), 4.

23. Shoked, "An American Oddity," 975.

24. Shoked, 981.

25. Shoked, 983.

26. J. Cooley, Charles E. Stuart v. School District No. of the Village of Kalamazoo (Supreme Court of Michigan, July 21, 1874).

27. Briffault, "The Local School District in American Law," 39–40.

28. Christopher R. Berry, "School District Consolidation and Student Outcomes: Does Size Matter?," in *Besieged: School Boards and the Future of Education Politics*, ed. William G. Howell (Washington, DC: Brookings Institution Press, 2005), 57–58; Shoked, "An American Oddity," 988–993.

29. William G. Howell, ed., *Besieged: School Boards and the Future of Education Politics* (Washington, DC: Brookings Institution Press, 2005), 3.

30. William J. Reese, "The Control of Urban School Boards during the Progressive Era: A Reconsideration," *The Pacific Northwest Quarterly* 68, no. 4 (1977): 164–174.

31. Shoked, "An American Oddity," 991.

32. Howell, *Besieged*, 4.

33. "Browse the Constitution Annotated: Fourteenth Amendment—Equal Protection and Other Rights," Library of Congress, accessed June 11, 2024, https://constitution.congress.gov/browse/amendment-14/.

34. Henig, *The End of Exceptionalism in American Education*, 84.

35. "Brown v. Board of Education (1954)," Milestone Documents, National Archives, https://www.archives.gov/milestone-documents/brown-v-board-of-education.

36. "Radio and Television Address on the Situation in Little Rock," September 24, 1957, recording, Dwight D. Eisenhower Presidential Library, Museum & Boyhood Home, National Archives, https://www.eisenhowerlibrary.gov/media/3883.

37. Justice Brennan, Green v. County School Board, No. 391 U.S. 430 (Supreme Court of the United States, May 27, 1968), https://www.law.cornell.edu/supremecourt/text /391/430.

38. "U.S. Reports: Swann et al. v. Charlotte-Mecklenburg Board of Education et al., 402 U.S. 1 (1971)," Library of Congress, https://www.loc.gov/item/usrep402001.

39. W. Arthur Garrity, Jr. Chambers Papers on the Boston Schools Desegregation Case, Digital Collections, Joseph P. Healey Library, Open Archives at UMass Boston, accessed February 8, 2024, https://openarchives.umb.edu/digital/collection /p15774coll33.

40. Henig, *The End of Exceptionalism in American Education*, 88–89.

41. Wiles and Bondi, *The School Board Primer*, 70–71.

42. Henig, *The End of Exceptionalism in American Education*, 98.

43. "Frequently Asked Questions: Section 504 Free Appropriate Public Education (FAPE)," U.S. Department of Education, accessed January 18, 2025, https://www.ed .gov/laws-and-policy/civil-rights-laws/disability-discrimination/frequently-asked -questions-section-504-fape; "A History of the Individuals with Disabilities Act," U.S. Department of Education, accessed January 18, 2025, https://sites.ed.gov/idea/IDEA -History.

44. "An Overview of the U.S. Department of Education," U.S. Department of Education, September 2010, https://www2.ed.gov/about/overview/focus/what.html.

45. Howell, *Besieged*, 4.

46. "How Is K-12 Education Funded?" (Peter G. Peterson Foundation, August 19, 2024), https://www.pgpf.org/article/how-is-k-12-education-funded/.

47. Wiles and Bondi, *The School Board Primer*, 170–171.

48. Henig, *The End of Exceptionalism in American Education*, 87–88.

49. San Antonio School District v. Rodriguez, Library of Congress (U.S. Supreme Court, 1973).

50. "Digest of Education Statistics," Table 235.10, 2023 Tables and Figures, National Center for Education Statistics, accessed February 8, 2024, https://nces.ed.gov /programs/digest/d23/tables/dt23_235.10.asp?current=yes.

51. "Digest of Education Statistics, 2022," Table 98, 2012 Tables and Figures, National Center for Education Statistics, accessed February 13, 2024, https://nces .ed.gov/programs/digest/d12/tables/dt12_098.asp; Table 214.20, 2022 Tables and Figures, National Center for Education Statistics, accessed February 13, 2024, https:// nces.ed.gov/programs/digest/d22/tables/dt22_214.20.asp.

52. Wiles and Bondi, *The School Board Primer*, 222.

53. Howell, *Besieged*, 4–5; Henig, Jacobsen, and Reckhow, *Outside Money in School Board Elections*, 31–34.

54. "An Overview of the U.S. Department of Education," U.S. Department of Education, September 2010, https://www2.ed.gov/about/overview/focus/what.html.

55. "Federal Role in Education," U.S. Department of Education, accessed May 23, 2024, https://www2.ed.gov/about/overview/fed/role.html.

56. Myron Atkin, *The Government in the Classroom* 109, 3 vols., Daedalus (The MIT Press on behalf of the American Academy of Arts & Sciences, 1980), 93.

57. *A Nation at Risk: The Imperative for Educational Reform*, National Commission on Excellence in Education, April 1983, https://www.reaganfoundation.org/media/130020/a-nation-at-risk-report.pdf.

58. Henig, *The End of Exceptionalism in American Education*, 56.

59. "IES: National Center for Education Statistics—Staff Employed in Public Elementary and Secondary School Systems," National Center for Education Statistics, Tables and Figures 2017, https://nces.ed.gov/programs/digest/d17/tables/dt17_213.10.asp.

60. "H.R.1—No Child Left Behind Act of 2001," 107th Congress (2001–2002), Library of Congress, accessed February 8, 2024, https://www.congress.gov/bill/107th-congress/house-bill/1/text.

61. Henig, *The End of Exceptionalism in American Education*, 119–159.

62. Russell Pustejovsky and Jeffrey Little, "Annual State and Local Government Finances Summary: 2021," United States Census Bureau, August 2023, https://www2.census.gov/programs-surveys/gov-finances/tables/2021/2021alfinsummarybrief.pdf.

63. Stacey Decker, "Which States Banned Mask Mandates in Schools, and Which Required Masks?," *Education Week*, August 20, 2021, https://www.edweek.org/policy-politics/which-states-ban-mask-mandates-in-schools-and-which-require-masks/2021/08.

64. Jordan Williams, "Judge Tosses Florida School Districts' Lawsuit over Mask Mandate Ban," *The Hill*, November 5, 2021, https://thehill.com/policy/healthcare/580363-judge-tosses-florida-school-districts-lawsuit-over-mask-mandate-ban/.

65. J. D. Allen, "Nassau County Calls for New York's Highest Court to Expedite Ruling on the State Mask Mandate," WSHU, February 1, 2022, https://www.wshu.org/long-island-news/2022-02-01/nassau-county-calls-for-new-yorks-highest-court-to-expedite-ruling-on-the-state-mask-mandate.

66. Mark Lieberman, "Can Governors Really Take Money from Schools over Masks?," *Education Week*, August 13, 2021, sec. Policy & Politics, Education Funding, https://www.edweek.org/policy-politics/can-governors-really-take-money-from-schools-over-masks/2021/08.

67. Adam Harris, "School Boards Are No Match for America's Political Dysfunction," *The Atlantic*, April 27, 2022, https://www.theatlantic.com/politics/archive/2022/04/parents-partisan-school-board-meeting-covid/629669/.

68. Gino Spocchia, "Parent Tells School Board That Vaccines Are Deep State Conspiracy to Depopulate the World," *The Independent*, September 6, 2021, https://ca.movies.yahoo.com/parent-tells-school-board-vaccines-172213872.html.

69. Jeri Chadwell, "Public Commenters Continue to Spout Conspiracy Theories at School Board Meetings," *This Is Reno*, August 25, 2021, https://thisisreno.com/2021

/08/public-commenters-continue-to-spout-conspiracy-theories-at-school-board
-meetings/.

70. Tawney Beans, "Do Schools with Masked Students Get More Funding? No, U.S. Department of Education Says," *Akron Beacon Journal*, October 1, 2021, sec. News, https://www.beaconjournal.com/story/news/2021/10/01/does-masking-students
-mean-more-funding-schools-united-states-department-education-stow/5897040001/.

71. Rich Allen, "Are ESSER Funds Dependent on Mask Mandates?," *Post Independent*, October 1, 2021, sec. News, https://www.postindependent.com/news/are-esser
-funds-dependent-on-mask-mandates/.

CHAPTER 5

1. Alexis de Tocqueville, *Democracy in America* (New York: Harper & Row, Publishers, 1969), 262–263.

2. Tocqueville, *Democracy in America*, 63.

3. Oleksandr Pankieiev, "Weaponizing Education: Russia Targets Schoolchildren in Occupied Ukraine," *Atlantic Council* (blog), September 20, 2022, https://www
.atlanticcouncil.org/blogs/ukrainealert/weaponizing-education-russia-targets
-schoolchildren-in-occupied-ukraine/.

4. Anton Troianovski, "Putin Aims to Shape a New Generation of Supporters, Through Schools," *New York Times*, July 16, 2022, sec. World, https://www.nytimes.com/2022
/07/16/world/europe/russia-putin-schools-propaganda-indoctrination.html.

5. Troianovski, "Putin Aims to Shape a New Generation of Supporters."

6. "Everyday Life" (see Education), *The Holocaust Explained*, The Wiener Holocaust Library, accessed February 3, 2024, https://www.theholocaustexplained.org/life-in
-nazi-occupied-europe/controlling-everyday-life/controlling-education/.

7. Chester E. Finn Jr., "Leadership Makes a Difference: Lamar Alexander and K–12 Education," *Education Next* 21, no. 2 (Spring 2021), https://www.educationnext.org
/leadership-makes-difference-lamar-alexander-and-k-12-education/.

8. Viola Garcia and Chip Slaven, "NSBA Letter to President Biden," September 29, 2021, https://s3.documentcloud.org/documents/21094557/national-school-boards
-association-letter-to-biden.pdf.

9. Merrick Garland, "Letter from Office of Attorney General to Director, FBI & Director, Executive Office for U.S. Attorneys Assistant Attorney General, Criminal Division, US Attorneys," October 4, 2021, https://www.justice.gov/d9/pages/attachments/2021
/10/04/partnership_among_federal_state_local_tribal_and_territorial_law_enforce
ment_to_address_threats_against_school_administrators_board_members_teach
ers_and_staff_0_0.pdf.

10. Todd Rokita et al., "Letter from State Attorneys General to President Biden and Attorney General Garland," October 18, 2021, https://content.govdelivery
.com/attachments/INAG/2021/10/18/file_attachments/1968225/Letter%20to%20
Biden%20on%20parents'%20First%20Amendment%20rights.pdf.

11. Andrew Ujifusa, "National School Board Group's Apology for 'Domestic Terrorism' Letter May Not Quell Uproar," *EducationWeek*, October 24, 2021, https://www.edweek.org/policy-politics/national-school-board-groups-apology-for-domestic-terrorism-letter-may-not-quell-uproar/2021/10.

12. "COSSBA—Members," COSSBA, accessed February 3, 2024, https://www.cossba.org/members.

13. Caroline Downey, "Ohio, Missouri, Pennsylvania School Board Groups Leave National Association over Letter Likening Parents to Domestic Terrorists," *National Review*, October 26, 2021, https://www.nationalreview.com/news/ohio-pennsylvania-school-board-groups-leave-national-association-over-letter-likening-parents-to-domestic-terrorists/.

14. Laura Meckler, "National School Board Group Says It Wrongly Took Sides in Political Debate," *Washington Post*, May 21, 2022.

15. Patrick McGuinn and Ashley Jochim, "The Politics of the Common Core Assessments," *Education Next* 16, no. 4 (July 12, 2016), https://www.educationnext.org/the-politics-of-common-core-assessments-parcc-smarter-balanced/.

16. Jennifer Reingold, "Everybody Hates Pearson," *Fortune*, January 21, 2015, https://fortune.com/2015/01/21/everybody-hates-pearson/; McGuinn and Jochim, "The Politics of the Common Core Assessments."

17. McGuinn and Jochim, "The Politics of the Common Core Assessments."

18. McGuinn and Jochim, "The Politics of the Common Core Assessments."

19. McGuinn and Jochim, "The Politics of the Common Core Assessments."

20. "Interim Findings: Union Officials Wrote Key Portions of the Biden Administration's School Reopening Guidance," Staff Report—Select Subcommittee on the Coronavirus Crisis—Minority (U.S. House of Representatives, March 30, 2022).

21. Bianca Quilantan, "GOP Probe Fails to Prove Teachers Union Influence on CDC Guidance, Democrats Say," *Politico*, July 31, 2023, https://www.politico.com/newsletters/weekly-education/2023/07/31/gop-probe-fails-to-prove-teachers-union-influence-on-cdc-guidance-democrats-say-00108922.

22. "New Jersey Passes Bill Requiring Diversity and Inclusion Courses for K-12 Education," *Insight into Diversity*, April 13, 2021, https://www.insightintodiversity.com/new-jersey-passes-bill-requiring-diversity-and-inclusion-courses-for-k-12-education/.

23. Rashawn Ray and Alexandra Gibbons, "Why Are States Banning Critical Race Theory?," Brookings, November 2021, https://www.brookings.edu/articles/why-are-states-banning-critical-race-theory/.

24. "Florida Department of Education Letter Regarding AP African American Studies," January 12, 2023, https://drive.google.com/file/d/1A7ooiX-5pyiCxxLbmrvyPKcD9rpo1u3H/view.

25. Matt Lavietes, "Florida Appears to Reverse Course on AP Psych, But Some Schools Still Won't Offer It," *NBC News*, August 8, 2023, https://www.nbcnews.com/nbc-out/out-politics-and-policy/florida-appears-reverse-course-ap-psych-schools-still-wont-offer-rcna98812.

26. "Indiana General Assembly | House Bill 1608—Education Matters," accessed February 9, 2024, https://iga.in.gov/legislative/2023/bills/house/1608/details.

27. "Creating a Safe, Supportive, and Affirming School Environment for Transgender and Gender Expansive Students," New York State Education Department, June 12, 2023, https://www.nysed.gov/sites/default/files/programs/student-support-services /creating-a-safe-supportive-and-affirming-school-environment-for-transgender-and -gender-expansive-students.pdf.

28. "Education Legislation Bill Tracking," National Conference of State Legislatures, accessed February 9, 2024, https://app.powerbi.com/view?r=eyJrIjoiOGUyM2E2NjIt ZGQzMS00MTU0LWExMGQtMmMyMDI5NWFhMjI2IiwidCI6IjM4MmZiOGIwLTR kYzMtNDEwNy04MGJkLTM1OTViMjQzMmZhZSIsImMiOjZ9.

29. Beth Schueler and Joshua Bleiberg, "Evaluating Education Governance: Does State Takeover of School Districts Affect Student Achievement?," *Journal of Policy Analysis and Management* 41, no. 1 (2022): 162–192.

30. Amelia Nierenberg, "The Conservative School Board Strategy," *New York Times*, February 15, 2023, sec. U.S., https://www.nytimes.com/2021/10/27/us/the-conservative -school-board-strategy.html; Brittany Shepherd, "Progressives Launch Their Own Campaign to Flip School Board Seats Nationwide," *ABC News*, June 23, 2023, https://abcnews.go.com/politics/progressives-launch-campaign-flip-school-board -seats-nationwide/story?id=100246945.

CHAPTER 6

1. "Organization" definition, *Cambridge Dictionary* online, accessed on February 7, 2024, https://dictionary.cambridge.org/us/dictionary/english/organization.

CHAPTER 7

1. Lorraine Levy, Advice for Board Service, August 2015. Text in author's personal collection.

2. Douglas B. Reeves, *The Daily Disciplines of Leadership: How to Improve Student Achievement, Staff Motivation, and Personal Organization* (Jossey-Bass, John Wiley & Sons, 2002), 83–84.

3. Ken Robinson and Lou Aronica, *Creative Schools: The Grassroots Revolution That's Transforming Education* (New York: Viking, 2015), xxiii.

4. Henig, *The End of Exceptionalism in American Education*, 2.

5. "Merrimack College Teacher Survey 2023," School of Education and Social Policy, Merrimack College, 2023, https://www.merrimack.edu/academics/education-and -social-policy/about/merrimack-college-teacher-survey/.

6. Merrimack College Teacher Survey 2023.

7. "1st Annual Merrimack College Teacher Survey: 2022 Results," Merrimack College & EdWeek Research Center, https://guinote.wordpress.com/wp-content /uploads/2024/02/merrimack_teachers_are_deeply_disillusioned_survey_data_con firms.pdf.

8. "1st Annual Merrimack College Teacher Survey: 2022 Results," 17.

9. Joseph Murphy, "The Five Essential Reasons for the Failure of School Reforms," *Journal of Human Resource and Sustainability Studies* 8, no. 1 (2020): 8, https://doi.org/10.4236/jhrss.2020.81001.

10. Liz Mineo, "Reason So Many Teachers Joining Great Resignation," *Harvard Gazette*, March 15, 2022, sec. Nation & World, https://news.harvard.edu/gazette/story/2022/03/ed-school-panel-examines-u-s-teacher-exodus/.

11. Amanda Olsen and Erica Mason, "Perceptions of Autonomy: Differential Job Satisfaction for General and Special Educators Using a Nationally Representative Dataset," *Teaching and Teacher Education* 123 (March 2023).

12. Ethan Siegel, "How America Is Breaking Public Education," *Forbes*, December 6, 2017, https://www.forbes.com/sites/startswithabang/2017/12/06/how-america-is-breaking-public-education/.

13. Henig, *The End of Exceptionalism in American Education*, 2–3.

14. Murphy, "The Five Essential Reasons for the Failure of School Reforms," 8.

15. Rose Hollister and Michael D Watkins, "Too Many Projects: How to Deal with Initiative Overload," *Harvard Business Review*, September–October 2018, https://hbr.org/2018/09/too-many-projects.

16. "Engage NY Grade 5: Building Background Knowledge on Human Rights," UnboundEd, n.d., https://lessons.unbounded.org/ela/grade-5/module-1/unit-1; Nicholas Tampio, "Why Are Parents Revolting against the Common Core? Start With the English Curriculum," HuffPost, March 18, 2014, https://www.huffpost.com/entry/why-are-parents-revolting_b_4590041.

17. Jessica Bakeman, "Teachers Wait for Next Chapter of $28.3 Million Curriculum," *Politico*, November 21, 2013, https://www.politico.com/states/new-york/albany/story/2013/11/teachers-wait-for-next-chapter-of-283-million-curriculum-013046.

18. Ted Dintersmith, *What School Could Be* (Princeton, NJ: Princeton University Press, 2018), 216.

19. Henig, Jacobsen, and Reckhow, *Outside Money in School Board Elections*, 41.

20. Heinrich Mintrop and Gail L. Sunderman, "Predictable Failure of Federal Sanctions-Driven Accountability for School Improvement—and Why We May Retain It Anyway," *Educational Researcher* 38, no. 5 (June 2009): 353–364, https://doi.org/10.3102/0013189X09339055.

21. Murphy, "The Five Essential Reasons for the Failure of School Reforms," 4–6.

22. Eric Abrahamson, *Change without Pain: How Managers Can Overcome Initiative Overload, Organizational Chaos, and Employee Burnout* (Boston: Harvard Business School Press, 2004), 2–4 and 23.

23. David B. Tyack and Larry Cuban, *Tinkering Toward Utopia: A Century of Public School Reform* (Cambridge, MA: Harvard University Press, 1995), 55–56.

24. D. L. Fixsen et al., *Implementation Research: A Synthesis of the Literature* (Tampa: University of South Florida, Louis de La Parte Florida Mental Health Institute Publication No. 231, 2005).

25. Greg McKeown, *Essentialism: The Disciplined Pursuit of Less* (New York: Crown Business, 2014), 5.

26. Douglas B. Reeves, *Finding Your Leadership Focus: What Matters Most for Student Results* (New York: Teachers College Press, 2011), 1–6.

27. Reeves, *Finding Your Leadership Focus*, 10 and 27.

28. Reeves, 3.

29. "Evidence for RULER," the RULER approach to SEL, Yale Center for Emotional Intelligence accessed January 18, 2025, https://www.rulerapproach.org/about/what -is-the-evidence/.

30. Hill and Davis, "The Board's New Innovation Imperative."

31. "1939: Westinghouse Students at the World's Fair," Society for Science Centennial Project, accessed February 11, 2024, https://centennial.societyforscience.org /entry/1939-westinghouse-students-at-the-worlds-fair/.

32. George Robinson, "Replicating a Successful Authentic Science Research Program: An Interview with Dr. Robert Pavlica," *Journal of Secondary Gifted Education* 15, no. 4 (Summer 2004): 148–154.

33. Robinson, "Replicating a Successful Authentic Science Research Program," 149.

34. Robinson, 149.

35. Robinson, 149.

36. Robinson, 148.

CHAPTER 8

1. Marc A. Brackett, *Permission to Feel: Unlocking the Power of Emotions to Help Our Kids, Ourselves, and Our Society Thrive*, First edition (New York, NY: Celadon Books, 2019), 191.

2. Scott Levy, "Byram Hills Central School District Staff Development Day Speech" (H.C. Crittenden Middle School, Armonk, NY, August 29, 2018). Text in author's personal collection.

3. "What Is School Climate and Why Is It Important?," *National School Climate Center*, May 27, 2021, https://schoolclimate.org/school-climate/.

4. Kalee De France and Jessica Hoffmann, "Disparities in School Experience for Minoritized Students during the COVID-19 Pandemic," *Research Square*, October 10, 2022.

5. Ming-Te Wang and Jessica L. Degol, "School Climate: A Review of the Construct, Measurement, and Impact on Student Outcomes," *Educational Psychology Review* 28 (June 23, 2015): 315–352.

6. Scott Keller, "McKinsey Quote of the Day," McKinsey & Company, accessed February 4, 2024, https://www.mckinsey.com/featured-insights/quote-of-the-day /february-16-2022.

7. Levy, "Byram Hills Central School District Staff Development Day Speech."

8. Marc Brackett and Christina Cipriano, "Teachers Are Anxious and Overwhelmed. They Need SEL Now More Than Ever," *EdSurge*, April 7, 2020.

__ 5

9. Levy, "Byram Hills Central School District Staff Development Day Speech."

10. Brackett, *Permission to Feel*, 191.

11. "Youth Risk Behavior Survey," Centers for Disease Control and Prevention, 2021, https://www.cdc.gov/healthyyouth/data/yrbs/pdf/YRBS_Data-Summary-Trends_Report2023_508.pdf.

12. "Roughly Half of Public Schools Report That They Can Effectively Provide Mental Health Services to All Students in Need," National Center for Education Statistics, May 31, 2022, https://nces.ed.gov/whatsnew/press_releases/05_31_2022_2.asp.

13. Daniel C. Ehlman et al., "Changes in Suicide Rates—United States, 2019 and 2020," *Morbidity and Mortality Weekly Report* 71 (2022), https://doi.org/10.15585/mmwr.mm7108a5.

14. Elizabeth M. Gaylor et al., "Suicidal Thoughts and Behaviors Among High School Students—Youth Risk Behavior Survey, United States, 2021," *Morbidity and Mortality Weekly Report* 72, no. 1 (April 28, 2023): 45–54), https://www.cdc.gov/mmwr/volumes/72/su/su7201a6.htm?s_cid=su7201a6_w.

15. "Challenge Success," Challenge Success, accessed February 4, 2024, https://challengesuccess.org/.

16. Alan Schwarz, "Risky Rise of the Good-Grade Pill," *New York Times*, June 9, 2012, sec. Education, https://www.nytimes.com/2012/06/10/education/seeking-academic-edge-teenagers-abuse-stimulants.html.

17. "Ivy League Schools and Top Universities Acceptance Rates from Spark Admissions," Spark Admissions, March 21, 2020, https://www.sparkadmissions.com/blog/ivy-league-acceptance-rates/.

18. Jack Schneider, "Privilege, Equity, and the Advanced Placement Program: Tug of War," *Curriculum Studies* 41, no. 6 (December 2009): 813–831; "Number of AP Exams Per Student," College Board AP Central, n.d., https://apcentral.collegeboard.org/media/pdf/number-of-ap-exams-per-student-2023.pdf.

19. "Most Public Schools Face Challenges in Hiring Teachers and Other Personnel Entering the 2023-24 Academic Year," Institute of Education Sciences, National Center for Education Statistics, October 17, 2023, https://nces.ed.gov/whatsnew/press_releases/10_17_2023.asp.

20. Matthew Kraft, William Marinell, and Darrick Shen-Wei Yee, "School Organizational Contexts, Teacher Turnover, and Student Achievement: Evidence from Panel Data," *American Educational Research Journal* 53, no. 5 (October 2016): 1411–1449.

21. Jonathan Cohen et al., "School Climate: Research, Policy, Practice, and Teacher Education," *Teachers College Record: The Voice of Scholarship in Education* 111, no. 1 (January 2009): 180–213, https://doi.org/10.1177/016146810911100108; "School Climate and Educator Well-Being in Kentucky," Kentucky Department of Education, n.d., https://files.eric.ed.gov/fulltext/ED618565.pdf.

22. Marc Brackett and Scott Levy, "2020 NSBA School Safety Summit—Yale Center for Emotional Intelligence Keynote Presentation," September 16, 2020 and uploaded October 12, 2020, 0:21;01, https://community.nsba.org/css/viewdocument/2020

-nsba-school-safety-summit-day?CommunityKey=b0da5370-8d95-446f-ab49
-894267e383d0&tab=librarydocuments.

23. Brackett and Levy, "2020 NSBA School Safety Summit," 0:24:43.

24. Brackett and Levy, "2020 NSBA School Safety Summit," 0:32:48.

25. Brackett and Levy, "2020 NSBA School Safety Summit," 0:25:44.

26. "NYS Education at a Glance," Data.NYSED.gov, accessed February 4, 2024, https://data.nysed.gov/; U.S. Census Bureau data, accessed December 18, 2024, https://www.census.gov/quickfacts/fact/table/rochestercitynewyork/PST045223.

27. Raj Chetty, John N. Friedman, and Jonah E. Rockoff, "Measuring the Impacts of Teachers I: Evaluating Bias in Teacher Value-Added Estimates" (working paper, National Bureau of Economic Research, September 2013), http://www.nber.org/papers /w19423; Raj Chetty, John N. Friedman, and Jonah E. Rockoff, "The Long-Term Impacts of Teachers: Teacher Value-Added and Student Outcomes in Adulthood" (working paper, National Bureau of Economic Research, December 2011), http://www .nber.org/papers/w17699.

28. "ASA Statement on Using Value-Added Models for Educational Assessment," American Statistical Association, April 8, 2014, https://www.amstat.org/asa/files /pdfs/POL-ASAVAM-Statement.pdf.

29. "ASA Statement on Using Value-Added Models for Educational Assessment."

30. Bruce Baker, "Fire First, Ask Questions Later? Comments on Recent Teacher Effectiveness Studies," *School Finance 101*, January 7, 2012, https://schoolfinance101 .com/2012/01/07/fire-first-ask-questions-later-comments-on-recent-teacher -effectiveness-studies/.

31. "ASA Statement on Using Value-Added Models for Educational Assessment"; David Morganstein and Ron Wasserstein, "ASA Statement on Value-Added Models," *Statistics and Public Policy* 1, no. 1 (December 22, 2014): 108–110, https://doi.org/10 .1080/2330443X.2014.956906.

32. "ASA Statement on Using Value-Added Models for Educational Assessment."

33. Levy, "Opt-Out Reflects the Genuine Concerns of Parents."

34. Roger McDonough, Lederman v. King, No. 5443-14 (New York State Supreme Court, Albany County May 10, 2016); Matt Barnum, "NY Teacher Wins Court Case against State's Evaluation System, But May Appeal to Set Wider Precedent," *The74*, May 11, 2016, https://www.the74million.org/article/ny-teacher-wins-court -case-against-states-evaluation-system-but-she-may-appeal-to-set-wider-precedent/.

35. Barnum, "NY Teacher Wins Court Case."

36. Cathy Woodruff, "LI Teacher's Lawsuit on Evaluation Rating Is Microcosm of Issues of APPR Fairness," New York State School Boards Association, *On Board Online*, August 31, 2015, https://www.nyssba.org/news/2015/08/27/on-board-online-august-31-2015 /l.i.-teacher-s-lawsuit-on-evaluation-rating-is-microcosm-of-issues-of-appr-fairness/.

37. *K-12 Education: Students' Experiences with Bullying, Hate Speech, Hate Crimes, and Victimization in Schools*, U.S. Government Accountability Office, November 24, 2021, https://www.gao.gov/products/gao-22-104341.

38. "CDC Adolescent Behaviors and Experiences Survey," Centers for Disease Control and Prevention, June 2021, https://www.cdc.gov/healthyyouth/data/abes.htm.

39. "Social and Emotional Learning Market by Component—Global Forecast to 2028," Markets and Markets, November 2023, https://www.marketsandmarkets.com/Market-Reports/social-emotional-learning-market-245017024.html?gclid=CjwKCA jw49qKBhAoEiwAHQVTo33hMwkOCCRVAw6MOuTHhTtFV4ros5guDjQxhMGYm Uh2VallLe1ahhoC8O0QAvD_BwE.

40. George Anderson, "In a New Era for Boards, Culture Is Key," SpencerStuart, April 2018, https://www.spencerstuart.com/research-and-insight/in-a-new-era-for-boards-culture-is-key.

41. "Legal Fight between Superintendent and Wellesley School Committee in 1930s Was One for the Ages," *Wellesley History*, November 5, 2015, https://wellesleyhistory.wordpress.com/townsman-articles/superintendent-graves/.

42. Rachel White, "Ceilings Made of Glass and Leaving En Masse? Examining Superintendent Gender Gaps and Turnover over Time across the United States," *Educational Researcher* 52, no. 5 (July 2023): 272–285.

43. Evie Blad, "High Pace of Superintendent Turnover Continues, Data Show," *Education Week*, September 19, 2023, sec. Leadership, School & District Management, https://www.edweek.org/leadership/high-pace-of-superintendent-turnover-continues-data-show/2023/09.

44. Christopher Peak, "Ed Board: Birks Is Done," *New Haven Independent*, October 2, 2019, https://www.newhavenindependent.org/article/superintendent_birks_buyout; Rich Scinto, "New Haven BOE Meeting Ends with Duel Threat: Report," *Patch* (New Haven, CT), November 22, 2017, https://patch.com/connecticut/newhaven/new-haven-boe-meeting-ends-duel-threat-report.

45. Brackett and Levy, "2020 NSBA School Safety Summit," 0:45:16.

46. "Corporate Culture and the Role of Boards," *Harvard Law School Forum on Corporate Governance*, August 13, 2016, https://corpgov.law.harvard.edu/2016/08/13/corporate-culture-and-the-role-of-boards/.

47. Linda Liu, Robyn Bew, and Friso van der Oord, "Building Board-Management Dynamics to Withstand a Crisis: Addressing the Fault Lines," McKinsey & Company and NACD, September 2019, https://www.mckinsey.com/~/media/mckinsey/business%20functions/risk/our%20insights/building%20board%20management%20dynamics%20to%20withstand%20a%20crisis%20addressing%20the%20fault%20lines/building-board-management-dynamics-to-withstand-a-crisis-addressing-the-fault-lines.pdf.

48. Liu, Bew, and Oord, "Building Board-Management Dynamics to Withstand a Crisis."

CHAPTER 9

1. Michael Melia, "Ban on Parents at School Lunchrooms Roils Connecticut Town," *AP News*, November 28, 2018, https://apnews.com/article/4f8d1f12797f4cb39e21f0 7972140f81.

2. Colleen Grablick, "How Loudoun County Schools Ended Up at the Center of Virginia's Election," NPR, October 26, 2021, https://www.npr.org/local/2021/10/26/1049266808/how-loudoun-county-schools-ended-up-at-the-center-of-virginias-election.

3. "CNN Election Center 2021: Virginia Exit Polls," November 2021, https://www.cnn.com/election/2021/november/exit-polls/virginia/general/governor/0; Zack Beauchamp, "Did Critical Race Theory Really Swing the Virginia Election?," Vox, November 4, 2021, https://www.vox.com/policy-and-politics/2021/11/4/22761168/virginia-governor-glenn-youngkin-critical-race-theory.

4. "NYSED.Gov District-Level Test Refusal File Released August 12, 2015," https://www.p12.nysed.gov/irs/pressRelease/2015800/home.html; "NYSED.Gov Enrollment Data 2014–2015," https://data.nysed.gov/enrollment.php?year=2015&instid=800000055804.

5. Levy, "Opt-Out Reflects the Genuine Concerns of Parents."

6. "NYS Board of Elections Governor Election Returns Nov 4, 2014 (Revised 4/3/2015),"; "NYS Voter Enrollment by County (November 01, 2014)," https://elections.ny.gov/system/files/documents/2023/10/11-01-2014.pdf.

7. "NYSED.Gov Enrollment Data 2014–2015"; "NYSED.Gov District-Level Test Refusal File Released August 12, 2015"; Levy, "Opt-Out Reflects the Genuine Concerns of Parents."

8. "Measuring Student Progress in Grades 3–8 English Language Arts and Mathematics," New York State Education Department, August 2015, https://www.p12.nysed.gov/irs/pressRelease/2015800/documents/20153-8TestResultsCommunicationsDeck.pdf.

9. "District-Level Test Refusal File," NYSED IRS release of data, 2015, https://www.p12.nysed.gov/irs/pressRelease/2015800/home.html; "NY State Public School Enrollment 2014-2015)," https://data.nysed.gov/enrollment.php?year=2015&state=yes.

10. Levy, "Opt-Out Reflects the Genuine Concerns of Parents."

11. Governor Andrew Cuomo and Robert Megna, "NYS Division of the Budget 2015 Opportunity Agenda," January 21, 2015, https://www.budget.ny.gov/pubs/press/2015/pressRelease15_eBudget.html.

12. Elizabeth Harris and Ford Fessenden, "Opt Out Becomes Anti-Test Rallying Cry in NYS," New York Times, May 20, 2015.

13. "Civil Rights Groups: 'We Oppose Anti-Testing Efforts,'" press release, The Leadership Conference on Civil and Human Rights, May 5, 2015, https://civilrights.org/2015/05/05/civil-rights-groups-we-oppose-anti-testing-efforts/.

14. Levy, "Opt-Out Reflects the Genuine Concerns of Parents."

15. Levy, "Opt-Out Reflects the Genuine Concerns of Parents."

16. Valerie Strauss, "Arne Duncan: Why Can't We Be More Like South Korea," Washington Post (blog), January 18, 2014.

17. National PTA, The PTA Story: A Century of Commitment to Children (Marceline, MO: Walsworth Publishing Company, 1997), 14–17 on National Congress of Mothers.

18. National PTA, The PTA Story, 11, 17.

19. "The Congress of Mothers: Great Crowds Attracted to the Sessions of the Convention in Washington," *New York Times*, February 19, 1897, 2.

20. "The Congress of Mothers," *New York Times*, February 18, 1897, 6.

21. National PTA, *The PTA Story*, 17, 23–25.

22. National PTA, 26.

23. National PTA, Reports & Financials, "One PTA," Annual Reports, 2022 and prior years, https://www.pta.org/home/About-National-Parent-Teacher-Association/PTA-Reports-Financials.

24. National PTA, *The PTA Story*, 35, 40–43, 85, 108.

25. Diana Hiatt-Michael, "Parent Involvement in American Public Schools: A Historical Perspective 1642–2000," *The Community of the School*, ed. Sam Redding and Lori G. Thomas (Lincoln, IL: Academic Development Institute, 2001), 247–258, https://www.adi.org/journal/ss01/chapters/Chapter18-Hiatt-Michael.pdf.

26. Jonathan Collins, "Should School Boards Be in Charge?," *Peabody Journal of Education* 96, no. 3 (July 16, 2021), 341–355, https://www.tandfonline.com/doi/full/10.1080/0161956X.2021.1943239.

27. "PDK Poll of the Public's Attitudes Toward the Public Schools: The 55th Annual PDK Poll," 2023, https://pdkpoll.org/2023-pdk-poll-results/.

28. Megan Brenan, "K-12 Education Satisfaction in U.S. Ties Record Low," August 31, 2023, https://news.gallup.com/poll/510401/education-satisfaction-ties-record-low.aspx.

29. Bob Lamm and Chris Ruggeri, "Activist Shareholders: How Will You Respond?," Deloitte CFO Program, CFO Insights, 2015, https://www2.deloitte.com/content/dam/Deloitte/tr/Documents/finance-transformation/wallace-cfo-insight-activist-shareholder.pdf.

30. Leah Malone, Maria Moats, and Paul DeNicola, "The Director's Guide to Shareholder Activism," Harvard Law School Forum on Corporate Governance, June 11, 2021, https://corpgov.law.harvard.edu/2021/06/11/the-directors-guide-to-shareholder-activism/.

CHAPTER 10

1. "Our View: Put Blame for Failing Schools on State," *Utica Observer Dispatch*, March 14, 2016, https://www.uticaod.com/story/opinion/editorials/2016/03/13/our-view-put-blame-for/32398509007/.

2. "Testing in American Schools: Asking the Right Questions," U.S. Congress, Office of Technology Assessment, OTA-SET-519 (Washington, DC: U.S. Government Printing Office, February 1992), chapter 4, 103, 107, 115–116, https://files.eric.ed.gov/fulltext/ED340770.pdf.

3. "Testing in American Schools," 119, 125–126.

4. Maris A. Vinovskis, *The Road to Charlottesville: The 1989 Education Summit* (Washington, DC: National Education Goals Panel, 1999), 13.

5. Vinovskis, *The Road to Charlottesville*, 38.

6. President George H. W. Bush, "Remarks at the University of Virginia Convocation in Charlottesville," The American Presidency Project, UC Santa Barbara, September 28, 1989, https://www.presidency.ucsb.edu/documents/remarks-the-university-virginia -convocation-charlottesville.

7. Vinovskis, *The Road to Charlottesville*, 18.

8. "High Stakes Testing," Massachusetts Teachers Association, accessed February 4, 2024, https://massteacher.org/current-initiatives/high-stakes-testing; Molly Farrar, "Yes on 2: MCAS Will No Longer Be High School Graduation Requirement," Boston.com, November 6, 2024, https://www.boston.com/news/politics/2024/11/06/yes-on-2-mcas -no-longer-be-high-school-graduation-requirement/.

9. Joanne Jacobs, "School Board Shakeup in San Francisco," *Education Next* 22, no. 3 (May 24, 2022): 36–43, https://www.educationnext.org/school-board -shakeup-san-francisco-arrogance-incompetence-woke-rhetoric-trigger-successful -recall-effort/.

10. Jacobs, "School Board Shakeup in San Francisco."

11. Jacobs, "School Board Shakeup in San Francisco"; Gary Kamiya, "The Meaning of San Francisco's School-Board Recall," *The Atlantic*, February 18, 2022, https:// www.theatlantic.com/ideas/archive/2022/02/meaning-san-franciscos-school-board -recall/622854/.

12. Isaac Chotiner, "How San Francisco Renamed Its Schools," *New Yorker*, February 6, 2021.

13. Thomas Fuller, "In Landslide, San Francisco Forces Out 3 Board of Education Members," *New York Times*, February 16, 2022, sec. U.S.

14. Kamiya, "The Meaning of San Francisco's School-Board Recall."

15. Aaron Mak, "Why San Francisco's Asians Voted to Recall 'Progressive' Members of the School Board," *Slate*, February 17, 2022.

16. Kamiya, "The Meaning of San Francisco's School-Board Recall."

17. Ida Mojadad, "Money and Motives: Who Is Paying for the School Board Recall?," *San Francisco Standard*, February 12, 2022, https://sfstandard.com/2022/02 /11/money-and-motives-school-board-recall/.

18. Kamiya, "The Meaning of San Francisco's School-Board Recall."

19. Jacobs, "School Board Shakeup in San Francisco"; "United Educators of San Francisco Oppose Board of Education Recall," United Educators of San Francisco, October 18, 2021, https://uesf.org/news/uesf-statement-on-board-of-education-recall /?doing_wp_cron=1734785013.6633388996124267578125.

20. Ethan Freedman, "In a NY Town, Increasing Haredi Influence Turns a School Board into a Battleground," *Times of Israel*, April 9, 2022, https://www.timesofisrael .com/in-a-ny-town-increasing-haredi-influence-turns-a-school-board-into-a -battleground/.

21. Freedman, "In a NY Town."

22. Henry Greenberg, Fiscal Monitor for the New York State Education Department, *East Ramapo: A School District in Crisis—Report of Investigation*, November 17, 2014, https://www.p12.nysed.gov/docs/east-ramapo-fiscal-monitor-presentation.pdf; Lanning Taliaferro, "Rockland Clergy Group Asks State to Take Over East Ramapo Schools," *Patch* (New City, NY), April 29, 2014, https://patch.com/new-york/newcity/rockland-clergy-group-asks-state-to-take-over-east-ramapo-schools.

23. Ben Calhoun, "A Not-So-Simple Majority," *This American Life*, episode 534, September 12, 2014, https://www.thisamericanlife.org/534/a-not-so-simple-majority.

24. Greenberg, 6, 22–23.

25. Greenberg, 15, 21, 33.

26. Greenberg, 8–9.

27. Greenberg, 18.

28. Greenberg, 20, 34–35.

29. Thomas Zambito and Nancy Cutler, "Cuomo Signs East Ramapo Monitor Bill in Victory for District's Public School Advocates," *Rockland/Westchester Journal News*, June 30, 2021, https://www.lohud.com/story/news/education/2021/06/30/east-ramapo-monitors-veto-power-cuomo-signs-bill/7810716002/.

30. Senate Bill S6052B, "Relates to the Powers and Duties of Monitors in the East Ramapo Central School District," New York State Senate, Pub. L. No. S6052B (2021), https://www.nysenate.gov/legislation/bills/2021/S6052.

31. New York State Education Department, "State Education Department Appoints Mary Fox-Alter as State Monitor for the East Ramapo Central School District," press release, April 5, 2022, https://www.nysed.gov/news/2022/state-education-department-appoints-mary-fox-alter-state-monitor-east-ramapo-central.

32. Bruce Singer, fiscal monitor, and Dr. Shelley Jallow, academic monitor, "East Ramapo Central School District Findings and Recommendations Regarding the 2024–2025 School Year Budget," Letter to NYS Commissioner of Education, April 11, 2024, https://resources.finalsite.net/images/v1720481100/ercsdorg/zachok0wua6stl4l5vcl/Comm_Rosa_24-25Budget_Analysis_Final.pdf.

33. Singer and Jallow, "East Ramapo Central School District Findings and Recommendations."

34. Singer and Jallow, "East Ramapo Central School District Findings and Recommendations."

35. Senate Bill 9833 (2024), New York State Senate, https://legislation.nysenate.gov/pdf/bills/2023/S9833.

36. Assembly Bill 10407-A (2024), New York State Assembly, https://legislation.nysenate.gov/pdf/bills/2023/A10407A.

37. "'Misguided and Counterproductive': Agudath Israel of America's Rockland Regional Office Statement on Proposed East Ramapo Takeover," May 28, 2024, https://agudah.org/misguided-and-counterproductive-agudath-israel-of-americas-rockland-regional-office-statement-on-proposed-east-ramapo-takeover.

38. Nancy Cutler, "Jewish Group: State's East Ramapo Tax Order 'Inflames Already Dangerous Racial Tensions,'" *Lohud*, August 28, 2024, https://www.lohud.com/story /news/local/rockland/2024/08/28/unfair-taxes-and-specter-of-antisemitism-seen-by -jewish-group-in-ny-order-in-east-ramapo-schools/74886900007/.

39. Cutler, "Jewish Group: State's East Ramapo Tax Order."

40. Kogan, "Locally Elected School Boards Are Failing."

41. "What Is a KPI?," KPI.org, accessed February 12, 2024, https://www.kpi.org/.

42. Robert Kaplan and David Norton, "Linking the Balanced Scorecard to Strategy," *California Management Review* 39, no. 1 (Fall 1996): 53–54.

CHAPTER 11

1. Roger Martin, "Yes, Short-Termism Really Is a Problem," *Harvard Business Review*, October 9, 2015, https://hbr.org/2015/10/yes-short-termism-really-is-a-problem.

2. John Graham, Campbell Harvey, and Shiva Rajgopal, "The Economic Implications of Corporate Financial Reporting," *Journal of Accounting and Economics* 40, no. 1 (September 2005): 3–73.

3. Matt Orsagh, Jim Allen, and Kurt Schacht, "Short-Termism Revisited," *Harvard Law School Forum on Corporate Governance*, October 11, 2020, https://corpgov.law .harvard.edu/2020/10/11/short-termism-revisited/#4b.

4. "U.S. Census—Public Elementary-Secondary Education Finances—Fiscal Years 2006 and 2022," Table 13, https://www.census.gov/data/tables/2022/econ/school -finances/secondary-education-finance.html and https://www.census.gov/data /tables/2006/econ/school-finances/secondary-education-finance.html.

5. IES / NCES, "Nearly One-Third of Public Schools Have One or More Portable Buildings in Use," National Center for Education Statistics, February 15, 2024, https://nces .ed.gov/whatsnew/press_releases/2_15_2024.asp.

6. ASCE, "Schools," 2021 Report Card for America's Infrastructure, American Society of Civil Engineers, https://infrastructurereportcard.org/wp-content/uploads/2020 /12/Schools-2021.pdf.

7. *Financial State of the States 2023*, Truth in Accounting Project, Daniels College of Business, University of Denver, https://www.truthinaccounting.org/library/doclib /FSOS-Booklet-2023.pdf.

8. Adrienne Lu, "States Intervene When School Districts Hit Financial Trouble," *HuffPost*, May 28, 2014, sec. Politics, https://www.huffpost.com/entry/school-districts -bankrupt_n_5404845.

9. Lu, "States Intervene When School Districts Hit Financial Trouble."

10. Pennsylvania Statutes Title 24 P.S. Education 5–508 (n.d.), https://codes .findlaw.com/pa/title-24-ps-education/pa-st-sect-24-5-508/#:~:text=Majority%20 vote%20required%3B%20recording&text=Fixing%20length%20of%20school%20 term,Adopting%20textbooks.

11. Kasia Lundy, *How to Assess the Financial Health of US K-12 Public School Systems*, EY-Parthenon report, February 16, 2021.

12. Lundy, "How to Assess the Financial Health."

13. Lundy, "How to Assess the Financial Health."

14. Philip Bromiley et al., "Enterprise Risk Management: Review, Critique, and Research Directions," *Long Range Planning* 48 (2015): 265–276.

15. Paul Sobel and Kurt Reding, "Aligning Corporate Governance with Enterprise Risk Management," *Management Accounting Quarterly* 5, no. 2 (Winter 2004): 29.

16. "CPI-U and Medical Care in US City Avg, All Urban Consumers, Not Seasonally Adjusted," U.S. Bureau of Labor Statistics, June 1944, https://data.bls.gov/pdq/Survey OutputServlet.

17. "CPI-U and Medical Care in US City Avg, All Urban Consumers, Not Seasonally Adjusted," U.S. Bureau of Labor Statistics, June 1944, https://data.bls.gov/pdq /SurveyOutputServlet.

18. Alicia Munnell, Jean-Pierre Aubry, and Caroline Crawford, "How Big a Burden Are State and Local OPEB Benefits?," State and Local Pension Plans, No. 48, Center for Retirement Research at Boston College, March 2016.

19. Munnell, Aubry, and Crawford, "How Big a Burden Are State and Local OPEB Benefits?"

20. Marc Joffe, "Survey of State & Local Government OPEB Liabilities," Reason Foundation, February 22, 2021, https://reason.org/policy-study/survey-of-state-and -local-government-other-post-employment-benefit-liabilities/.

21. Joffe, "Survey of State & Local Government OPEB Liabilities"; Peter Warren, *New York's Growing Debt Iceberg*, Empire Center for Public Policy, November 2021.

CHAPTER 12

1. Kelly Devine, "Visualizing Voter Turnout in Local and School Board Elections," *Carnegie Reporter*, Carnegie Corporation of New York, no. Winter 2022 (November 2, 2022), https://www.carnegie.org/our-work/article/visualizing-voter-turnout-local -school-board-elections/.

2. Michael Hartney, "Revitalizing Local Democracy: The Case for On-Cycle Local Elections," *Issue Brief*, Manhattan Institute, October 2021, https://manhattan .institute/article/revitalizing-local-democracy-the-case-for-on-cycle-local-elections.

3. Brian Jacob, "How Did the COVID-19 Pandemic Influence School Board Elections?," Annenberg Institute, Brown University EdWorkingPaper No. 24-906 (February 2024), https://edworkingpapers.com/sites/default/files/ai24-906.pdf.

4. Michael T. Hartney, "Teachers' Unions and School Board Elections: A Reassessment," *Interest Groups & Advocacy* 11, no. 2 (January 21, 2022): 237–262, https://doi .org/10.1057/s41309-022-00152-5.

5. Michael T. Hartney, *How Policies Make Interest Groups: Governments, Unions, and American Education* (Chicago: University of Chicago Press, 2022), 150–152.

6. Hartney, *How Policies Make Interest Groups*, 152.

7. Terry Moe, "Political Control and the Power of the Agent," *Journal of Law, Economics, and Organization* 22, no. 1 (April 2006): 1–29.

8. Hartney, *How Policies Make Interest Groups*, chapter 2.

9. Hartney, 114.

10. Hartney, "Revitalizing Local Democracy."

11. Vladimir Kogan, Stephane Lavertu, and Zachary Peskowitz, "Do School Report Cards Produce Accountability Through the Ballot Box?," *Journal of Policy Analysis and Management* 35, no. 3 (2016): 639–661.

12. Vladimir Kogan, Stéphane Lavertu, and Zachary Peskowitz, "Performance Federalism and Local Democracy: Theory and Evidence from School Tax Referenda," *American Journal of Political Science* 60, no. 2 (April 2016): 418–435, https://doi.org/10.1111/ajps.12184.

13. Julia Payson, "When Are Local Incumbents Held Accountable for Government Performance? Evidence from US School Districts," *Legislative Studies Quarterly* 42, no. 3 (n.d.): 421–448.

14. Vladimir Kogan, Stephane Lavertu, and Zachary Peskowitz, "Election Timing, Electorate Composition, and Policy Outcomes: Evidence from School Districts," *American Journal of Political Science* 62, no. 3 (July 2018): 637–651.

15. "School Board Elections, 2023," Ballotpedia, accessed February 1, 2024, https://ballotpedia.org/School_board_elections,_2023.

16. "Today's School Boards & Their Priorities for Tomorrow," 2018 Survey, National School Boards Association & K12 Insight.

17. "Analysis of School District and Board Member Characteristics, 2022," Ballotpedia, accessed February 1, 2024, https://ballotpedia.org/Analysis_of_school_district_and_board_member_characteristics,_2022.

18. "Women in State Legislatures 2018," Center for American Women and Politics (CAWP), Eagleton Institute of Politics, Rutgers University–New Brunswick, 2025, https://cawp.rutgers.edu/facts/levels-office/state-legislature/women-state-legislatures-2018; "Women in U.S. Congress 2018," Center for American Women and Politics (CAWP), Eagleton Institute of Politics, Rutgers University–New Brunswick, 2025, https://cawp.rutgers.edu/facts/levels-office/congress/women-us-congress-2018.

19. "The Condition of Education 2020," Institute of Education Sciences, U.S. Department of Education, https://nces.ed.gov/pubs2020/2020144.pdf, 32 (Indicator 1.7, "Racial/Ethnic Enrollment in Public Schools); "Today's School Boards & Their Priorities for Tomorrow"; New American Leaders, "State of Representation 2020: New Americans in State Legislators," 2020, 7, https://www.newamericanleaders.org/wp-content/uploads/2017/05/State-of-Representation-2020-New-American-Leaders.pdf.

20. "Today's School Boards & Their Priorities for Tomorrow."

21. Melissa Marschall, "Minority Incorporation and Local School Boards," in *Besieged: School Boards and the Future of Education Politics*, ed. William G. Howell (Washington, DC: Brookings Institution Press, 2005), 173–198.

22. Kenneth J. Meier and Eric Gonzalez Juenke, "Electoral Structure and the Quality of Representation on School Boards," in *Besieged: School Boards and the Future of Education Politics*, ed. William G. Howell (Washington, DC: Brookings Institution Press, 2005), 224.

23. Stephen B. Billings et al., "Self-Interest in Public Service: Evidence from School Board Elections," National Bureau of Economic Research, February 2022, http://www.nber.org/papers/w29791.pdf.

24. William McGurn, "Trump Endorsements vs. DeSantis on Endorsements," *Wall Street Journal*, August 29, 2022, sec. Opinion, https://www.wsj.com/articles/trump-vs-desantis-endorsements-elections-school-boards-teachers-union-politicized-institution-children-candidates-party-rival-11661804037.

25. Eric Oliver, *Local Elections and the Politics of Small-Scale Democracy* (Princeton, NJ: Princeton University Press, 2012), 8.

26. "Today's School Boards & Their Priorities for Tomorrow," 9.

27. "Today's School Boards & Their Priorities for Tomorrow," 15.

28. Hartney, "Revitalizing Local Democracy."

29. "Rules Governing Party Labels in School Board Elections," Ballotpedia, accessed June 12, 2024, https://ballotpedia.org/Rules_governing_party_labels_in_school_board_elections.

30. Evan Crawford, "How Nonpartisan Ballot Design Conceals Partisanship," *Political Research Quarterly* 71, no. 1 (March 2018): 143–156.

31. "Today's School Boards & Their Priorities for Tomorrow," 3, 5.

32. "Today's School Boards & Their Priorities for Tomorrow," 13.

33. Jon Fullerton, "Mounting Debt," *Education Next*, July 13, 2006, https://www.educationnext.org/mountingdebt/.

34. "Student Member of the Board," Student Leadership, Montgomery County Public Schools, MD, montgomeryschoolsmd.org, accessed January 17, 2025, https://www.montgomeryschoolsmd.org/departments/student-leadership/smob/index/#:~:text=The%20SMOB%20can%20vote%20on,this%20position%20full%20voting%20rights.

CHAPTER 13

1. "Most Important Problem," Gallup, July 2024, https://news.gallup.com/poll/1675/most-important-problem.aspx.

2. Lisa Lerer and Jeremy W. Peters, "Republicans Seize on Schools as a Wedge Issue to Unite the Party," *New York Times*, November 3, 2021, sec. U.S., https://www.nytimes.com/2021/11/03/us/politics/school-republican-campaign-issue.html.

3. Stephen Groves, "House Republicans Pass 'Parents' Rights' Bill in Fight over Schools," *PBS News*, March 24, 2023, https://www.pbs.org/newshour/education/house-republicans-pass-parents-rights-bill-in-fight-over-schools#:~:text=McCarthy%20made%20the%20bill%20a,rights"%20activists%20largely%20fell%20short; Lerer and Peters, "Republicans Seize on Schools."

4. Evan Goodenow, "School Board Candidates Endorsed by Loudoun Democratic, Republican Committees," *Loudoun Times-Mirror*, July 18, 2023, https://www.loudountimes.com/news/education/school-board-candidates-endorsed-by-loudoun-democratic-republican-committees/article_829a9868-25b3-11ee-ad52-d7351527b136.html.

5. Chris Higgins and Phillip Sitter, "Conservative, Progressive Groups Wade into Central Iowa School Races. Who Are They Backing?," *Des Moines Register*, October 30, 2023, sec. Elections, https://www.desmoinesregister.com/story/news/politics/elections/2023/10/26/why-political-groups-weigh-in-on-des-moines-metro-school-board-races-johnston-ankeny-west-des-moines/71219091007/.

6. Amber Jo Cooper, "DeSantis Endorses 23 School Board Candidates in 2024 Election," *Florida Voice News*, July 19, 2024, https://flvoicenews.com/desantis-endorses-23-school-board-candidates-in-2024-election/.

7. Dana Goldstein, "In School Board Elections, Parental Rights Movement Is Dealt Setbacks," *New York Times*, November 8, 2023, sec. U.S., https://www.nytimes.com/2023/11/08/us/parental-rights-school-board-elections.html.

8. Thomas Beaumont and Stephen Groves, "Tea Party 2.0? Conservatives Get Organized in School Battles," AP News, September 1, 2021, https://apnews.com/article/business-health-coronavirus-pandemic-3157002e9d011e5283f55886b1c7078a.

9. Kiara Alfonseca, "How Conservative and Liberal Book Bans Differ amid Rise in Literary Restrictions," *ABC News*, January 12, 2023, https://abcnews.go.com/US/conservative-liberal-book-bans-differ-amid-rise-literary/story?id=96267846.

10. Katie J. M. Baker, "When Students Change Gender Identity, and Parents Don't Know," *New York Times*, January 22, 2023, sec. U.S., https://www.nytimes.com/2023/01/22/us/gender-identity-students-parents.html.

11. "Majority Support Parental Notification for Gender Identity," Monmouth University Polling Institute, August 22, 2023, https://www.monmouth.edu/polling-institute/reports/monmouthpoll_nj_082223/.

12. Rachel M. Cohen, "How Education Issues and 'Parents' Rights' Are Shaping the Midterms," Vox, November 4, 2022, https://www.vox.com/policy-and-politics/2022/11/4/23436470/education-crt-parents-schools-midterms-desantis.

13. Jonathan Weisman and Benjamin Rasmussen, "Divided by Politics, a Colorado Town Mends Its Broken Bones," *New York Times*, November 30, 2023, sec. U.S., https://www.nytimes.com/2023/11/30/us/politics/silverton-division.html.

14. Weisman and Rasmussen, "Divided by Politics."

15. "Navigating Political Tensions over Schooling: Findings from the Fall 2022 American School District Panel Survey," Center on Reinventing Public Education, January 26, 2023, https://crpe.org/asdp-2023-politics-brief/.

16. "2023 S&P 500 Compensation Snapshot," Spencer Stuart, accessed January 17, 2025, https://www.spencerstuart.com/research-and-insight/sp-500-compensation-snapshot.

17. Scott Levy, "Byram Hills High School Graduation Speech," Byram Hills High School graduation video, June 2020. Text in author's personal collection.

INDEX

Publisher contact:
The MIT Press
Massachusetts Institute of Technology
77 Massachusetts Avenue, Cambridge, MA 02139
mitpress.mit.edu

EU Authorised Representative:
Easy Access System Europe, Mustamäe tee 50,
10621 Tallinn, Estonia
gpsr.requests@easproject.com

Printed by Integrated Books International,
United States of America